SOMEWHERE FURTHER NORTH

Elgar and the Morecambe Festival

Geoffrey Hodgkins

Canon Gorton on the steps of the Morecambe Rectory

SOMEWHERE FURTHER NORTH

Elgar and the Morecambe Festival

Geoffrey Hodgkins

PONEKE PRESS

Published in Great Britain by

Poneke Press

an imprint of

Triflower Publications
20 High Street, Rickmansworth, Herts WD3 1ER

© Geoffrey Hodgkins, 2003

First Published : January 2004

British Library Cataloguing in Publication Data
A Catalogue record for this book
is available from the British Library

ISBN 0-9546301-0-6 (Triflower Publications)

Printed and bound in Great Britain by Antony Rowe Ltd,
Bumper's Farm, Chippenham, Wiltshire

*Cover: Adapted from the central panel of the Morecambe Festival
certificate design. Normally, the date of the event would appear
above the panel, with the name of the competitor, the marks
gained and the competition class being written in below.*

CONTENTS

In memory of

Gareth Lewis,

true Elgarian
and
true friend

FOREWORD

It is a particular pleasure to welcome a book by Geoffrey Hodgkins because as editor of the *Elgar Society Journal* between 1991 and 2002 and of *The Best of Me: the Gerontius Centenary Companion* (1999) he acted as midwife and nurse to other writers' projects. We are, however, already indebted to him for *Providence and Art* (1979), his sensitive study of Elgar's religious beliefs, and for his ever-useful Elgar Bibliography (1993).

Now comes a work of major research. Time was when history was mostly about great figures. Things change, and today there is more emphasis on links, trends, and hidden musicians. The stimulus behind the Morecambe Festival in Lancashire was idealistic, social as much as musical. As a singer himself, who took part in Boult's recording of *The Apostles*, Geoffrey knows about singing in choirs. He tells of the rise and fall of the Festival, which briefly became famous – infamous, even – as a result of a comment (… 'somewhere further north…') by Elgar. Elgar attended the Festival as adjudicator and conductor, and composed for them the part-song 'Weary Wind of the West'; the Festival's founder, Canon Gorton, wrote commentaries on *The Apostles* and *The Kingdom*. The friendship between the two men and the previously unpublished letters between them are what give the book a special interest for Elgarians.

Diana McVeagh

INTRODUCTION

"Four factors of importance to the [English musical] renascence must not be overlooked: the revival of folksong,....the growth of competition festivals, a renewed concern with musical scholarship, and notable developments in musical performance". So wrote the distinguished musicologist Eric Blom in *Music in England* (1942); and whereas three of those four have since been widely acknowledged, little attention has been given to the competition festivals. No detailed appraisal has ever appeared; usually the most they can hope for is a footnote in a musical biography. Yet for the thirty years leading up to the First World War, competitions were a major element in the musical life of the nation, so much so that in 1908 *The Musical Times* was forced to bring out a supplement entitled *The Competition Festival Record*, as reports of festivals were taking up so much space. The main festivals drew large numbers of competitors and huge audiences; they received considerable coverage in the national press; and all the leading composers of the day wrote test pieces for them.

Elgar's association with the movement began in the 1890s with the Madresfield Festival near his Worcestershire home, organised by Lady Mary Lygon, the thirteenth of the *Enigma Variations*. However it is his links with Morecambe which are of far greater significance. Four of his finest part-songs received their premieres there; and the complexity of his later part-songs are a response to the abilities of the top choirs, which led to greater accomplishment among amateur singers generally. William McNaught, the doyen of competition adjudicators and editor of *The Musical Times*, realised something of the significance of what was happening when he said in 1911: "I question whether the country would be in its present position musically but for the Morecambe Festival".

Elgar's links with the Festival are set in the context of his friendship with Charles Gorton, Rector of Morecambe, and founder and President of the Festival (Elgar dedicated his part-song 'There is Sweet Music' to Gorton). Elgar's relationships with other personalities at the Festival - McNaught, Arthur Johnstone, and Walford Davies - are explored, as is the controversy which developed in the press following his comments on music in London and the

North of England; this rumbled on for several years. Two important aspects of Elgar's career are also dealt with in detail – the 1905 Worcester Festival, at which he received the Freedom of the City; and the holiday on Capri which the Elgars and Gortons took two years later.

Elgar's years at Morecambe cover the composition of his two great biblical oratorios – *The Apostles* (1903), and *The Kingdom* (1906). Canon Gorton was of inestimable help to the composer at this time, advising him on the use of biblical texts, and writing an interpretation of the libretto of each work. This aspect of their friendship is only mentioned where it relates to the main argument of the book. (I am currently writing a book on the oratorios' libretti in conjunction with the American musicologist and author, Dr Charles E McGuire).

For the sake of neatness and completeness I have extended the narrative beyond Elgar's personal involvement at Morecambe to include details of Gorton's untimely death in 1912, and to conclude in 1914 with the cessation of festivals at the outbreak of the First World War. *Somewhere Further North* thus deals with a major friendship of Elgar's most creative period in the context of the leading pre-war musical competition.

Some works regularly quoted are mentioned in abbreviated form in footnotes. These are:

E Wulstan Atkins: *The Elgar-Atkins Friendship*
(Newton Abbot: David & Charles, 1984)
Musical Criticisms by Arthur Johnstone
(Manchester: University Press, 1905)
Jerrold Northrop Moore: *Elgar and his publishers*
(Oxford: Clarendon Press, 1987)
Percy M Young (ed): *Letters of Edward Elgar & other writings*
(London: Geoffrey Bles, 1956)
Percy M Young (ed): *A Future for English Music*
(London: Dennis Dobson, 1968)

I would like to acknowledge the great help I have received from many people during the writing of this book, especially Canon Gorton's daughter, the late Mrs Priscilla (Ella) Thouless; his grandson, Stephen Gorton; and other members of the Gorton family. The staff of several libraries and record offices have been of great assistance, especially the Worcester Record Office, Chris Bennett of the Elgar

Birthplace Museum, and Lynn Wilman of the Morecambe Public Library. Permission to quote Elgar's letters has been kindly given by the Sir Edward Elgar Will Trust. Thanks are also due to Felix Aprahamian, Alice Bolitho, James Brandreth, Alan Chatham, Rev Anthony Clegg, Mr C R Lavenell of Alfred Lengnick & Co, Prof John Marshall, James Money, and Alan Shaw. Derek Collins and Stella Redburn were kind enough to read the text and make comments. Perhaps the greatest debt of all is to fellow Elgarians: the late Gareth Lewis, Vivienne and the late Jack McKenzie, Diana McVeagh, Ronald Taylor, Michael Trott, and many others too numerous to mention. Jerrold Northrop Moore's generous help and wise counsel has been of inestimable benefit. I am particularly grateful to John Norris for his assistance in preparing this book for publication.

Finally I would like to pay tribute to my wife Eluned and daughters Elizabeth and Sarah for their forbearance during the book's long gestation.

                                                      Geoffrey Hodgkins

CHAPTER 1

MORECAMBE - 'THE PREMIER COMPETITION'

The enormous social upheaval brought about by the Industrial Revolution alarmed many nineteenth-century thinkers. Some of the Romantic poets believed that such "progress" would lead to spiritual impoverishment. In 1821 Shelley wrote: "Poetry, and the Principle of Self, of which Money is the visible incarnation, are the God and Mammon of this world". Disraeli thought that material prosperity meant nothing for man - a spiritual being - if not accompanied by moral purpose and enlightenment. John Ruskin held that a society built on competition was in direct conflict with the concept of community, in which people cared for each other (this belief was also central to the teaching of the early Christian Socialists such as Frederick Denison Maurice and Charles Kingsley).

As the century progressed and the economy thrived, the lower classes began to share in the benefits. Advances in medicine, and improvements in housing and sanitation, gradually led to a healthier population. Inventions of many kinds reduced physical chores, both domestic and industrial. Trade unions began to negotiate for better working conditions and shorter hours. Many more children went to school after the passing of the 1870 Education Act.

Yet an increasingly educated working class, with time on its hands and money in its pockets was an uncomfortable prospect for a society which was aware of revolution across most of Europe and could still remember the Chartist riots of the late 1840s. How could the people's energy be channelled into positive recreations instead of leading to antisocial behaviour? An important development was the emergence of team games from the 1860s onwards. Sport encouraged "manliness" and a sense of team spirit; moreover it was competitive, and competition was one of the principles of middle-class life. It would not only teach moral lessons but provide an outlet for physical energy. National leagues soon began in cricket and football, assisted by cheap and rapid transport via the railway system.

Sport might take care of man's physical needs, but culture and religion were needed to make him whole. The difficulty was to turn this ideal into a reality. The written word was valueless to the thousands of adult illiterates, and although some large towns now had libraries and art galleries the visual arts were generally the preserve of a privileged minority. But the appeal of music, and its potential benefits for the masses, had long been recognised. George Hogarth wrote in 1835:

> The cultivation of musical taste furnishes...to the poor, a 'laborum dulce lenimen', a relaxation from toil, more attractive than the haunts of intemperance...Wherever the working classes are taught to prefer the pleasures of the intellect, and even of taste, to the gratification of sense, a great and favourable change takes place in their character and manners...Sentiments are awakened in them which make them love their families and their homes; their wages are not squandered in intemperance, and they become happier as well as better...In the densely populated manufacturing tracts of Yorkshire, Lancashire and Derbyshire, music is cultivated among the working classes to an extent unparalleled in any other part of the kingdom.

The widespread extension of musical appreciation and performance was facilitated by two further developments. In 1861, after a long battle, excise duty was finally removed from paper. This reduced the price of publications and made widely available music of all kinds - not just the great choral masterpieces, but anthems, glees and part-songs, at the cost of just a few pence. The pioneer in this fight was J Alfred Novello, proprietor of the music-publishing company which bore his name.

Eight years earlier, in 1853, John Curwen set up the Tonic Sol-Fa Association, to promote his system of notation which he devised to help those who wanted to sing but who had little or no knowledge of musical theory. Sol-Fa was a tremendous success, and by 1890 over 2½ million children (some sixty per cent of the total) were learning singing by this method. To publicise his "invention", Curwen organised competitions for choirs at the Crystal Palace, beginning in 1860; and it soon became clear that harnessing the Englishman's love of sport and competition to the cause of musical education was highly popular. A choir bearing the name of its conductor, Henry Leslie, set new standards in choral singing, and in 1878 won first prize in the Paris International Contest. In 1880 the *Musical Times* declared: "The rise of artistic and refined part-singing in this country is undoubtedly to be dated from the formation of Mr Henry Leslie's Choir".

Among Leslie's friends was Mary Wakefield (1853-1910), a remarkable lady. She had studied music with the famous singing teacher Alberto Randegger, and was an accomplished soloist who appeared at the leading festivals. She wrote several popular drawing-room songs, and lectured and wrote books on music. Ruskin was a close friend, and a great influence on her thinking. One of his maxims - "Music fulfils its most attractive and beneficial mission when the masses of people enjoy it as a recreation and solace" - came to stand for a summary of her life's work. Like Ruskin, she came to believe that the role of the upper classes was not merely to govern their inferiors, but to "raise them always to the nearest level with themselves of which those inferiors are capable".

Leslie introduced Mary Wakefield to the concept of musical competitions and its realisation in the Welsh Eisteddfod, and while disapproving of certain elements of it, she saw the possibilities for good. She concluded: "We both felt that the stimulus of competition was a valuable vital initiative, and we thought that the many evils that follow in its wake might be to a great extent avoided".[1] The festival which she proposed was to have three distinguishing features. First, competition must be seen as a stimulus to the study and practice of music. Second, there were to be no money prizes. And finally, to encourage camaraderie and to allay hostility, the competitors would unite in a common cause - the combined performance of a longer and more elaborate piece, for musical and not competitive ends.

The first Westmoreland Festival in 1885, at the Wakefields' house just outside Kendal, was a modest affair, but it became an annual event and soon grew in size and prestige. Meanwhile Curwen's son John had begun a similar event at Stratford in East London in 1883, and this too quickly established itself. Gradually other centres followed suit, including in 1891 the seaside resort of Morecambe. The Morecambe Festival began as an afternoon event as part of a six-day 'Bazaar, Sale of Work, Tournament and Athletic Sports' put on by Holy Trinity Church in July of that year to raise funds for building a daughter church at the west end of the parish. The Rector, Charles Vincent Gorton, later wrote: "It proved delightful to escape from the over-heated and mercantile atmosphere of the bazaar into this region of fresh air and sweet sound. At the close of the week, while we vowed as usual that we would never hold another bazaar...we still more fervently resolved to repeat the contest of song".

1. Newmarch, Rosa: *Mary Wakefield : a memoir* (Atkinson & Pollitt, 1912), 81

Gorton was born in India in 1854, the son of a clergyman who later became Archdeacon of Madras. The young boy was sent home to England for his schooling, and at Oxford in the 1870s he, like many other undergraduates, was fired by the socialist teachings of Maurice and Kingsley. As the first warden of Toynbee Hall, Samuel Barnett, later wrote: "Men at the universities were conscious of something wrong underneath modern progress : they realised that free trade, reform bills, philanthropic activity, and missions had made neither health nor wealth". Gorton was ordained in 1882 and after a curacy at Altrincham was made vicar of St Barnabas in Crewe in 1885, where he began to turn his convictions into action. When Gorton and his wife Ella moved on to Morecambe in 1889, one leading church member wrote that they were "...universally loved by their parishioners: they have been instrumental in bringing about a very marked improvement in the parish, which was previously in bad condition".

Like many Victorian clergy, Charles Gorton was a man of determination, wide interests, and boundless energy. He discovered at Morecambe that much needed to be done to keep pace with the growth brought about by its popularity as a seaside resort, as a ferry port to Belfast, and as a dormitory town for the West Riding of Yorkshire. (At one time it was fashionable to work in Bradford and live in Morecambe; the commuting took less than two hours on what became known as the 'Residential Express'. For a number of years the town acquired the nickname 'Bradford-by-the-Sea'). During his years as Rector, Gorton served on the School Board, and campaigned vigorously for a new school; he founded an Art School, and was chairman of the Morecambe Technical Instruction Committee. In 1896 he called a meeting of doctors which led to the building of a hospital six years later. He developed a scheme for putting the local fishing industry on to a sound financial basis.

In November 1892 Gorton called a meeting in Lancaster and invited all those interested in establishing a music competition on a permanent basis. A number of notable local people attended, and those assembled were addressed by Mary Wakefield. The declared aim of the committee was "to stimulate the musical education of Morecambe and district", and Miss Wakefield was adamant that the competition should be limited to local performers. "In an open competition it is very unlikely that choirs will come any distance unless they are extremely good", she said. This would have a discouraging effect upon local choirs. Gorton believed the opposite - that hearing talented choirs would be a spur to self-improvement for

The start of it all: the Church Bazaar, July 1891. Ella Gorton is seated immediately to the right of her husband.

local musicians. Both local and open classes were therefore necessary, he argued.

As a later report confirmed, Mary Wakefield "differed considerably from the Committee as to its methods, and publicly advocated the abandonment of open classes". She took part in the 1893 Festival, conducting the final concert, but by the following year was no longer involved. Yet the Festival continued to flourish. Years later Gorton identified three important factors contributing to its growth:

> We had access to one of the finest halls in the country, which we might reasonably expect to rent out of season for a small sum. As a holiday resort we were in touch with four different railway lines; placing us in communication with the whole of the North of England. What was of still greater value we discovered that we included in our committee a musician of quite singular genius, of unerring sense of what was best in music, and of ambition coupled with sound judgment.

The person referred to was Robert Howson, a local bank manager, and organist of Holy Trinity's daughter church, St Laurence's. He was the conductor of the Morecambe Madrigal Society, and in full agreement with the views of Gorton, who later summarised them as follows:

Our aim was to open a School for music which should commence
with sight reading for the smallest child, and have its climax in the
Challenge Choir and full Orchestra, nor should we be content until
every step between these classes had been filled in. It was not our aim
to be merely an examining board. A School, as we understand it...is a
Society and involves a Fellowship. We strove therefore to promote a
spirit of comradeship between the various conductors, their choirs,
and ourselves...

Howson operated a strict regime with the Madrigal Society, insisting
not only on a rigorous musical audition to join, but also on
attendance every week from October to May, unless unavoidably
prevented. The Society's stature and reputation grew rapidly, and in
1896 it held its first Open Night, when a choir of thirty-two voices
sang a programme of glees and part-songs to an audience of 140.
Howson later commented:

Many musical people predicted failure for such a scheme. 'A concert
programme', they said, 'unrelieved by any instrumental music or
solos, would be too monotonous for anything'. But, as I say to the
choir, when we cannot present our part-songs,&c. in a sufficiently
artistic manner to really interest our audience, we will drop it. The
result, however, is that the invitations...are eagerly sought after...[2]

The 1890s saw phenomenal growth in the Morecambe Music
Competition, as it was called. Between 1893 and 1898 the number
of classes, of entries, and of competitors all more than doubled, and
in 1897 it was extended to two days. That same year the Winter
Gardens was enlarged and refurbished, where a Grand Pavilion,
holding 6000 people, was built. The former People's Palace was
converted into a ballroom; and the former ballroom, below ground,
became a restaurant capable of seating 500. The new ballroom
became the marshalling area for competitors.

Railway companies began to run special excursion trains on the
Saturday. *The Musical Times* carried increasingly detailed accounts
of the proceedings. William Gray McNaught (1849-1918), an
inspector for the Board of Education, and the most highly regarded
and popular adjudicator in the country, began to attend each year
and was enthusiastic about what he heard.

In November 1898 the Executive changed the name to the
Morecambe Musical Festival and Competition. The 1899 event was

2. *The Musical Times*, vol xliii, June 1902, 388

extended to four days, and more new classes were introduced. A syllabus was published for the first time; and the number of entries rose from 117 to 173, and the competitors from 1200 to more than two thousand. Sir Frederick Bridge, the organist of Westminster Abbey, and McNaught were the adjudicators, and at the close Bridge said: "I have never known a competition so featureful, so excellent, and so well conducted". McNaught declared: "I have exhausted on my mark-sheet all the English epithets of praise at my command". The *Musical Times* commented: "The greatest doubter of the value of competitions could hardly fail to be converted when brought face to face with the splendid results achieved at Morecambe. The Festival may justly claim to be the premier competition in the North of England".[3] Given that the largest and most prestigious competitions were in the North, that last remark had national significance.

For the first time the event was reported in the North-West's own daily newspaper, the *Manchester Guardian*. Its chief music critic, Arthur Johnstone, was a very gifted man of forthright views. He was greatly impressed with what he heard, but that did not stop him from being brutally frank about several aspects of the Festival. McNaught may have exhausted all the epithets of praise at his command; but Johnstone was free in his use of such words as "inferior", "second-rate", "amateur", "hackneyed", and so on. He also urged that evening concerts should be "finished performances and ...not...a mere continuance of the day's competitions... The evening concerts are very like the proceedings earlier in the day - full of tiresome iterations and tiresome interruptions, given over to the ting-ting of the adjudicator's bell and the voices of harassed committee-men who wander about shouting instructions, and, worst of all, given over to the crudities of amateur singing and playing". Finally, he warned of the danger in allowing such contests to "degenerate into a vulgar, pot-hunting business".

Gorton was aggrieved by the attack, but characteristically did not take it lying down. "We had grown accustomed to unstinted praise,....composers told us that they had never heard their part-songs so perfectly rendered. Then came a bomb from the critic. He was not in touch with us or cognisant of our aims, nor did he allow for our limitations...I do not claim to know much about music, but I recognise good English when I see it. I replied at once in the *Manchester Guardian* rejecting his interpretation of our motives,

3. vol xl, June 1899, 400

and still more the motives which brought choirs to our festival".[4] His letter, published on 4 May, was certainly no less direct than Johnstone's attack had been, particularly in its repudiation of the charge of "pot-hunting": "As to the concluding sentence of the article...it is unjust, because the sole object of the competition is the development in this locality of music...On the last occasion on which I heard this offensive word used I was at pains to make an enquiry on what object the winning choir had spent their prize-money. I found to my great satisfaction that it had been given to their own infirmary. There was this year a choir of forgemen from Whitehaven, a distance of some 70 miles. These men last year walked seven miles and then spent some of the night in Carnforth railway station. The prize in their class was six guineas only. This year one of the orchestras was formed out of a body of miners from Rothwell, near Leeds, and I would ask how far a prize of seven guineas would go towards meeting the expenses of these men, or of the winning orchestra, which included 53 players from Colne. These illustrations, some among many which might be given, ought once for all make it impossible for anyone to attempt to tarnish such enthusiasm with so offensive a phrase".

Shortly after this, Gorton called on Johnstone at the Reform Club in Manchester, and so began a close friendship between the two men, "the memory of which I shall always hold as a matter of pride", Gorton wrote. "He henceforth became for us 'the critic'"[5].

It became clear to Gorton and Howson that if the "premier competition" status were to be maintained they needed to be much more progressive and enterprising in the choice of test pieces, especially in the open classes. Johnstone's charge of "inferior music" was true not only of many of the old glees and part-songs, but also of some by contemporary composers. Howson recalled that when Brahms had died in 1897, an obituary had referred to his "many beautiful part-songs" as a branch of his art that was practically unknown in England. On investigation they found that there were two good reasons for this: in Gorton's own words, "the price was prohibitive, and the translation incomprehensible". He persuaded Brahms' publisher, Simrock, to bring out a new translation to his own words, and at a lower price. The actual translations were done by Gorton's wife, Ella, who as a child had had a German governess. Gorton put them into metrical form to fit the notes. Over the next ten

4. Johnstone, lxxxiii-iv
5. op cit., lxxxiv-v

Two views of the Winter Gardens:

(left) looking north along the Promenade;

(right) during the Musical Festival - notice the competitors entrance through the ballroom.

years nearly thirty of his settings of German texts were published, and received their first performances at the Morecambe Festival.

Further expansion took place at the 1900 Festival. Sir John Stainer joined Bridge and McNaught as an adjudicator. The most important competition, the Open Choir class, was renamed the Challenge Shield class, as a local businessman had presented a shield valued at one hundred guineas. The renowned baritone Plunket Greene was engaged to sing at the concert on the first evening; and on the second evening McNaught lectured on 'Musical Competitions'. The number of classes rose by twelve to 32, including a £5 prize for "original composition" of a part-song. A programme book containing the events, competitors' names, and the words of the songs was published for the first time.

The growth and success of the Festival was not lost on Morecambe's great rival just down the coast, Blackpool. At the end of May it was announced that a music festival would be held there the following spring. It was the brainchild of a councillor, J L Smith, a keen lover of music, whose two daughters had sung at Morecambe. One of them later wrote:

> In 1900 my sister & I were members of the [Blackpool] Glee & Mad[rigal Society] & we went to Morecambe & won the Silver Shield there (the biggest trophy they had won so far) & I think that spurred my father to get a musical festival in Blackpool. He thought if Morecambe could have one, Blackpool ought to be able to have a better one.[6]

Clearly Morecambe could not rest on its laurels. The following month at the annual meeting of the Morecambe Festival Arthur Johnstone was voted on to the Executive. All future criticism was thus pre-empted; but far more important, Johnstone could now be relied upon to use his perceptive mind and musical contacts to lead the Festival in the right paths. In October 1900 Johnstone attended the first performance of Edward Elgar's *The Dream of Gerontius* at the Birmingham Festival, and was much impressed by the work, despite the shortcomings of the performance. On his recommendation therefore the same composer's *Serenade for Strings* was chosen as the test piece in the string orchestra class the following year. Howson and the Morecambe Madrigal Society had already given Elgar's part-song *My love dwelt in a northern land* at their Open Night concert in 1900, and the next year they sang another of his compositions, *O Happy Eyes*.

6. Lancashire Record Office: DDX 706

The 1901 Festival was larger than ever, and another great success. But two weeks later came the Blackpool Festival, held over four days, and with three evening concerts given by the famous Hallé Orchestra conducted by the great Hans Richter. Some of the country's leading singers took part, and works given included Beethoven's *Choral Symphony*, Brahms' *Requiem*, and Elgar's *Enigma Variations*. The deficit of £400 - underwritten by the local council - was largely due to the artists' fees; nevertheless, Blackpool had made an impressive start, as *The Musical Times* was led to comment:

> Capital organisation and a policy of judicious enterprise have certainly marked this first festival at Blackpool, and there can be little doubt that a strong effort will be made to perpetuate the event.[7]

Blackpool had obviously learned from Morecambe, and the onus was on the older festival to show it could match the newcomer in initiative. But how could this be done? There was a good deal to occupy the thoughts of the Morecambe Executive as it pondered the form and content of its next Festival. The president, Charles Gorton, was in no doubt. He was "fired with the ambition to bring the Festival still more prominently before the public, and recognised Dr Elgar as a 'coming man'".

7. vol xlii, June 1901, 401

CHAPTER 2

'WEARY WIND OF THE WEST'

When Elgar arrived home in Malvern after conducting the successful first performance of the overture *Cockaigne* in London on 20 June 1901, he found a letter from Dr McNaught waiting for him.

Board of Education, Edinburgh.
11 June 1901

My dear Elgar
Of all the festivals combining competitions and joint performances that are held in this country I think *Morecambe* ranks highest

Certainly I have heard there year after year the finest choral performances I have ever heard. This year there were three thousand competitors. Their magnificent Hall holds more than five thousand people. It was full on the last day. The whole affair is well managed by a local committee of the best sort. The Rector of Morecambe Mr.C.L.[*sic*] Gorton is the active guiding spirit. I want to give the affair the highest character. Last year Sir John Stainer judged with me. This year Sir Frederick Bridge was with me. All of us greatly admire the results.

The best of the Choirs unite on the last day to perform some work with Band. This year [*Stanford's*] Phaudrig Crohoore was given

The Council now very strongly desire to get you to come for once and further to get you to compose something for them. So far as `judging' during the competition you would be simply asked to be with me during the most important competitions.

The great point is to get a first performance of some short choral work from your pen[.] They would all work *con amore* for you if you can see your way to meet them[.] Unlike more pretentious Festivals they don't expect composers to work for nothing. I am commissioned to say that they are prepared to pay you Fifty Guineas for your attendance and the right of first performance. If this is not enough I daresay they will pay more[.] The event will take place next year about the first week in May

I enclose a letter just received from The Rev.C.L.Gorton[.] He makes some suggestions which may be deemed of value.

I earnestly hope you will entertain the proposition. If you will do so I can see you after my return to town on the 22nd and then I can tell you much more

With Kind regards to Mrs.Elgar and yourself
Believe me,
Yours sincerely,
W.G.McNaught[8]

Elgar must have had mixed reactions on reading this. McNaught was a man he trusted and admired: but Elgar had endured years of amateur performances of his music. Musicians of international stature were now taking up his cause and performing works by him. On that basis, it would be a step backwards to write something for an amateur choral competition.

Judging such an enormous number of competitors would be tiresome. Besides, Elgar had several large projects pending, including a symphony on the life of General Gordon, and two choral works - one for the 1902 Norwich Festival, plus the exciting possibility of an ode to celebrate the coronation of Edward VII.

Against all this was, according to McNaught, the assurance of a warm and genuine reception from the Morecambe people, which would be a welcome change from the oppressive atmosphere of the musical scene Elgar experienced in London and Worcestershire. The deciding factor could well have been the offer of at least fifty guineas for a "short choral work" and his attendance at the festival.

Elgar wrote back to Gorton in encouraging vein, and the Rector was able to report to the Festival Executive on 17 July:

> Our chief hope is that Dr. Elgar, who by his 'Dream of Gerontius' has placed himself in the very first rank of European composers, may be enabled to compose a work for our festival. He writes that he is 'taken with the idea'. If our hope is realised, Dr. Elgar will not only be one of the judges at the next Festival, but will also conduct his own work. If we are thus honoured in being able to bring out a work by Dr.Elgar we must spare no efforts to be worthy of the honour. We must make every effort to secure a full rehearsal of choirs and orchestras on the Friday night preceding the performance.

On 27 July the conductors gathered in Morecambe for their conference, and Gorton told them: "The Executive hopes to have their syllabus out by October, but much depends on what is being done by Dr Elgar". But what *was* being done by Dr Elgar?

8. Moore, 298-9

Aware that time was slipping by, Gorton determined to follow up the composer's initial enthusiasm by paying him a personal visit, and increasing the financial incentive. In early August therefore the two men met, Gorton arriving unannounced at Elgar's summer retreat, the cottage called Birchwood, two miles north of Malvern. (The actual date is uncertain, as Alice Elgar's diary refuses to dignify this discourteous intrusion with any comment[9]). Without any formal introduction, Gorton entered Elgar's study, and in his bluff manner came straight to the point. "My name is Gorton, of the Morecambe Festival", he said, "and I want you to write me a piece of music. The executive are anxious to secure from you a short choral work to last about fifteen minutes. For such a work the committee will give you one hundred pounds". The ever-sensitive Elgar was taken aback by this aggressive approach, and gave a cool, non-committal reply. "You come to me 'advocatus diable'", he countered. "I will sell myself neither to you nor anyone else. I will not write except I am moved to write".[10]

Gorton had come upon Elgar in a depressed mood, caused by the fact that he had no large-scale composition in progress, and deepened by the feeling that no-one wanted his music. Several years later in a letter to Gorton, Elgar spoke of the "pessimistic views" he had poured into Gorton's "unwilling ears". However, Gorton was not one to be easily discouraged, and despite this unpromising beginning to their relationship Elgar's sympathies were gradually aroused, although he refused to commit himself to anything definite at this stage.

Gorton duly reported back to McNaught, who wrote to Elgar on 17 August:

> I have had a visit from Rev.C.V.Gorton today. He told me of his having visited you and of the conversation he had with you. We all very much hope that there is still a chance of getting a short choral work out of you. Mr.G. suggests Bottreau from the volume (p.84) I send with this note.
> The poem is a suggestive one. I hope that failing anything else that may have struck you this will attract you.
> Novellos will surely give you a decent sum for the copyright especially

9. "...no mention was ever made in a diary of anything disagreeable or vexing" (Mrs Richard Powell, *Edward Elgar: Memories of a Variation* (3rd edn., Methuen, 1949), 64)

10. The details of this first meeting between the two men were contained in Gorton's speech of welcome at the 1904 Morecambe Festival.

in view of the fact that Morecambe will at once want three or four hundred copies.[11]

Elgar was on holiday in Wales when this letter was written, and when he returned he was soon immersed in other things - the Three Choirs Festival at Gloucester, and the writing of some incidental music for George Moore's play *Grania and Diarmid*. Realising that he would not now be able to supply the work as requested, Elgar suggested that the Morecambe authorities might approach Percy Pitt, organist at the Queen's Hall, and an up-and-coming conductor and composer. But Pitt's reputation was not great enough for this suggestion to be taken up; and his reply to Elgar shows that he was not very successful with any of his compositions at this time:

> Many thanks...for your kindness in having mentioned my name to the Morecambe man.
> But I am unlucky in most things, witness the Suite de Ballet Competition (Chappell & Co) which has been carried off by a man who writes coon songs! And the two Morecambe part-songs (1900-1901). However never say die.[12]

Gorton replied to Elgar, giving details of what had been planned so far. He was determined to obtain the services of a well-known composer, and had opted for the Principal of the Royal Academy of Music.

> The Rectory, Morecambe
> Oct 4 [1901]
>
> Dear Dr.Elgar -
> Mr. Pitt is doubtless a clever man, but the gap between him & Dr.Elgar is too wide - Sir Alex[ander] Mackenzie has promised to come, and we shall probably take portions of the Rose of Sharon - Meanwhile we must wait in hope -
>
> I wish we could persuade you to come for the next Festival - It would give us so much pleasure if you would stay with us - I hope you will keep us at the back of your mind, so that we may yet have the honour of giving a new work of yours.
> With kind regards
> Yours sincerely
> C.V.Gorton[13]

11. Elgar Birthplace Museum letter (EBML) 8266. The poem was likely to have been *The Silent Towers of Bottreaux*, written in 1831 by Robert Stephen Hawker (1803-75)
12. British Library (BL) Egerton MS 3303 fos. 95 & 96v [5 October 1901]
13. EBML 2462

From now on Gorton periodically sent Elgar possible texts for him to set. "I dosed him with libretto, including some of my own, but it all went into the waste paper basket", Gorton said later.

The Morecambe executive went ahead with its plans for 1902. Sir Frederick Bridge was once again commissioned to write a humorous cantata for combined performance by the children's choirs. Agnes Nicholls was engaged as the solo artist, and as well as a recital she was to sing the solo part in a choral work during the Friday evening concert.

A week before the Festival began Gorton wrote to Elgar.

> The Rectory, Morecambe
> April 24 [1902]
> Dear Dr. Elgar
> I send you our Festival Book - In the hope that it may next year include a work of yours - I once more try some words - Do they not embody the [Boer] war sorrow which saddens many hearts - and could you not go where words fail to comfort -
> Yours vy truly
> C.V.Gorton[14]

The 1902 Festival began on 30 April. The number of competitors had increased by over seven hundred to almost four thousand. Gorton's disappointment at his failure to secure Elgar's attendance at the Morecambe Festival was in part tempered by the presence of F G Edwards, editor of *The Musical Times*, who wrote a highly complimentary article entitled 'The Morecambe Musical Festival, by one who was there', for the June issue.[15]

The first day was devoted to children, and at the evening concert the combined choirs of some four hundred voices under Dr McNaught gave the first performance of Bridge's cantata *The Spider and the Fly*. Edwards was favourably impressed: "The children followed their conductor in a manner that would have put many an adult choir to blush, if not to shame".

The second day was without competition, but in the afternoon Kendrick Pyne, the organist of Manchester Cathedral, gave a recital at St Laurence's church, at which Agnes Nicholls also sang. In the evening Dr Pyne lectured on 'The organ and its evolution'.

14. EBML 2449
15. vol xliii, 388-391

The large increase in the number of competitors placed an unbearable strain on the arrangements for the Saturday, with the result that some of the smaller open classes, such as trios and quartets (both vocal and instrumental) were now included into Friday's "local" competitions. Mackenzie, who was adjudicating, said that one of the highlights of the Festival was the accompanied mixed voice quartet class. The tests were Brahms's Op 92 quartets, and the winners were the Manchester Orpheus Quartet, in which the soprano was blind. "The unity and expressiveness of the rendering of those beautiful compositions calls for high commendation", Edwards remarked. At the evening concert, when the various winners performed, Agnes Nicholls gave a recital, and was the soloist in Schubert's *Song of Miriam*, given by the combined local choirs under McNaught.

There was an audience of 6000 for the open day on Saturday, when "the muster...was on an even more imposing scale than usual", as Arthur Johnstone reported. In the open female voice class the winners with 118 out of 120 were the Southport Vocal Union, but great interest was shown in the choir finishing second. They were the Manchester Girls' Institute choir, who beat the formidable opposition of the Blackpool ladies into third place. The girls were mill-workers from the Ancoats district of Manchester, one of the poorest areas of 'Cottonopolis', and so impressed was Edwards with their performance that he asked the conductor, Miss Ashworth, to provide some particulars of the choir, as "the philanthropic potentialities of music, as exemplified in the achievements of these Manchester girls, appealed to me so strongly". Miss Ashworth's remarks, together with those of Mr Townsley, conductor of the Nelson Congregational Orchestra, formed the basis of an article entitled 'Millian Music', which also appeared in the June issue of *The Musical Times*. In his introduction to this article, Edwards took the London music critics to task:

> Popular music - of a good kind, of course - does not receive the attention it deserves by writers on music. Take, for example, the musical critics of the London press, with their circumscribed beat and their pathetic experiences. Excepting the provincial festivals in the gooseberry season, when editors are glad of copy, these important gentlemen of the press, like the old Christy Minstrels, 'never perform out of London'. If some of them could have found their way to the recent Festival at Morecambe they would have had their eyes opened to an important and far-reaching educational movement.[16]

16. loc.cit., 391

The smaller mixed-voice choir class was won by Kendal Madrigal Society from an entry of no less than fifteen choirs. This year saw a division of the male-voice choirs into two classes: the smaller class (sixteen to thirty voices) with an alto lead; and a larger open class (twenty-four to forty voices) with a tenor lead. The Kendal choir won the smaller class, and Southport completed a double in the larger class with a one-point victory over the redoubtable Manchester Orpheus. Ten choirs took part in each class, and the *Manchester Guardian* reported: "A very high standard [was] reached not only by the winning choirs but by several others as well".

In the string orchestra class, the *Serenade* by Goetz was the test for the two entries, Nelson Congregational and Colne, the former winning by a convincing nine marks. However the positions were reversed in the full orchestra class, for which Weber's *Oberon* overture provided the test. Edwards, while acknowledging that "the playing of all three orchestras was exceedingly creditable" felt that "the wisdom of the choice...as a test piece for amateur orchestras is doubtful". Johnstone, on the other hand, found *Oberon* "an admirably well-chosen piece", and the renderings by the orchestras from Nelson and Colne "were in the highest degree interesting...It is most extraordinary that with ranks partly filled up with quite young people, girls and boys, such results as these two orchestras achieve should be possible. Both conductors are evidently most effective disciplinarians, besides being intelligent musicians, and the performances that they get from their players have nothing in common with the ordinary half-hearted amateur work, with shifting intonation, ragged entries, happy-go-lucky phrasing, and clogged rhythm. Their renderings of the beautiful *Oberon* music were both most enjoyable".

Only five choirs competed for the Challenge Shield in 1902. Presumably the extremely high standards now being achieved by the top choirs deterred many would-be entries. In the afternoon session the test pieces were Ward's five-part madrigal *Hope of my heart* and Brahms's *The Maiden*, "an amazingly difficult part-song", according to Johnstone. In the evening were added Elgar's *O happy eyes* and Brahms's *O lovely May*. Both the Brahms pieces were published by Simrock especially for the Festival to translations by Charles Gorton. Edwards wrote in *The Musical Times*:

> It is no exaggeration to say that the singing of these choirs reached the high-water mark of choral excellence.

Johnstone eulogised in a similar vein:

> With three out of the five choirs - those of Blackpool, Saltaire, and Morecambe - the adjudicators had a difficult task, the performances of all three being of such excellence that they left very little scope for fault-finding of any kind.

In Johnstone's opinion the Morecambe Madrigal Society under Howson should have won:

> At the evening concert the two unaccompanied part-songs were sung by the Morecambe choir...without the slightest loss of pitch. The keys were quite different, the Brahms piece being in C major and the Elgar piece in E flat, and in each case the singers ended in exactly the right key. This particular technical feat I have only heard accomplished on two former occasions, the singers in the one case being the Manner-Gesangverein of Cologne, and in the other the choir of Magdalen College, Oxford. But besides the marvellous exactness of intonation, there was every other quality of fine choral singing in the performance of the Morecambe choir, the dynamic gradations, phrasing, and style being almost unimpeachable. Yet their performance was not considered the best, and the first prize went to Blackpool, who had not kept the pitch quite exactly but had appealed to the adjudicators more strongly than any other choir by their absolute beauty of tone. Very possibly the decision was just, but I suspect that had the prize been something divisible the adjudicators would have divided it between Morecambe and Blackpool.

As it was, Blackpool retained the Shield, and thus won the trophy for the third year running. The margin of victory, even allowing for Johnstone's remarks, was seven marks, 233 to 226, with Nottingham third on 223 and Saltaire fourth with 221. Morecambe gained some consolation by winning the Novello prize - music to the value of £5. This was awarded for an aggregate mark in the open choir class and competition music, which this year was 'The Procession of the Ark' from Mackenzie's oratorio *The Rose of Sharon*. The performance of this piece, conducted by the composer, was the chief feature of the concluding concert on the Saturday evening. The day had been so full that the Weber overture had to be abandoned in the concert, as there had been no time for the combined orchestras to rehearse it.

Arthur Johnstone's conclusions must have delighted Gorton and Howson:

> It may be doubted whether the observer can lay his finger on any single event or institution more typical of our recent musical progress than the spring meeting at Morecambe. Year by year the standard improves, and the open competitions on the final day acquire greater interest...The arrangements - necessarily very complex, owing to the great number of the competitors - all worked satisfactorily, and the impression left by the day's proceedings was of the best possible kind...One feels that there must be a future for the music of this country when such a festival is possible.

Similarly, the impressions gained by Edwards were just the sort of national advertisement that Morecambe required:

> The apparent good feeling which prevailed between the victors and those who were unsuccessful was a marked feature of the contests. There appeared to be a total absence of 'bad blood'. The good of the cause (of music) seemed to animate all who competed and took part; the sporting element was, happily, conspicuous by its absence. In this respect, and also from the educational point of view, the Welsh people at their Eisteddfodau may learn a valuable lesson from the fine spirit of the competitors at Morecambe.

For his Festival sermon the following day, Gorton took as his text the words of St Paul: "Whatsoever things are lovely, think on these things". He referred to the 4000 performers who had attended the Festival: "What have these people to occupy their leisure hours? What have they to 'think on'? You have little test of a man to judge him by his occupation. He may be in garden, or farm, or bank, or mill, or forge, or warehouse. He does the work of his profession or trade. You cannot differentiate man from man thus. But the buzzer sounds, or the clock strikes, and he goes home. What does he do with his leisure hours, on what are his thoughts fixed, what interests him? Surely it is something to provide ever so indirect an influence to lead him to tune his instrument, to join with his fellows in chorus, glee or orchestra, to aid in putting before him subjects of thought which elevate him - such action lies within the circle of St Paul".

The national recognition afforded by the *Musical Times* article established beyond doubt that Morecambe was indeed the "premier competition". Blackpool had reduced the scope of its festival for 1902, moving it to the autumn, cutting it down to three days, and confining it to competition rather than ambitious concerts.

It was a happy coincidence that the town of Morecambe celebrated the granting of its civic charter on the same day in June 1902 that

Morecambe seafront looking south. The old Midland Hotel is on the left.

Charles Gorton was made a canon of Manchester Cathedral[17]; seeing how much he had done in thirteen years to advance the name and reputation of Morecambe as a resort: not least through the success of the music festival.

It was imperative that to retain its supremacy the momentum created by the success of the 1902 Festival should not be lost, and so Canon Gorton determined to try again with Dr Elgar. During that summer McNaught was forced to take a complete break from work for three months owing to ill-health, so Gorton was forced to go it alone. The executive was due to meet on 4 July, but try as he might Gorton could not evoke a definite response from the composer before then. At the meeting therefore it was hoped that "Dr Elgar would be seen in the adjudicators' box at the next Festival and that he would write something for competition".

The Canon had every reason for optimism. Elgar had been greatly impressed by Edwards' complimentary article in *The Musical Times*, written by a man whose musical views he knew and trusted. And in May that year the Lower Rhine Festival at Düsseldorf had given a wonderful performance of *The Dream of Gerontius*, after

17. Morecambe is now in the Diocese of Blackburn, which was formed from part of the old Manchester diocese.

which Germany recognised that Elgar was a composer to be reckoned with. Richard Strauss, speaking at the reception following the concert, said:

> I raise my glass to the welfare and success of the first English progressivist, Meister Edward Elgar...

The German musical journal, *Allgemeine Musik-Zeitung* commented:

> With that work England for the first time became one of the modern musical states.

Among the English people attending the performance was Robert Howson. Arthur Johnstone, who was covering the Festival for the *Manchester Guardian*, and who had persuaded Howson to go to Düsseldorf, introduced him to Elgar, and the two men had a long conversation. Elgar, whose experience of amateur musicians was not always favourable, was impressed by Howson's perceptive musicianship, and promised to consider carefully the possibility of attending the next festival at Morecambe.

The growing reputation of *Gerontius*, with forthcoming performances of it at the Three Choirs and Sheffield Festivals helped to dispel the depression of 1901 and to create in Elgar a happier frame of mind than for some time. In response to a commission from Birmingham for a new work for the 1903 Festival, he had decided to write a large-scale oratorio on the life of Christ, called *The Apostles*. It was a theme that had been in his mind since childhood. At the end of July Elgar spent a week at Bayreuth, and soon after his return he received a letter from Gorton:

> The Rectory, Morecambe
> July 31 [1902]
>
> Dear Dr.Elgar -
> The Shakespeare Society under the guidance of Dr.[Frederick] Furnivall [1825-1910] elected Robert Browning as their president, he would not accept the post so for 10 years the list of officers was printed, headed with
>
> ["]President (vacant till R.Browning accepts the post)["]
>
> patience & faith were rewarded, and at last Rob. Browning became President, which things are an allegory - for so we must importune you, till we see you at our Festival, and render some work by you -

To get a work for next May may now be hopeless, but will you write a part song, and will you occupy judges seat with Dr. Macnaught[sic], for two or three of the events -

We do not wish to tie you down to any scheme of marks[.] We simply want [you] to give your impressions on a few of the competitions on the Saturday -

As to fees, I think I may say we shall be glad in this matter to do what you think right -

For the adjudication only I would suggest 20 guineas, or 30 guineas for this & part song.

There are 3 songs to be selected[:] the other two usually Brahms - Mr.Arthur Johnstone promised to put our plans before you -

So please write & say you will come.

We are asking Mr. Plunket Greene also -

We thought of taking a Väter Gruft by Cornelius [for] baritone and unaccompanied chorus - If you would prefer to write a work of this nature to part song we should be equally glad. The Festival will take place last 3 days of April, first day of May -

Some assistance in adjudication [on] May 1st is all we ask -

If you can come I trust that you and Mrs.Elgar would stay with us - and permit us to defray railway fares -

We were rejoiced to hear of the fame of Gerontius at Dusseldorf.
I remain yours vy truly
C.V.Gorton[18]

Craeg Lea, Wells Road, Malvern
Augt 1: 02

Dear Mr. Gorton :
Many thanks for your letter : I am going to take a few days to 'consider' - I should like to [do] all you wish but dates are filled up, & brains are empty - I'll try and equalise things somehow & let you hear.

Our warmest thanks for your kind hospitable offers & kindest regards.
Yours sincly
Edward Elgar

18. EBML 2452

The Rectory, Morecambe
Aug 5
recd.Aug 6.02[in Elgar's hand]

Dear Dr. Elgar -
Many thanks for your kind letter -

If you could come we should propose to take your Banner of
St.George, and lest we should give anything but a satisfactory
rendering - we should bring orchestras & choirs to Morecambe on the
Friday night, so as to get a sufficient rehearsal - As this will mean a
reorganisation of our Festival, we should be very thankful to know if
this is possible for you - and whether you would conduct the work -

If this were arranged, it would prevent you being tied down in any way
as an adjudicator - only we should hope you would give your
impressions on two or three classes - also we should much like the
part song -

We propose to take as one subject [for the orchestral class], the
intermezzo Dorabella [from the Enigma Variations].

As you are hesitating on the brink, I am trying to give you an extra
push -
I remain yours vy truly
C.V.Gorton[19]

Elgar was preparing to go on holiday in Cheshire, but before he went
he wrote to Gorton finally agreeing to come, and to write a part-song.
However, he suggested that Morecambe might consider the
Coronation Ode as the work to be performed.

The Rectory, Morecambe
Aug 8 [1902]

Dear Dr.Elgar -
The good news makes us feel very elated -

We have not absolutely made choice between the Coronation Ode, and
the Banner of St.George -

At the Kendal Festival which is close to ours they are taking the Ode -

The advantage of the Banner is the absence of soloists - We should
have to engage these for this work alone as we have no time on
Saturday for solos of any kind. Again the soloists would be imported,
and we wish to produce on Saturday only what is home grown -

19. EBML 2448

The earlier in the Festival, which begins on the last Wednesday in April ending on May 1st, you can come the better we shall be pleased - the rehearsal will be on Friday night, about 8 o'clock.

On the Saturday we would ask you to assist Dr.Macnaught and Mr.Percy Pitt (if we can arrange with him) in two or three classes - As to the part song, as choirs will have the two songs of Brahms [*The Dirge of Darthula* and *Dim-lit Woods*] to commence with[,] if we could have it by the end of November it would be soon enough, We will at least wait hoping your spirit may be moved.

As to fees, I suggest 20 guineas clear of all expenses, and 10 guineas more if we have the part song. If this is not satisfactory you must kindly let me know what you wish -

Again thanking you most sincerely
I remain
Yours vy truly
C.V.Gorton[20]

The Morecambe executive reaffirmed Gorton's views, and on 3 September the *Morecambe Visitor* noted:

It was Dr.Elgar's wish that his new work the Coronation Ode should be performed, but seeing that the Kendal Festival Executive have already announced this work for performance it has been decided, subject to Dr.Elgar's consent, to substitute The Banner of St.George.

Elgar's decision to attend the Festival was now made public and appeared in the musical press. On 13 September the *Musical News* commented:

The executive of the Morecambe Musical Festival have been successful in securing the co-operation of Dr.Elgar as conductor for next year, and it has now been decided that the magnum opus of the 1903 Festival shall be a performance of that eminent composer's Banner of St.George by the combined amateur choirs and orchestras which have given the Morecambe gathering the prominent position it has come to occupy in the musical world...With Dr.Elgar will be associated at least two other musicians of note as adjudicators and conductors, including W.G.McNaught...

This was a busy time for Elgar, with many conducting engagements. A slightly abridged performance of *The Dream of Gerontius* was given at the Three Choirs Festival at Worcester on 11 September, and some of the more explicitly Roman Catholic sections of the text

20. EBML 2464

were changed. The success of this work in Germany led to its reappraisal in this country, and Hans Richter decided to conduct it again the following spring in Manchester.

There was also the composition of *The Apostles*, for which Elgar had decided to compile his own libretto with the help of some of his clergy friends.

By the beginning of October Gorton had heard nothing from Elgar, but was still optimistic about a new part-song.

> The Rectory, Morecambe
> Oct 8[1902]
>
> Dear Dr.Elgar
> I send you the Brahms which will be taken at the Festival -
>
> Have you been able to find any words which may lead us to hope that we may have something from you to go with the Brahms -
>
> How strange it is that the best pastiche songs do not seem to ally themselves to music - except with Shakespeare -
>
> We shall publish our syllabus leaving blank spaces, in the hope that before the end of the year we may get something from you -
>
> I enclose words of a song which I published in some magazine when I was a lad -
>
> Please do not laugh at them -
>
> I have watched with keen interest the growing knowledge of Gerontius and hope to hear a worthy rendering in Manchester in March - I know none of my fellow clergy who were not horrified at the preposterous action of the committee at Worcester in bowdlerising the Dream -
> With kind regards
> Yours sincerely
> C.V.Gorton[21]

Within three weeks Elgar had selected some words by the Manx poet T E Brown (1830-97)[22], which Gorton had sent to him, and wrote to the Canon with the news that he had written a new part-song. However, he was also angry that as a result of press reports, several other competitive festivals had sought to obtain his services. Elgar complained to Gorton and asked for the situation to be clarified in the syllabus.

21. EBML 2447
22. Brown's collected poems were published in 1900.

The Rectory, Morecambe
Oct 28 [1902]

Dear Dr.Elgar -
I received your welcome telegram - I am glad to know that the Weary Wind of the West caught you - and now we are all anxiety to hear it translated into song –

I have written to Macmillans [for permission to use the words] -

I have acted on your instructions as to syllabus altering the first page - The newspaper reports had no authorisation from us[.] I am sorry to know that you have been so bombarded thro' the post - But may I state what we have hoped you would do -

We do not offer large pecuniary prizes, but we have secured the presence of musicians of note - and for this reasons[sic] choirs & orchestras come to us - Sir John Stainer & Sir Alex Mackenzie had both refused to attend Eisteddfods, but they came to us because they believed we were educationalists[.] After attending Sir Alexander said he would come whenever we asked him -

We should not consider that we had offered the choirs and orchestras what they might expect if we had only added to Dr.MacNaught (a master as a judge) Mr.Percy Pitt - In three or four of the chief classes, we want to know that Dr.MacNaught and Mr.Percy Pitt are free to know your impressions - Without blazing it broadcast it is enough for us to know that you will be good enough to assist to this extent -

I quite understand that you have chosen your field of work - and do not want to be pestered to be either judge, or conductor - but I trust you will not therefore feel that it is beyond your wishes to express an opinion, on our chief events if there is occasion -

When you publish your part song, if I may advise on the matter - I would suggest you keep a royalty on it - for it is certain to obtain a very large circulation - We issue 3000 syllabuses - and other Festivals borrow freely from our choice of music -
With many thanks for your great kindness
I remain yours very truly
C.V.Gorton[23]

23. EBML 2457

The Rectory, Morecambe
[no date, c.31 October]

Dear Dr. Elgar -
I enclose Macmillan's answer - You will see that they ask for acknowledgement -

How do you propose that the part song should be published - We should be thankful for it as soon as is possible in order to issue it to the choirs -
I remain
Yours very truly
C.V.Gorton -
When you come here I shall beset you with 'words' for music - [24]

Elgar in turn sent the letter from Macmillan to Henry Clayton at Novello on 2 November:

Here's the Morecambe part-song: we can talk about terms later: also enclosed is the 'permit' from Macmillan, this, you will see, is addressed to Mr.Gorton - but I suppose that's all right.
I send the copy of the words supplied to me by Mr.Gorton: you will see the punctuation is left to the imagination - I could not get a copy of the poem during my hurried visit to town, consequently the words, in the music, are not punctuated at all.
I send the M.S. (mine I mean) now because the printers may be able to go on (Can they without the stops?)
I have sent to Mr.G. asking him to let me have a caveat copy; or to send it direct to you...[25]

It is clear that Gorton had sent Elgar the words of the poem in his own hand.

[Worcestershire Philharmonic Society notepaper]
Malvern
Sunday [2 November 1902]

Dear Mr.Gorton.
I have been away - I send to Novello the pt song this day. but the punctuation of the poem you sent me is vague.

Will you kindly correct the enclosed & make it correspond exactly with the poem in the volume & send it direct to Messrs Novello.

The part song is not bad I think & not easy!
Yours ever
Ed. Elgar

24. EBML 2463
25. Moore, 378

Gorton's reply to the composer shows that, given the distinction of an Elgar première, he was keen that nothing should go wrong.

> The Rectory, Morecambe
> Nov 4 [1902]
>
> Dear Dr. Elgar -
> I corrected the punctuation, and forwarded the words to Dr.MacNaught at Novellos -
> I enclose you a cheque for ten guineas - as I first suggested -
>
> I should be obliged if you could give instructions to Novello's that the song is to be first sung at our May Festival - We have before published music at considerable expense - and found that at other festivals and concerts the work has been given before we gave it - If Novellos cannot insist on this they might issue to us the music in the first instance until after our Festival and we would insist on this condition -
> I remain yours very truly
> C.V.Gorton[26]

Elgar was conducting a performance of the *Coronation Ode* at Leeds, from where he wrote to Henry Clayton on 6 November:

> Mr.Gorton writes from Morecambe that they expect the first performance of the part-song for their festival: so will you please reserve it for them & issue the copies to them only for the present.[27]

Alice Elgar wrote to Canon Gorton the same day, acknowledging receipt of the cheque.

> [Queen's Hotel notepaper]
> 6 Nov.1902
>
> Dear Mr.Gorton
> My husband is much pressed for time & asks me to write for him & thank you very much for the cheque you kindly enclose £10.10.0 - for the partsong for your Festival for its first performance.
>
> He has written to Novello & asked them to keep it for you & it can be issued after your Festival.
>
> My husband also asks me to say he concludes you leave all commercial matters regarding publishing the Pt.Song with him.
>
> He also begs me to thank you so much for altering the announcement of conductors &c, he will of course be very pleased to help adjudicate

26. EBML 2446
27. Moore, ibid.

the principal events as you wished. He has been so rushed with sudden calls upon him to conduct at Queen's Hall[28] that he has had no time to write wh. he hopes you will forgive. We are to be here till Saturday A.M.
With united kind regards
Yrs sincy
C.A.Elgar

The Rectory, Morecambe
Nov 12 [1902]

Dear Dr.Elgar -
Of course we have nothing to do with any financial claims on the Song - We look on the ten guineas as a 'retaining fee' assuring us that we have the right to be the first to give a public rendering -

We anxiously await the music
Yours vy truly
C.V.Gorton
Please to thank Mrs. Elgar for her kindness in writing [29]

By the end of the following month Novello had completed the printing, and Elgar sent a copy to Arthur Johnstone:

Craeg Lea, Wells Road, Malvern
Dec: 28. 1902

Dear Johnstone :
Many - all, good wishes from us here to you for the New Year.

You are somewhat responsible for the enclosed - lay it amongst your crimes -

The thing is not bad perhaps & there are not many partsongmongers' harmonies.

'Twill serve.
Yrs sincerely
Edward Elgar

28. Due to the indisposition of Henry Wood.
29. EBML 2465

CHAPTER 3

THE 1903 FESTIVAL

The turn of the century heralded a large increase in the number of competitive festivals as the movement continued to expand. Apart from Blackpool, the festivals at Kensington, Hunstanton, York, Brigg, Northampton, Ilfracombe, Shepton Mallet, Ipswich, Barrow, Petersfield, Whitby and Nottingham all date from this period, and the wide geographical spread of these venues indicates that the movement was indeed becoming nationwide. Composers were now commissioned to write test pieces: for instance, the young Ralph Vaughan Williams wrote a part-song for ladies' voices entitled *Sound Sleep* for the East Lincolnshire Festival in April 1903.

The outstanding performance of the Blackpool Glee & Madrigal Society at Morecambe and elsewhere led to their appearance at the Schiller Anstalt in Manchester in January 1903. When the concert was first announced, Arthur Johnstone took the opportunity to challenge the musical establishment of the city about its attitudes:

> Little or nothing has yet been done by the leaders of music in Manchester to encourage the musical revival that has for a good many years been going on in the north of England, and more particularly in Lancashire...If in consequence of this engagement musical people in Manchester began to take a little more interest in the remarkable doings in neighbouring places, they might find therein less cause for sarcasm or superior smiling and more stimulus to improvement in themselves than they anticipated.

The concert was a great success, and the *Musical Times,* after congratulating the choir, went on to give credit where it was due:

> It ought to be mentioned that they have greatly profited, especially as regards their exceptionally interesting repertory, by the labours of Canon Gorton and Mr Howson of Morecambe. The Choral Society conducted by Mr Howson is no doubt one of the best and most enterprising in the kingdom. I send the programme of the annual 'Open Night'...as it may well interest readers...[30]

30. vol xliv, February 1903, 121

The nineteen songs included Elgar's *As Torrents in Summer*.

The renewed rivalry at Morecambe in 1903 of these two old adversaries was keenly anticipated, and was heightened by the knowledge that the Hanley Cauldon Vocal Society would be competing for the first time. Singers from the Potteries were no strangers to Elgar's music, the first performance of *King Olaf* having been given by the North Staffordshire Chorus at Hanley in 1896; and in March 1903 they gave what was only the fifth performance in England of *The Dream of Gerontius*, with Elgar conducting.

The continuing success of the Morecambe Festival produced further expansion and refinement. The number of competitors in the thirty-seven classes exceeded 4000. Since the programme book first appeared in 1900 the title page had comprised a daffodil motif, designed by Mrs Rawnsley, wife of the vicar of Crosthwaite near Keswick. But the increasing prestige of the event led Gorton on to more ambitious schemes. When setting up the art school at Morecambe in the early 1890s the Canon had met Walter Crane (1845-1915), then director of design at the Manchester Municipal School of Art. Crane was a distinguished painter and engraver, having produced a number of picture books for children. In the 1880s he had come under the influence of William Morris and began to produce works of a socialist nature. Gorton thus found in him a kindred spirit, with the cultural betterment of the working classes at heart. Late in 1902 Gorton approached Crane, who was now Principal of the Royal College of Art in South Kensington, with the idea of providing a new design for the Festival book. Crane duly complied, and in February 1903 Gorton was able to explain the meaning behind the design, which was entitled *Sources of Song among the People*:

> We were at pains to explain to him the aims which we had set before us, namely, the re-awakening of musical life among the people, and the recognition of the rightful part music should play in worship and in work. Mr.Crane's natural social sympathies, aided by his artistic genius, enabled him at once to embody one phase of this, our effort. His design will not only beautify our Syllabus, but it will interpret it...It must win for us the sympathy and support of all who care, if not for music, then for the social well-being of their fellows.
>
> What are the sources of song among the people?
>
> How does song help to lighten the burden, or to quicken the joy of life?

There is the cradle song; the mother lifts her head in song, whilst she clasps her babe in arms, strong, as they are loving.

There is the song of the pit; a brave, stalwart, grimy figure emerges from the earth's bowels, miner's lamp in hand, undaunted he grips his mother earth and sings a song of labour. There is the song, not of the spinning wheel, which makes its own music, but of the factory; the mill girls in clog and apron take their parts in the fellowship. There is the child, as ready for dance as for song. There is the fisherman with the sou'wester, a sou'wester which has proved an aureole, he lifts the song of the sea. There is huntsman with horn, the shepherd with pastoral pipe, the harvestman who sings at close of day. These, music claims, blesses and crowns.

All this might seem an artist's ideal, yet it is an ideal aimed at our festival. It is an ideal realised just where most would deem it visionary. Who is the chief of song among the English workers? Does the song issue from amidst the country lanes or village pastures, or from the coal begrimed lanes and streets? Walter Crane's design answers this question, and his answer is true to fact. That grimy head, which breaks the line, is the head of the chief singer. It is the miner of the North, or of Wales. It is the mill girl, the mill worker, the dweller in dark cities, not those who dwell softly by copse and brook, who leads the chorus of song among the people.

How is this? Smoke does not strengthen the vocal chords, dirt does not make for music. Music exists in spite of and not on account of these surroundings. What does exist in the towns is fellowship, and a few "who care".

Our aim then is to help those "who care", and to promote fellowship. At our Festival, town and country meet, workers in forge & workers in field. The towns lead the way, we set the music, open out things new and old, and they interpret. Year by year the singing from country villages and hamlets advances in merit, the children are caught up by the movement.

Surely those who have aided in the movement are thankful to know that they too have played their part, and will continue to assist; and those who are thankful to recognise that a good work is going forward will be willing to aid us in opening out fresh "sources of song & music among the people".

The presence of Elgar at the 1903 Festival obviously overshadowed everything else. Gorton gave due prominence to his chief guest in the Preface to the programme book.

We look back to the last century and respect the names of the men who will for all time be linked with the Victorian era - Carlyle, Ruskin, Tennyson, Browning, Holman Hunt, Watts, Darwin, and Herbert Spencer. We have fallen upon dull times. We ask of the present age, but ask in vain for men with any message. But those who have heard *The Dream of Gerontius* must be thankful to recognise the fact that, if in the other arts and sciences no one rises above the level, yet in music we have one who, as his fellow-workers will be the first to recognise, has created a master work, a work which must live, for it opens to those who hear fresh regions of thought...

But such an one as Dr Elgar is not an accident. What is, is never an accident. What is, is ever the outcome of what has been.

A great statesman is the product of a nation of patriots, a great general is the product of a nation of soldiers. Dr Elgar is an Englishman, and he *is*, because the English *are becoming* a people who love music.

But this love of music we must associate chiefly with the North country. *The Dream of Gerontius* has as yet, not been rendered in London, not because the greatness of the work is doubted, but because it makes too great demand on chorus and audience.

On the other hand several renderings have been given in the North.

There were last minute problems with the judging at Morecambe, Percy Pitt having been forced to withdraw.[31]

The Rectory, Morecambe
April 16 [1903]

Dear Mrs. Elgar -
I have avoided troubling Dr. Elgar with programmes - I will early next week send him [a] Festival Book, and some of the Saturday's music -

The rehearsal of the Banner of S George will be on Thursday April 30th in the evening - But we much hope you both will come early in the week - He promised me that you would come - and part of our arrangement is that we take your tickets. It is a disappointment to us that Mr. Percy Pitt cannot come, as we understood that he was a friend of your husbands -

---

31. Pitt wrote to Elgar on 5 August 1903: "I was extremely annoyed that I couldn't manage the Morecambe Festival after all: originally [Harry] Higgins [*managing director of Covent Garden*] promised to let me get off Covent garden for the days in question, but when the time arrived, said he could not spare me!" (BL Egerton MS 3303 fo.109)

I think it is most likely that we shall obtain the help of Mr.Acton of Manchester College of Music, & a friend of Mr.Johnstone's - but we have not yet definitely settled -

Mrs.Gorton will write tomorrow - Morecambe is usually very pleasant in May, at present the Lakes mountains which we see across the Bay are covered with snow -

With kind regards -
I remain
Yours vy truly
C.V.Gorton

Dr.Macnaught telephoned to your husband, because we did not wish to bring any one likely to get on his nerves -[32]

Elgar had a good deal on his mind at the time. Work on *The Apostles* had been held up by a large number of conducting engagements in the first few months of 1903, and he was still a long way from completing his original scheme. As so often with Elgar, anxiety showed itself in physical illness - a chill on the liver, sciatica, lumbago, influenza, rheumatism - and he had been unwell during the week before he and Alice were due to go to Morecambe. On the first day of the Festival Alice wrote in her diary:

E. raser[rather] tired and vesy porsley[very poorly]. Dr. East came. Did not know if we shd. really go or not.

But go they did.

*   *   *

Wednesday 29 April, the opening day of the Festival, was taken up by the children's competitions. These included musical theory; two-part sight reading; piano solo; cantata solo; church choir boys' solo; Girls' Friendly Society choir (for the Challenge Banner); maypole dancing; action songs; village elementary school choir; and public elementary school choir. At the evening concert the combined choirs sang Moonie's cantata *A Woodland Dream*.

The Elgars travelled to Morecambe on 30 April. The weather was bad, with heavy storms. They had to change trains at Shrewsbury (where according to Alice the lunch was "horrid"), and Crewe. Canon Gorton met them at Morecambe Station and took them to the Rectory where they were to stay. The other guests were Arthur

32. EBML 2455

Johnstone and his fiancée; and a niece of the Gortons and her husband. Elgar, who was a poor traveller and not in the best of health, would have been happy to rest after his journey, but Gorton was keen for him to savour the festival atmosphere, and so after a light meal they went to the evening concert at what Alice called "the wonderful Town Hall" - actually the Winter Gardens. The local competitions had been held that day, and the concert included the prize winners. These included Mr Bleasdale's orchestra from Lancaster, the only entry in their class, playing Weber's overture to *Peter Schmoll*. The *Morecambe Times* commented kindly: "They gave a tuneful and interesting performance and gained first prize, no marks, however, being announced". It is not hard to imagine the effect the performers' imperfections had on Elgar's sensitive ear. The combined local choirs gave Bach's *O Light Everlasting*, and the amateurish performance did not please him much either, as his subsequent comments showed. The recital was given by Plunket Greene, who had been the bass soloist at the ill-fated *Gerontius* première two and a half years earlier. He was the soloist in *Vätergruft* by Cornelius, in which he was accompanied by the Morecambe Madrigal Society. This revived painful memories of Birmingham in 1900, as Greene had sung in this same work on the evening before he performed so badly in both his solos in *Gerontius*. No wonder Alice's diary recorded: "Rather depressed at Morecambe at first. E. did not like it at all - the first evening".

"Nothing going on in morning", Alice wrote on Friday 1 May. The Elgars were able to relax after their exertions of the previous day, and to enjoy the warmth and hospitality of the Gorton household. "Canon & Mrs.Gorton very nice, very interesting. Nice pictures and books", Alice wrote. Of all the pictures one in particular caught Elgar's eye. It was a photographic reproduction of a painting by the Russian artist, Ivan Nikolayevich Kramskoi, entitled *Christ in the Wilderness*. He later called it "my ideal picture of the Lonely Christ"[33], and said that it depicted visually what he was endeavouring to put into music in *The Apostles*. Seeing that Elgar liked the picture so much, Gorton gave him the copy.

33. In a letter of 14 September 1903 to David Ffrangcon-Davies, who sang the role in the first performance of *The Apostles*. See *David Ffrangcon-Davies: His Life and Book* by Marjorie Ffrangcon-Davies (Bodley head, 1938), 39

*Charles and Ella
Gorton, May 1903
(photographed by Elgar)*

The afternoon programme was taken up by another innovation - a church choir festival, held in St Laurence's church. A service book was produced, and the Bishop of Burnley preached a sermon. The Elgars decided not to attend this and, in company with Arthur Johnstone, set out to walk to Heysham, but the poor weather continued and in the face of persistent rain they were forced to return.

Before the rehearsal of *The Banner of St George* in the evening, there were a few of the smaller open classes, and Elgar was in the judges' box for the first time. The number of judges was now four: apart from Elgar, McNaught, and John Acton, the Morecambe authorities had obtained the services of Frederick Corder, professor of composition at the Royal Academy of Music, as a late replacement for Percy Pitt.

Then at eight o'clock the rehearsal began. The proficiency with which the choir and orchestra acquitted themselves can be judged from the reaction of Elgar, never the most patient or tactful conductor when dealing with amateur singers and players. Alice's verdict on the rehearsal was "very good". Arthur Johnstone wrote in the *Manchester Guardian*: "He had plenty to say to the choir and orchestra... and soon placed himself on excellent terms with them". The *Morecambe Times* reported that "Dr Elgar was accorded a great reception", while the *Visitor* said that Elgar was "so favourably impressed with the success that had attended his efforts that he told them they had done 'splendidly'". Supper was served in the ballroom for everyone afterwards.

A full rehearsal on the eve of the concert involved considerable administrative difficulties. The three choirs from Blackpool, Kendal and Southport (who with Morecambe made up the Festival chorus) and the orchestras from Colne and Nelson obviously had to stay in Morecambe overnight. The *Westmoreland Gazette* of 21 March reported how the problem was to be solved:

> ...The festival committee appealed to the lodging-house keepers for gratuitous quarters for 200 choristers, in order that the additional expense entailed need not be thrown on the festival funds. The appeal has succeeded; the choirs are to be entertained gratuitously; and the entertainers will of course be entitled to a share of the glory which attaches to the visit of Dr Elgar...

The excitement and interest shown in the Saturday of the Morecambe meeting was more intense than ever before. The evening edition of the *Lancashire Daily Post* reported:

> The partisans of both vocal and instrumental competitors were in great form this morning, and enthusiasm ran high.

But Arthur Johnstone, ruthlessly candid as ever, was prompted to call for a re-assessment:

> ...the concluding day has for some years past regularly brought a most remarkable revelation of the great and significant musical movement in the North of England. The experience of today seems to suggest that a sort of climax has now been reached, and that time is ripe for some kind of change in the lines on which the affairs of the meeting have thus far been conducted. For the simple truth is that the principal competitions have grown and developed till they have become unmanageable. If the crowding and excitement was only a

little greater than in former years there was one completely unwonted feature - namely, failure to carry out the evening programme in its entirety. Notwithstanding the very great and remarkable skill that Morecambe has gradually acquired in the management of such affairs, it was this year found impossible to deal with the Challenge Shield class without the sacrifice of other important business. No fewer than eleven choirs, each with two pieces to sing, claimed the attention of the adjudicators in the afternoon, and five of the eleven were selected to sing two more pieces in the evening. This was altogether too much, encroaching seriously on the time that should have been devoted to other events.

Elgar did not adjudicate at the morning competitions, but lunched at the Midland Hotel and then went from there to the Winter Gardens in time for the start of the Challenge Shield class in the afternoon. However Alice and Mr Curtis, the husband of the Gortons' niece, were present from the start. "Very interesting competitions", noted Alice, "most *beautiful* singing". The ladies of Blackpool, with 113 points, won the female voice class by one point from Barrow St James, with Miss Ashworth's girls from Ancoats third. The first three places in the open male voice choir class were exactly the same as in 1902 - Southport, Manchester, Sheffield - and the winning margin was again one point. Johnstone wrote: "The standard was quite as high as usual, and Manchester would probably have won had they sung in the evening as well as they did in the afternoon". Honours were even in the orchestral classes between the two old rivals, Nelson and Colne, the former winning the full orchestra class, while Colne won the string class by four points.

In the Challenge Shield class, the afternoon tests for the eleven choirs were the madrigal *So saith my fair* by Marenzio; and *The Dirge of Darthula* by Brahms. The five choirs who won through to the evening session were Blackpool, Hanley, Kendal, Morecambe, and Southport. The congestion caused by the large number of entries meant that Elgar was late getting back to the Rectory, and he found that everyone else had dined. However, Alice helped him dress, and they were quickly back at the hall for the climax of the Festival, the evening concert, which began forty-five minutes late. The Elgars thoroughly enjoyed themselves: "Wonderful evening, huge hall crowded, music beautiful", Alice wrote. The occasion was, of course, the first public performance of Elgar's new part song. "Weary Wind *most* beautiful", was Alice's comment. The judges' remarks on the performances of the song, later recorded in the Festival report, were as follows:

<u>Morecambe</u> Transfixed attention throughout. Surely as beautiful as possible! A delicious treatment of p.6, and the end diaphonous in the extreme. Loss of a semitone.

<u>Blackpool</u> Seemed beyond criticism in the way of fault. An extraordinarily impressive performance.

<u>Southport</u> Pages 1 & 2, execution slightly troubled, lacked ease. Fine tone and the greatest precision, pages 4 & 5. Magnificently dramatic here. The last page just slightly marred by a trifling misreading of the diminuendo mark, as though needing a previous crescendo. Kept pitch.

<u>Kendal</u> Beautiful tone and highly skilful treatment. "Fell and died at my feet" an excellent point not made by any other choir so far. Very fine expression. Altogether a rendering full of charm.

<u>Hanley</u> All three adjudicators considered this a wonderful performance. Vowels and tone generally gorgeous.

Elgar's new part-song was received very favourably. *The Musical Times* said simply: "The music is not exceptionally difficult, but it is exceptionally effective"[34]. In a letter to Gorton Dr McNaught called it "picturesque and beautiful", and added that it "affords the most virtuoso choir a chance of displaying splendid technique and fascinating expression. The fact that this fine part-song was written for the occasion will always be a distinctive feature of the 1903 Festival". The *Yorkshire Post* was most enthusiastic: "Dr Elgar's latest contribution to the nation's store of part-songs is a very welcome addition to a branch of music in which there is so much that is commonplace. That is the last word that can be applied to *Weary Wind of the West*; it is musicianly from the first bar to the last, yet the composer of *The Dream of Gerontius* has once more proved that cleverness is not inconsistent with beauty, and there is a real charm in his highly descriptive setting of lines that are at once poetic and picturesque. It depicts moods rather than scenes, and the music is in thorough keeping with the words".

The point has often been made that Elgar's musical thinking was primarily for the orchestra, even when he was writing purely choral music; and this was picked up by one of the perceptive singers, as an observer later remembered: "There was a festival supper at Morecambe the night before 'Weary Wind of the West' was first sung, and I can see still the quiet amusement in Elgar's eyes as one of the basses, in allusion to that descending octave figure in the bass part "Fell and died at my feet", said, in blunt Lancastrian doric, "Making bloomin' double-bass fiddles of us"[35]

34. vol xliv, June 1903, 403

35. 'Düsseldorf & Morecambe Reminscences', *Manchester Guardian*, 2 June 1927.

The other test in the final part of the competition was Brahms's Op.62, no.3 - *Dim-lit Woods* in Gorton's translation. Elgar read out the judges' comments and announced the result. Commenting on the singing of the Southport choir Elgar said: "I wish I could find singing like that down south", at which McNaught shouted, "But you cannot!" The huge audience roared its approval. The final result was extremely close: Hanley 232, Blackpool 231, Morecambe 229. Possibly the wider experience of the Blackpool and Hanley singers gave them a slight edge over Morecambe, but there was a good deal of sympathy and high regard for the local choir, as Arthur Johnstone noted:

> Notwithstanding Mr Howson's wonderful powers of interpretation and the exceptionally fine material and perfect discipline of his choir, they have never succeeded in winning the Shield. That much-desired trophy has hitherto been held by Blackpool - a choir that is perhaps stronger in certain virtuoso qualities. On the other hand, Morecambe never fails to give, in the course of the competition, some performance so exquisite that it dwells delightfully in the memory of attentive listeners. Their rendering today of the Marenzio madrigal was certainly unsurpassed and perhaps unsurpassable.

The Musical Times summarised the respective merits of the four leading choirs:

> Morecambe is pre-eminent in artistic repose and in the faculty of penetrating the secret of different styles, and Blackpool in smartness and the virtuoso qualities...The Blackpool singers have a certain peculiar alertness which they naturally and legitimately cultivate...But while Blackpool is pre-eminent in qualities that appeal to the voice expert, a person primarily interested in the due drawing forth of the composer's meaning would be likely to prefer Morecambe. In the other two choirs, Southport and Hanley, it is all-round efficiency, or high average, rather than any differentiating point of excellence, that challenges attention.[36]

"Great excitement. Conductor hoisted up on shoulders on platform", wrote Alice. Then: "E. immensely applauded. Excellent performance S.George". *The Musical Times* was particularly impressed with the quality of the orchestra:

> The standard of the orchestral playing on the whole could only be considered astonishingly high, for one remembered that the performers were mostly working men from small manufacturing towns in North Lancashire. In rehearsing and performing his cantata

36. *Musical Times*, ibid.

Dr Elgar did not find it necessary to make much allowance for the amateur status of the instrumentalists.[37]

Arthur Johnstone agreed that the Colne and Nelson players had "acquitted themselves strikingly well". The *Manchester Courier* also endorsed the performance:

The setting would not of itself have placed Dr Elgar upon the pinnacle of fame...but when rendered with such spirit as on Saturday its excellent qualities are manifest.

No doubt because of the lateness of the hour, no speeches were made at the close of the concert at Elgar's request. While Alice returned to the Rectory, Elgar went for supper with the other dignitaries at the Midland Hotel, and after changing, walked home with Canon Gorton in the dark "thro' the mud", as Alice noted.

The appalling weather continued on the Sunday morning. Elgar stayed in bed, but Alice got up and went to the 10.30 am Mass. In the afternoon it brightened up and the Elgars went for a walk by the sea with Arthur Johnstone and Lucy Morris. Robert Howson came in after supper and spent the evening with the Elgars and the Gortons. Elgar revelled in the cultured, intelligent company and spoke at length about *The Apostles*. As composer and librettist, he struck a sympathetic chord in the musician and the clergyman, who were both delighted with the news of another Elgar oratorio. Elgar also discovered that Gorton was a regular contributor to an educational monthly called *The Parents' Review*. He had written a number of articles on nineteenth-century art and literature, including Browning and Holman Hunt, and had recently completed a critique of Tennyson's *In Memoriam*, due for publication in the autumn, a copy of which he lent to Elgar for his comments. The subject of the next Morecambe Festival was raised. Elgar provisionally agreed to attend, and was asked whether further test pieces might be forthcoming. The previous autumn he had completed a set of five male voice part-songs to words from the Greek Anthology, and on hearing this, Gorton and Howson declared an interest, and asked to see copies. But although Novello had had the manuscript for some time, there was no sign yet of their publication. (On his return home, Elgar wrote to the firm: "Could the printing of the *TTBB* things be hastened? I am asked a great deal about things for next season's competitions & have suggested these pt-songs - shortly people will be wanting to *see* them before deciding. I

37. ibid.

think they will include the whole set at Morecambe")[38]

Canon Gorton had persuaded the Elgars to stay over on the Monday so as to have a day in the Lake District, but when they woke it was once again pouring with rain. They were somewhat uncertain about going but in the end were persuaded by Mrs Annie Gandy, who lived at a country house called Heaves near Sedgwick, just south of Kendal. She was a purposeful and vivacious lady who had been associated with the Morecambe Festival from the beginning. The rain showed no signs of abating but they drove first to Kendal, and then after lunch at Heaves they visited the picturesque village of Levens, finally returning on the train via Lancaster. Alice recorded in her diary: "Pleasant day in spite of weather".

In the evening Gorton and Howson sprang a surprise on Elgar. Unknown to the composer, they assembled members of the Morecambe Madrigal Society in the hall at the Rectory, and the choir sang the part-song *O Happy Eyes*. The Gorton's twelve-year-old daughter Helen later recalled Elgar saying: "I never realised I had written anything so beautiful"[39]. The Gorton children successfully brought out the playful side of Elgar's character: he had a particular rapport with eight-year-old Christopher.

The sun finally appeared on Tuesday morning. Gorton was keen for Elgar to experience the beneficial effect which the Festival had had on the local children, so they went across the road to the Morecambe National School, whose choir had won the Challenge Shield in the public elementary school class the previous Wednesday. The children sang their test piece, and also a couple of anthems. Elgar wrote in the school log book: "Heard with the *greatest* pleasure (& surprise) the really beautiful singing of the school children: a revelation to me. Edward Elgar". Alice too thought that the children sang "quite beautifully". The weather broke again on their journey home. Immediately they returned Elgar sent Christopher a postcard showing a picture of himself with the words: "We are just safely home. I am sorry you had not a *real* card of the festival so I send you this".

The triumphant outcome of Elgar's attendance at the Morecambe Festival had not only exceeded all Charles Gorton's expectations but had opened up the possibility of new horizons, not only musically through the Festival but personally through his offer of help with *The Apostles*.

38. Moore, 433.

39. Young (1956), 344

The Rectory, Morecambe
May 5 *[Gorton mistakenly wrote May 4]*

My dear Mrs. Elgar -
After you left I could but express my feelings to my wife in a parable -

A little child was brought up on the banks of St.Laurence[.] Later in life aetate 12 she was taken by her mother to Geneva, her mother & friends were moved by this peak & this fall - the child remained in silence - at last her mother said "Elsie you don't seem to admire anything["] - sorrowfully said the child "I can't help it Mother - It's Niagara has done it" -

Not that Dr.Elgar is Niagara - but they whose eyes are opened know 'That God at the fountains far off has been raining'[40]

I cannot tell you how I value the privilege which has been ours, and in a singular degree mine, it must leave life the richer - We hope the journey has not tired you both - and that he may return to some extent refreshed to deliver his great message [ie. *The Apostles*] - I enclose a cheque, which I would ask you kindly to pay in to his account - I know he cares nothing for such things, but we on our part hope we are not imposing on him by the smallness of the sum -

I will send you some of our literature. Mr.Howson has already secured The Bavarian dances, & the Te Deum - the prospect of his consenting to come again, makes the way clear for next year -

There is so much that I leave unsaid
I remain with kindest regards
Yours vy sincerely
C.V.Gorton[41]

---

40. Words by Longfellow, set to music by Elgar in his part-song *As Torrents in Summer*
41. EBML 2458

CHAPTER 4

'SOMEWHERE FURTHER NORTH'

Back in Malvern, Elgar returned to *The Apostles*. He was now seriously behind schedule: more than half of the enormous project was still to be composed, let alone orchestrated, and Elgar feared a repetition of the disastrous première of *The Dream of Gerontius* three years earlier.

[Worcestershire Philharmonic Society notepaper]
Malvern
May 7 : 03

My dear Canon Gorton :
I have had no moment of peace since my return home or I wd. have written. Many thanks for the cheque safely recd. - I think the amount seems to be more than we decided upon, but I have no record & must leave it to you. I hope however the commercial results warrant your very generous enclosure.

I am *hoping* to write fully to you about your festival but really have no minute free. My wife thinks you may like to have a photograph so I have signed one.

With kindest regards to you all
Yrs ever
Ed.Elgar

The Rectory, Morecambe
[n.d., c.8 May 1903]

My dear Mrs.Elgar -
I received this morning to my great pleasure the most excellent photograph of your husband - I did not think a photograph could give so much - those I have seen before give the house but not a glimpse of the tenant - The kind words he has written at the back will prevent me putting it in a frame -

I send you a spare copy of the festival book - also a book of last year's report - Dr.Macnaught will issue details - but if between arrival of proofs Dr.Elgar would be good enough to write a few paragraphs of general impressions it would prove of the utmost possible value -

He would be amused at some press notices - the Manchester Courier writes that the Banner of S.George would not have in itself have [sic] placed Dr.Elgar on the pinnacle of fame - 'for indeed the words of the poem *are scarcely on the same level* as the Dream of Gerontius'!!

My wife & I send you a memorial of your damp day at Levens - in the hope that we may visit the spot again with you in the glory of sunshine -

We are looking forward to the Apostles - I should be so grateful for a copy of the libretto - The literary side appeals to me in the first instance - I have to grow to the other - Its fulness I can never hope for in this world - I stand now with the gates only ajar

With kindest regards from us all
Yours vy sincerely
C.V.Gorton[42]

A photograph of Elgar was also sent to Howson.

45 Lansdowne Cres, Leamington
May 26 1903

Dear Mrs Elgar,

I have been prevented through sickness from acknowledging your great kindness in providing for me Dr.Elgar's photograph. Will you please thank the Dr for his most welcome gift, which I shall always prize very much indeed?

His visit is a great event in our Festival annals, & it is gratifying to know that he enjoyed it. I do hope his mind will hold good as to coming again next year.

All the kind things he has said of us - & especially his promise to write a part song for the Madrigal Society - has I'm afraid given us what is known in the north as a 'keen edge' on ourselves. But at any rate we shall strive to deserve it all, & to live up to it.

I am looking forward to the Birmingham Festival & the production of the new work. I do hope the Chorus will rise to the occasion!

You hinted when you were in Morecambe that there was a possibility of my studying the short score beforehand. Is such a thing possible? But please don't hesitate to say if there is the smallest difficulty. I know it would be a most unusual privilege & I should never have dreamed of suggesting such a thing had you not mentioned it.

With kind regards to yourself & Dr Elgar
Believe me
Your very obedient Servant
R G W Howson

42. EBML 2459

P.S. I have got the Bav[arian].High[lands choral suite] which I venture to think will suit us 'down to the ground': & if you *do* favour us with a visit next year we should be only too delighted to sing you No.5[*On the Alm*], & the others as well
RGWH[43]

By the last week in May, and with the deadline for the festival report fast approaching, Gorton had received nothing from Elgar. He wrote again, this time to Alice, on the pretext of telling her how he obtained a replacement of the Kramskoi picture which he had given Elgar at Morecambe.

The Rectory, Morecambe
May 23 [1903]

Mr dear Mrs. Elgar

You will be glad to hear that I have received another copy of the picture - Some years since I had been lecturing on Browning [*at the Parents' National Educational Union College at Ambleside*] and afterwards drove to the train at Windermere with a Mrs. Dr.Webb - she had a very important engagement in London - When we reached the platform the train was disappearing - I seized the station Master & said ["]You *must* bring that train back["], and strange to say he did - Her friend has the only negative of the picture & as a token of gratitude, and also because I told her she was helping with the Apostles she has sent me a second copy -

I went in London on Wednesday last to an invitation concert of the Handel Society - The singing was extraordinarily bad - 80 trebles & 19 tenors, each one of the latter improvising[.] However they sang sufficiently near to the music of a cantata by Humperdinck - Die Wallfahrt nach Kevlaar - with which I was greatly impressed, and long to hear it well rendered -

I had the great pleasure of being introduced to Lady Mary Lygon - who is all that a most gracious lady can be - and she promised to come to next year's festival & give the prizes -

We are about to issue our Festival report - I hate other folk who disturb or bother your husband - but would you in an opportune moment ask him for some statement -
    (1) As to his opinion of the benefits of the movement
    (2) as to the standard attained by choirs & orchestras -
    (3) as to any further development -

43. Worcestershire Record Office (WRO) BA 5184/1(iii)

Any suggestion he might make would be of the utmost value - We have to face the indifference of the London press - but they must pay attention to what he says -

I hope this joy-to-be-alive weather has surrounded Malvern - Would that we had had such days when you were here -
With kind regards from all the household -

I remain yours vy truly
C.V.Gorton[44]

Gorton's reference to the London press finally stirred Elgar into action. It was two weeks before the first London performance of *Gerontius*, and the shame of this delay was compounded by the fact that the choir had to be imported from the Midlands, as no London chorus was sufficiently competent yet to take up the work. Elgar was also annoyed at the total neglect of the Morecambe Festival in the London press. He referred to this two years later in one of his Birmingham lectures:

I do not think the press has taken a sufficiently serious view of the importance of these gatherings. I ventured to point this out some two years ago and many things were said upon it. My point was this, the London papers - not the musical critics - make pretensions to give us the news of the country. Columns are headed with the names of districts, news is tabulated and so forth. I read concerning one watering-place the following remarkable news:- 'Another lovely day: the corpse of a foreign sailor was washed up on the foreshore this afternoon and will be buried on Sunday'. Whether this remarkable piece of information was worth telegraphing I know not; but it seemed strange that the fact that in another place nearly 10,000 people were gathered during four days for the making of music and good music too and not a word mentioned.[45]

The "telegraphing" was possibly a pun on *The Daily Telegraph*: however, on 4 May that paper *did* carry a report on Morecambe, albeit a mere seventy words at the foot of a column, which it seems Elgar did not see. Knowing that what he wrote would be published verbatim in the Festival report, Elgar seized the opportunity to draw attention to the wonderful results achieved at Morecambe, although he was not uncritical of several aspects of what he had heard.

44. EBML 2433

45. Young (1968), 215. Elgar never forgot this anecdote; he mentioned it in an interview for *The World* for 2 October 1912 (reprinted in *An Elgar Companion*, edited by Christopher Redwood (Sequoia, 1982), 139)

Craeg Lea, Malvern
May 26 1903

Dear Canon Gorton,

I should like to thank you and the Committee for the very pleasant time I spent at the Morecambe Festival.

I was delighted, and will add surprised, at the general excellence of the choral and orchestral work; the singing of the children especially was a revelation.

In all the advanced classes there was displayed a quite uncommon appreciation of the poetical possibilities of the music, and the words were pronounced and (apparently) understood by the singers in a refreshingly sure way. Soon - a good day for art when it arrives - we shall all know the difference between sentiment and romance, and between what is theatrical and what is dramatic: these distinctions are unknown to many critics and to more performers - all of whom might have listened to a considerable portion of the Morecambe Festival with advantage.

I cannot well express what I feel as to the immense influence your Festival must exert in spreading the love of music ; it is rather a shock to find Brahms' part-songs appreciated and among the daily fare of a district apparently unknown to the sleepy London press: people who talk of the spread of music in England and the increasing love of it rarely seem to know where the growth of the art is really strong and properly fostered. Some day the Press will awake to the fact, already known abroad and to some few of us in England, that the living centre of music in Great Britain is not London, but somewhere further North.

I thought the general effect of all was so good that it is the more necessary to point out what I did not like. A tendency to over-emphasise 'points' should be checked; the innocent p too often became pp, and occasionally the ff was translated into mere noise.

It cannot be too strongly insisted upon that the artistic climax of your Festival must be the 'combined piece' for choirs and orchestra. Naturally I could only feel flattered by the choice of a cantata of my own composition (The Banner of St.George) and I was delighted with the spirit and expression given to the performance: at the same time I regret that the splendid forces placed at my disposal were not employed upon some really noble piece of music, such as Brahms' Song of Destiny. I trust some work of this class may find a place in next year's programme.

The Bach cantata on Thursday evening did not satisfy me; there was a suggested feeling of "getting it over" which was irritating. The broad, manly style of the choral writing seemed too virile for the chorus; they were too much inclined to sing it in ordinary part-song fashion. This tendency to confuse styles should be guarded against; by all means refine and elaborate the reading of the madrigals and part-songs, but do not allow ultra-refinement and elaboration of effect to weaken the broader and more masculine music written for chorus and orchestra. I am aware that the choirs singing in O Light Everlasting were drawn from smaller centres than those singing together on Saturday evening: to the latter performance the above remarks apply in a much less degree.

In conclusion I will say it was a unique pleasure to hear so much that was truly admirable, and I look forward to the next Morecambe Festival with keen pleasure; I think it amply worth a long journey to be a listener, and as the enthusiasm is somewhat unusual to the eyes of a chorally-starved southerner, may I say a spectator also?

I offer you a personal congratulation on the great organization you have called into being, and trust you may long be able to direct and advise your coadjutors.

Believe me,
Yours sincerely,
Edward Elgar.[46]

On 6 June *The Dream of Gerontius* was duly performed in the unfinished and unconsecrated Westminster Cathedral. The soloists were Ludwig Wüllner, Muriel Foster, and David Ffrangcon Davies; and the chorus was the North Staffordshire District Choral Society. The poor acoustics of the new building detracted from the performance, and many London critics were still far from convinced of the work's greatness. Fuller Maitland in *The Times* opined that the favourable comments made about the work by Richard Strauss had caused it to become a "prime favourite", whereas previously "there was no reason to doubt whether the oratorio would not meet the fate of many better works and be put straightway on the shelf".

In a letter of thanks to the choir secretary on 10 June Elgar wrote: "The whole of the work was splendidly done. The immense size of the building prevented our obtaining a great effect in the louder movements, but to those listeners who were sufficiently near, and whose opinion is worth having, the whole of the choral work was a great artistic success. Several critics who have been brought up to regard a mere shouting machine as an ideal chorus have naturally something absurd to say, but the real judges were more than satisfied, and so was I".

46. From the Report Book of the 1903 Morecambe Festival (EBM 1076).

The necessity of an imported chorus was not lost upon several of the critics. The writer in *The Star* said:

> I have often pointed out how discreditable it is that London has no organisation which can perform such a composition as part of a day's work.

The *Yorkshire Post* commented:

> It is little short of a scandal that choral music, unless it be of the hackneyed type, is so burked in the Metropolis.

It is worth remembering that most writers were agreed about two aspects of music in London: first, that amateur performances of choral music were of rather poor quality; and second, that the musical public was generally undiscerning and conservative in its taste. Several quotes from this period will suffice as examples.

Three years, earlier, in December 1899, *The Times* reviewed a concert given by the Victoria Madrigal Society: "The choir gave a certain number of inferior modern part-songs. As public taste is at the present moment, it may be difficult, if not impossible, to dispense with such things altogether".

In his comments on the 1902 Blackpool Festival, Arthur Johnstone wrote in the *Manchester Guardian* on 11 October: "Musical enthusiasm is very general in the neighbourhood, and amateur minstrels are not so backward in coming forward as they are in politer and more cockneyfied parts of the country".

The *Musical Standard* for 29 November 1902 reported that "matters are not running very smoothly with the re-organised Bach Choir. We regret it, especially as it seems to mark another stage in the decadence of London choral music. At the present rate there will soon be none at all. Happily, that form of art flourishes amain in the less frivolous provinces, where, indeed, it is strengthening its position year by year. Of course, we recognise a vast difference between the conditions of London and those prevailing elsewhere, but the metropolis should be first in everything...Many excellent concert-goers detest choral music. It is to be regretted. At the same time our lovers of choral music are impenetrably conservative. The result is the music they practise is fast becoming equivalent to a strange language".

The eminent critic Hermann Klein wrote the following in April 1903 in a prefatory note to his book *Thirty Years of Musical life in London 1870-1900*:

The English festival lives and flourishes, and remains perhaps the most characteristic feature of musical progress in the United Kingdom...As regards the future of the art in England, it is the great provincial centres that display the promise to be sought for in vain amid the invertebrate elements which constitute musical life in the huge, overgrown metropolis of the British Empire.

In a lecture given to the Incorporated Society of Musicians on 13 June 1903, W Harding Bonner spoke of the decline of choral singing; and on 16 June the *Daily News* linked public apathy to a surfeit of music:

It is all very well to gush on paper concerning the amount of music to be heard in London. Certainly it has been extraordinary, and in no year which I can remember have so many concerts of uncommon interest been arranged : but in no year has London so plainly shown that it does not want so much music. Even the concerts that have been well attended have not necessarily been a financial success. Things have come to such a pass that the average Londoner expects to get his music free, and in the future agents will find that to secure an audience at all they will have to give light refreshments gratis, and perhaps charter cabs for the convenience of concert-goers.

The *Orchestral Times* for July agreed with this and added:

The public soon get tired of music as they do of anything else, and it must be either a great novelty or a great favourite to fill the concert room now.

It is clear then that Elgar was no lone voice in his criticism, but was merely restating views which were already generally accepted among the discerning. Yet when his letter appeared in the *Musical Times* for July there was an immediate and widespread outcry, and his remarks were denounced. There are several reasons for this. First, Elgar was now England's leading composer, and his views could not be ignored, especially as they were reproduced in the most popular musical journal of the day. To make matters worse, F G Edwards had edited out the three paragraphs after the expression "somewhere further North", making it appear that Elgar's praise of Morecambe was completely without reservation. But what really seems to have goaded the musical writers into responding was the reference to themselves, especially the charge of being "sleepy"[47].

---

47. Yet Edwards himself had already berated the London critics for not attending the Morecambe Festival (see p.17)

The *Daily News* led the attack on 30 June:

> The sleepy London press, or London's sleepy press, ought to wake up after such a clarion challenge. Only too gladly would we have hied to Morecambe, where there is a bay, but there have been one or two little things to notice since the beginning of the musical season in London. Over and over again I am implored to journey to this, that, or the other provincial town to hear its choir sing, but the dates never fit in with my London work. Some day I mean to make a long provincial tour and visit all the provincial towns which have a reputation for their music. In the meantime would it not be a good thing for some of our provincial choral societies to visit London and show amateurs here what is being done in choral singing outside London?

This was mild compared with what was to come. Few of the later criticisms were as even-tempered and constructive. The following weekend the musical weeklies weighed in. *Musical Standard*, 4 July:

> London's musical critics are annually driven near crazy during the months of May, June and part of July in the process of deciding which of the forty (or more) concerts per week need their personal attention. Also, is it not to London that all the world's greatest musical artists come? Perhaps Dr Elgar would like to put the matter another way. He should remember at all events that there is other music besides part-songs and oratorios.

Musical News on the same day suggested the delay in *Gerontius* reaching London as a possible cause of Elgar's displeasure:

> Dr Elgar appears to have thought it necessary to belittle London in order to magnify Morecambe...By all means let us acknowledge the prowess of Morecambe and other towns in the north but these disparaging remarks as to musical activity in London read somehow oddly at the end of one of the busiest seasons on record, including the enlightenment of poor little London by a performance of Dr Elgar's *Dream of Gerontius*. Possibly the impatient Doctor thinks that London waited unduly long before drinking at this fount of inspiration. No matter! The Philistines have now imbibed freely, and entered the ranks of the initiated under the magic wand of Dr Elgar.

On 7 July Joseph Bennett of *The Daily Telegraph* joined the fray, obviously unaware that Elgar's letter was intended for publication.

> It seems a pity that Dr Elgar, when addressing a letter to the chairman of the Morecambe Musical Festival did not mark it 'private'. Failing this, the communication was of course published, and the world thus

got to know that the eminent composer accounts the London Press 'sleepy'. It also appears that some of Brahms' part-songs were sung at Morecambe: also that no reporters from London were present to hear them...We have not a ghost of a quarrel with Dr Elgar for expressing opinions which he honestly holds. He has a right to them and though we do not share the opinions, we respect the right. Nor are we under the necessity of defending Londoners, or any section of them, from the charge of sleepiness. But it may be put to Dr Elgar whether his attack on London was needful to the completeness of his congratulatory letter to the chairman of a festival at Morecambe.

Gorton wrote to Elgar: "Your remarks in our report tickled up the Telegraph Critic who made the most fierce rejoinder - I hope it will have a salutary effect"[48]. A week later Bennett added the observation that the "first duty" of a London newspaper "lies with the concerns of the five millions of people calling themselves Londoners".

One offended critic, Vernon Blackburn of the *Pall Mall Gazette*, wrote to Elgar personally to protest on 5 July:

Your letter of May 26 addressed to Canon Gorton (a propos of the Morecambe Festival) has been the source of great pain - I may even say, of real suffering to me. Your standpoint is so cruel that I will venture in justification to explain my position quite frankly.

You write music. I try to write literature. It matters not that my work appears in the daily papers...It has been part of my duty to appraise your work; and I have always written the thing I thought. But I as well as others, are, it seems, 'sleepy': one has it appears to go to Morecambe to find vigilance. And you give us consequently a very indifferent sort of character, because we don't go.[49]

On 10 July Blackburn's article appeared. Referring to Elgar's letter, he wrote:

It is from one point of view deplorable, from another irrational. Dr Elgar can never complain that he has been neglected...in the columns of this paper. We have always been among the outspoken and professed admirers of his later work...The fact is that Dr Elgar's scornful attitude towards London critics...is not only unkind; it is also uninformed. It is in that phrase 'the living centre of music in Great Britain' that any controversy which may be aroused will lie. The fact then remains, and you cannot get away from its truth, that the art of

48. EBML 2426
49. EBML 2821

music is cosmopolitan. Therefore, that place which illustrates the cosmopolitan art of music most successfully in any country must necessarily be the musical centre of that country...Where else but to London come the thousand and one great artists who desire the appreciation of the 'living centre of music in Great Britain'? Their name is legion; and each of these men is conscientiously discussed by London musical critics who...are always at work under the highest pressure during anything like a busy season...Anyway, when the new opera season, which opens at the end of next month at Covent Garden, calls sleepy London critics back from an undeserved holiday, we shall look also for the invasion of the critics who dwell in the musical centre of Great Britain, 'somewhere further North'.

Among Elgar's papers there is a draft for a letter in which many of these points are taken up:

'Somewhere further north' Unfairly quoted: had reference to the activity - 'living centre' & *diffusion* of music. The London critics appeared to take the reference to the press as referring to themselves:- herein showing less than their usual modesty: no reference was made to that hardworked body & I shd. be the last to suggest a wider sphere for their activity: the press reference was to the inept subeditor who prefers to give his readers something he can understand to educating them 'up' to something he cannot sympathise with. The question as to the actual state of music in London was not really opened by me: it was opened by the critics but one may be grateful to them for allowing us to find out that London (pop.5,000,000) cannot support twice twenty orchestral concerts while Manchester (pop.500,000) can. That Middlesbro' (100,000) has a concert hall practically as good as St James Hall with an organ tuned to concert pitch*: when Dr Strauss came this last summer a temporary organ had to be hired & it had to be explained that it was not worthwhile to alter the pitch of the old organ because the hall was sold to a restaurant or hotel company. There is at present no decent choral society in London although steps are being taken to remedy this under competent conductors.

*Newcastle, Sunderland, Leeds, Bradford, Liverpool, Bristol, Birmingham, &c,&c.[50]

But the torrent of disapproval was now in full spate. *The Musical News* for 11 July carried the following letter:

Londoners who are musical can afford to laugh at Dr Elgar's attempted depreciation of music in London. To a great extent he is ignorant of

50. WRO BA 5184/1(iii)

what goes on in the metropolis; he lives a long way off, and I venture to say that he has never been a regular attendant at, say, the concerts of the Philharmonic, Crystal Palace, Monday Pops, Royal Choral Society, to mention a few notable concerts, except and only when some new work from his distinguished pen is brought to a hearing. Brahms' songs are sung quite often enough in public, and are even popular among our cultivated amateurs, Dr Elgar may be surprised to hear...Morecambe is 'the living centre of music in Great Britain', so says an authority. Dear, dear me, who would have thought it!

On 13 July *The Morning Post* condescended to mention the affair:

We should not have taken any notice of this singularly ill-considered letter but that it has created a certain stir in musical circles, and very naturally has called forth unfavourable comments. It is indeed difficult to understand what can have induced Dr Elgar to commit himself to such unjustifiable assertions. No one has less reason than he to complain of the attitude of the London Press. In his journey towards fame his road has been made easy by the very journalists whom he now terms 'sleepy', seemingly because they have taken no notice of the performance of some part-songs by Brahms at Morecambe! The word 'sleepy' is indeed about the most inappropriate that could have been employed. One may well wonder if Dr Elgar has the faintest idea of the amount of work a London musical critic gets through during the year. His suggestion that London is a less important musical centre than Morecambe may be humorous, but certainly it is not worth discussing.

The Star on 17 July was milder in tone:

Several of my friends who live north of the Trent have written to me this week to tell me that Dr Elgar is right, and that the musical centre of England is not London: that if ever I came north I should have my eyes opened : that there is no choral singing in London : that music in London is merely a matter of fashion, and London fashions are hopelessly reactionary. Of course, I feel duly humbled, but am fortified by the support of London friends who find that there is after all some good music to be heard in London occasionally, and that there are some few people left in London who are not more than half a century behind the times. This seems to me to be one of the questions which never can be decided : and as long as Londoners do not persist in the irritating and unfounded belief that London has the monopoly of good music, there is no harm done.

The *London Musical Courier* devoted an editorial to the affair on 18 July. It began:

> There is always food for mirth when the artist and the critic or the author and the reviewer fall to wrangling. The most amusing example of it has just transpired. Dr Elgar has acquired great fame, and has achieved by right a position of the first importance among contemporary musicians, and yet for some reason he has gone rather out of his way to attack the London press, which has done so much for him. The occasion was a recent musical festival which is holden yearly, we believe, on the shores of Morecambe Bay, and is one of the not inconsiderable attractions of that charming locality. It is a music meeting of no great dimensions or pretensions; but it is the outcome of honest, hearty love of the art of music, and it enlists the sympathies of many music-lovers in northern England. Naturally, however, it fails to make quite the same amount of stir down here in the south, and a large proportion of concert-goers in London may be pardoned if they are almost unconscious of its existence.

Such damning with faint patronising praise must have confirmed the truth of Elgar's remarks to every northerner. The article went on:

> To speak of Morecambe as in any sense a rival to London is too absurd for serious discussion. What Dr Elgar was thinking about when he permitted himself to make such a comparison we can never hope to know, but that he is wrong entirely we have no doubt at all.

Thereafter the excitement largely died down, and the musical world turned its attention to other matters. But this skirmish was in reality only a curtain raiser to the main conflict between Elgar on one side and the press and musical establishment on the other. This took place two years later, when Elgar began his series of lectures from the Chair of Music at Birmingham University. He was an outspoken and forthright speaker: W H Reed, Elgar's biographer and one of his closest friends, once wrote: "Even in an ordinary short speech he would let a word or phrase drop which had the effect of annoying someone and which, if he had stopped to consider it, he might have left unsaid"[51]. Like many brilliant men Elgar was not always able to convey accurately what he wanted to say, and was often genuinely misunderstood : nevertheless from this time forward there were those who were not slow to oppose him if an opportunity presented itself.

51. Reed, *Elgar* (Dent, 1939), 89

CHAPTER 5

THE 1904 FESTIVAL

By the beginning of July 1903 the Morecambe executive had met and were making plans for the next festival. Elgar's provisional promise to attend, combined with the congestion in the open classes, caused the committee to opt for a five-day festival.

The Rectory, Morecambe
July 3 [1903]

Mr dear Mrs Elgar -

I enclose you the report of the Festival, it should have great educational value -

I do not like to break in upon your husband while he is brooding upon his great Theme - but we mundane people must make our plans - We have fixed our Festival next year for the week ending April 30th - To prevent crowding we propose to extend to 5 days -

This is somewhat what we propose -
Tuesday afternoon [-] Church Choir Festival -
evening - Stabat Mater of Palestrina etc
Wednesday - children's Day
Thursday - Local choirs
Friday - main rehearsal of work -   G.F.S. classes
    "   evening - work conducted by *Dr.Elgar*
Saturday - open competitions

All our hopes are centred on your husband's kind promise to come -

As to financial aspect I would suggest 30 guineas and if he can give us the part song he will

I will bombard him with 'words' later on -

Now will you kindly let me know if these proposals meet his wishes -

I hope your husband is keeping well - I am sure it is vital that he should not permit himself to be worried, or over worked -

I hope when you can you will permit me to see the remainder of the libretto - I am anxious to know the sequel & to see what he has done with the prayers from the Didache -

Gorton and Elgar, 4 August 1903 (photographed by Charles Grindrod)

We are trying to arrange for an exchange for the holidays into Herefordshire but have not succeeded as yet -

With our kindest regards
Yours vy sincerely
C.V.Gorton[52]

Minafon, Bettws-y-coed
July 6 [1903]

My dear Canon Gorton:
Many thanks for your letter: I will come to Morecambe with great pleasure - but as to a new partsong I cannot yet say.

I am finishing my orchestration here in the quiet.

I hope to send the libretto (proof) in a day or two.

Kindest regards
Yrs ever sincy
Edward Elgar

So the situation regarding a new part-song was unclear. However, the male voice part-songs could be used - provided they were ready. At the beginning of August Gorton stayed with the Elgars at Malvern to discuss an interpretation of the libretto of *The Apostles* which he had been asked to write for publication. During his visit, the Canon enquired of progress in the publication of the part-songs, and this reminded Elgar of the delay. On 4 August he wrote to Novello:

> The Men's voice things have been delayed so long that I fear they will be published too late for people to include them in big winter schemes.
> They are anxious to see them at Morecambe, to include them in the festival programme...
> Perhaps you wd. look into the matter sometime & if publication is likely to be put off for some time you might let the Morecambe people see a proof so that they can decide if the things shall be put in as [a] whole or a selection, or if they shall be for Quartet or Chorus in their Competition: - that's really what they want to know[53]

The competitive movement was still making news. On 5 October 1903 the *Manchester Guardian* published a letter from John

52. EBML 2432
53. Moore, 466

Spencer Curwen, founder of the Stratford Festival, and an experienced adjudicator of Welsh eisteddfodau.

> I read from time to time with interest your notes of the progress of various musical competitions in Lancashire. These meetings no doubt do good but I should like to point out how difficult it is to control the competitive and sporting spirit in music when once it has been awakened. Competitions in moderation may be stimulating and useful, but if they become a chronic condition of choral music they are exceedingly destructive of art and of higher music.
>
> Wales is an example. The best musical thought in Wales is more and more turning from the domination of the eisteddfod and the combative spasmodic spirit it evokes. A leading Welsh musician said the other day that there are only two permanent choirs in Wales; all the others - and how many! - are got up to learn a single piece and fall to pieces after a few months training. This is competition run mad. Works are seldom performed in their completeness. There are but few permanent orchestras or choirs. Competitions are useful in discovering solo performers and young composers. I doubt if they help choral music in the long run.
>
> I merely desire to show the organisers of these competitions that they are entering upon a dangerous path. The more success they have, the nearer will they approach to the condition of things that has done such mischief in Wales. This sporting spirit kills the pure love of art for its own sake.

Those who knew Arthur Johnstone would not have expected him to tolerate this; nor did he. In a leading article in the same issue, he countered Curwen's arguments in no uncertain terms.

> Mr John Spencer Curwen...is unquestionably an authority on choral singing, but his limitations are precisely those which recently provoked a certain famous protest from Dr Elgar...All the peculiar evils enumerated by Mr Spencer Curwen as being fostered by competitions were observed a good many years ago by those who were organising meetings in North Lancashire. Indeed, one may say that the observation of those evils was the point of departure in Lancashire, and we are therefore a little tired of strictures on the choir got up to learn a single piece, dispersing immediately afterwards, on fragmentary performances, and the rest of the things in Mr Curwen's black list. It is evident that Mr Curwen, who speaks of choirs having no permanence and with an absurdly limited repertory as a necessary result of competitions, is entirely without knowledge of the best Lancastrian choirs, formed by the influence of competitions in their own neighbourhoods. Those choirs have as strong a principle of cohesion as any in the world. Their repertory is extremely wide. Their

conductors show immense enterprise in unearthing the treasures of the old English and Italian madrigal writers, and of the very finest modern part-song writers, such as Schumann, Brahms, Cornelius and Elgar. Every musician that goes from London to hear them is astonished and delighted. The German periodical "Die Musik" has described the excellence with which one of them sang a long and varied selection of choral pieces by Brahms. Yet of all this the typical Londoner knows nothing whatever, and he habitually talks of musical competitions as though they were all like the one that, a good many years ago, disgusted Sir A.C.Mackenzie. This is the state of things against which Dr. Elgar protested after the Morecambe Festival of the present year. Let Mr.Curwen go to Morecambe next spring; his ideas on the subject of musical competitions will be pretty thoroughly revolutionised if he does. As to the sporting spirit of which Mr. Curwen complains, we are not sure that his own letter does not exemplify it. As a Yorkshireman he seems almost wilfully to ignore the musical movement in Lancashire. The best competitions, we would remind him, are not in Wales but 'somewhere further north'.

The originator of that last remark had been completely exhausted by the composition of *The Apostles* and the preparation for its first performance on 14 October. The Elgars had already decided to leave for Italy at the end of November to spend the winter there. But before they left two events of significance occurred. First, a three-day festival of Elgar's music was arranged for Covent Garden the following March: Elgar would be expected to write a new work for it, and Richter would conduct. Then on 9 November Elgar's close friend and champion, Alfred Rodewald, died suddenly at the age of forty-three. His death was a tremendous shock to Elgar, and threatened his precarious emotional equilibrium. He became depressed, and the situation was not helped by continuing financial problems. It was almost as if Elgar believed that every success and pleasure in life had to be paid for by corresponding failure and sorrow. Before he and Alice left for Italy on 21 November Edward wrote to his friend Ivor Atkins, organist of Worcester Cathedral: "I am sad at heart, and feel I shall never return".[54]

The plan of the Morecambe executive to hold a five-day festival in 1904 thus needed amending. There would be no new work from Elgar, although he had agreed to conduct part of the festival concert. Before the syllabuses went out in October the committee had decided to revert to a four-day meeting. The festival concert was moved to the Friday evening, to leave ample time on the final day for the open competitions.

54. Atkins, 107

Soon after the Elgars arrived in Bordighera Alice sent a postcard to the Gortons.

> Hotel Royal, Bordighera
> 6 Dec 03
>
> Just a line to tell you we are here in this most *lovely* place, may move further on, but this address wd. find us - We are both, so far, much better for this lovely air. The Archbp. of York is here & E. has lent him yr. little book [*An Interpretation of the Libretto of The Apostles*] - Trust you are all well, love & remembrances from us both. Hope Mr.Howson is much better.
>
> V.sincy
> C.A.Elgar

Within a week they *had* moved on, to a house in Alassio, from where Edward sent another postcard on 11 December.

> Villa San Giovanni, Alassio, Italy
>
> We have at last settled down & this is our new home; I have taken it! However I do not want to be worried so outsiders must think Hotel Royal, Bordighera is my address. We hope you are all well: this is only to bring kindest regards & a promise to write lucidly as soon as the piano comes & sundry other furnitures, which are fixing and fixed.
>
> Yours ever
> Ed.Elgar

The weather was poor over Christmas and on New Year's Eve the Elgars seriously considered coming home. No new music had been written, and on 3 January Elgar wrote to his great friend Jaeger: "I have never regretted anything more than this horribly disappointing journey; wasting time, money and temper".[55] Nevertheless, the weather brightened and he began to compose a concert overture *In the South*, bearing the sub-title *Alassio*. The Elgars eventually left Italy on 30 January, slightly earlier than they had intended, as Edward had been invited to dine with the King and Prince of Wales at Marlborough House on 3 February.

The second performance of *The Apostles* was to be in Manchester on 25 February, and Gorton had planned to take a small party of family and friends along. It was now less than three months to the

---

55. Moore, 529

Morecambe Festival, and Gorton was anxious to know Elgar's views on the tempi of the three works he was to conduct at the Friday concert: his own 'Wraith of Odin' from the cantata *King Olaf*: Bach's *Now shall the grace*: and the piece Elgar had suggested in his report the previous year, Brahms's *Song of Destiny*.

> The Rectory, Morecambe
> Feb 10 [1904]
>
> My dear Dr.Elgar -
>
> It was with great regret that I heard you had returned from Italy - to dine either with King or Emperor - I only hope you got some thorough rest - for you will be beset on all sides -
>
> Is there any possibility that you will be at Manchester on 25th[?] Olive & Helen have saved up their money for tickets, and I hope to take them - There are several questions I wish to put to you especially regarding tempo of the Bach, Brahms & Wraith of Odin - if you are coming to Manchester I will bring the music -
>
> We get information from time to time of the Covent Garden Elgar Festival - It all makes me very anxious to be there, but there is no hope of this -
>
> I enclose our Brahms [*"Memories", the test piece for the Challenge Shield*] - it opens out great possibilities, would that Howson were likely to be able to render it, he makes progress, but it is very slow -
>
> I have constantly in mind your future development of Apostles - What will you do with S.Paul? I much hope you may be coming to Manchester that you may enlighten me - The great Dr.Richter said to some friends of my sister all that one would wish him to say - about you & your music -
>
> I must only add all greetings from the united family - to you both -
> I remain
> Yours vy sincerely
> C.V.Gorton[56]

However, Elgar was very busy orchestrating *In the South*, and completing it as soon as possible was a priority for him. He felt unable to commit himself to going to Manchester; Gorton therefore sent him the scores of the three works.

56. EBML 2489

[Morecambe Musical Festival and Competition stationery]
Feb 20 1904

My dear Mrs. Elgar

I hope your husband will not add to his work by writing - We are very disappointed that he will not be at Manchester[.] Dr.Richter is sure to give a fine rendering, and an appreciative reception by a Lancashire audience would do you both good -

I am going to Neville's confirmation on March 13th, so that I quite hope I may get to the Festival. I shall go aloft, where I hope to hear quite well, and I greatly look forward to get an insight into further developments -

I hope he realises how vital it is to us all that he should not permit himself to be overworked - but alas the deplorable weather must give him few temptations to exercise -

Will you be good enough to get him to mark generally the tempo of the enclosed, 4 choirs and orchestras practising separately will prove a difficulty unless they adopt a common treatment -

We are all looking forward eagerly to Thursday next, the expectation helps the week along - I will write after my return -

I need not say that all join in all kind messages -
I remain
Yours vy sincerely
C.V.Gorton
I enclose too our Festival Service with a hymn I have written for Plain Song -[57]

[Worcestershire Philharmonic Society notepaper]
Malvern
Feb 22 04

My dear Canon Gorton:
Here are the M[orecambe] M[usical Festival] marks.

I am sorry I have left you so long without writing but my hand almost refuses to hold the pen at times - I have written so much:- now my present work is just finished & my picture of Italy has gone to the printer I may write letters instead of notes - this looks like a feeble pleasantry.

57. EBML 2470

I hope you will be in London for the festival - when I poured pessimistic views (not grumbling views remember) into your unwilling ears at Birchwood we little thought that the most serious music wd. be required in so many places: times change.

I trust Mr.Howson is better?

I *may* travel to M'chester tomorrow & *may* be there on Thursday - very subjunctive & nothing potential in my mood: then I may see you & the children: if I do shall I learn if Christopher is growing large as I told him he must - but in reality we all have to carry the Christ child - weak puny or sick; so he need not grow too big. My love to you all.

Thanks for your hymn; I am so glad you have chosen a bit of plain song for the Service: the words are excellently done.

In greatest haste
Yours ever
Edward Elgar

The pressure of completing a new work had once more taken its toll on Elgar, and in the event he did not feel able to travel to Manchester. The performance of *The Apostles* had been eagerly anticipated in that city, and in the *Manchester Guardian* on the day of the concert Arthur Johnstone contributed an introductory article. He contrasted the subsidiary role played by the libretto in traditional oratorio with the indissoluble marriage of words and music in *The Apostles.*

...For so long a time has that kind of oratorio been regarded by the general public as the only possible kind, that even now immense numbers of persons discuss works like "Gerontius" and "The Apostles" on the old lines. That a musician should have a mind, and a message to which notes and chords are subservient, is an idea so new as to be disquieting, if not at once dismissed as absurd...Yet now comes a composer and makes the subject the chief thing, writing music that gives no one the slightest encouragement to take an interest in it apart from the subject - in short, displaying the most complete indifference to everything that used to be expected of a composer, and giving us all to understand that, in a religious work, if the music does not in some clear manner contribute to the exposition of the subject, it is not justified at all. In this respect "Gerontius" and "The Apostles" are alike. People can take them or leave them, but they cannot make them out to be pretty music, such as one can enjoy without 'bothering about' the subject. For Elgar so orders that we have to enjoy with the head and the heart or not at all. He will not allow us to enjoy simply with the nerves or by recognising approved kinds of musical rhetoric.

Johnstone went on to pay tribute to the help which Canon Gorton's *Interpretation* would be to a fuller understanding and appreciation of *The Apostles*.

> Everyone intending to hear the work should read the short and clear account given in Canon Gorton's "Interpretation of the Text". The writer is remarkably successful in bringing out the profound consistency and psychological insight which distinguish this oratorio text so very sharply from most others.[58]

Johnstone found the performance "highly satisfactory", but the audience response was mixed. "There was applause, of course...but no scene of great enthusiasm such as the earlier and simpler oratorio evoked. Some persons seem to be of the opinion that the comparative reserve of the public was caused by the extreme solemnity of the subject; that they were really impressed by the music, but in such a manner that there was no inclination to be demonstrative. In this there may be some truth; but, as 'The Apostles' being unquestionably much more austere and difficult to understand than 'Gerontius' we are inclined to accept the simpler explanation that the audience did not like it so well".[59]

Naturally Canon Gorton was overwhelmed.

> The Rectory, Morecambe
> Feb 27 [1904]
>
> My dear Dr.Elgar -
>
> I have returned with haunting memories, and with many sacred truths made the more precious - Strange indeed is God's gift to you from your study not only to build the palace, or Temple of Sound, to open up a heaven for yourself, but to spread over such a vast audience of variously assorted folk a spirit of awe, and reverence -
>
> How many have gone home with your sinless Alleluias sounding within them - with your winning invitation 'Turn ye [sic] to the stronghold' - and with that wondering comment of love - What are these wounds!
>
> As to the rendering, orchestra & choir to me seemed finer than at Birmingham - that grubby old Brodsky wept, Agnes Nicholls was certainly in the Mary an advance on Albani - [Ffrangcon] Davis [sic]

58. Johnstone, 109-110
59. *op cit.*, 112, 113

again was all a man could be - M[uriel] Foster is heart & soul in the work, [Andrew] Black better, but lacking in bewilderment & tragic force[:] *Whither* shall I go etc. had little or no power - The other men without full understanding singing as for themselves, and not losing themselves - in the whole.

You will I hope have seen Johnstone's admirable article - It is hard to tell the effect on the audience as a whole, the fact that applause was out of place & was hushed held people back - I saw many others [-] Bishop of Burnley - Geoff Sadler - and many others, these felt it to be an advance even on Gerontius - Our lively friend Mrs.Gandy said she had never felt music so much -

At the end I took Olive & Helen into the Green room to see Miss Nicholls - where I had some talk with the great doctor, and all was excitement - Afterwards I went to supper with the Actons & Agnes Nicholls & had a great time going over the experiences of the evening -

I enclose you a notice of Johnstone[:] you will see his references to my Interpretation -

I had some months since called to see Mr.Forsyth [*secretary of the Hallé Concerts*] & asked him to arrange with Novello for sales on the day of the oratorio[.] He was very kind, said he would do all he could - I wrote to Novellos asking them to see copies were sent - On Thursday morning I called - saw Forsyth - he said we have about 6 copies of your book, have written to Novellos for a supply & they have no more! I wrote to Dr.MacNaught & told him what I feel about the firm - I said 'I felt very sore - I wrote the pamphlet not for the sake of the few pounds they might choose to give me - but for the privilege of aiding where I am sure aid is needed' - for there are spiritual subtleties in the libretto not obvious to any one at sight, nor does Jaeger's analysis, admirable as it is meet the need - so that they might as well have sold 400 copies as 4 - I have asked them to supply copies at Covent Garden, but they will probably do nothing of the kind - and have asked them to issue at sixpence - which also they will probably not do -

No copies of the words are issued apart from the whole score - Could they not print the words in front of the Interpretation or side by side on opposite pages[?] - I do not want to annoy you in the matter, but it is somewhat riling to have people come to you in the hall and ask where the book can be obtained -

I do hope you have made satisfactory financial arrangements[:] they must have made a fortune over Jaeger's Book, which of course is only the picking of your brains - Forsyth told me that he had sent order for 1500 copies of The Apostles, and they could only send him 1000 -

I hope to go to London on the 8th by a midnight train - and from thence to Marlborough, returning early on Monday morning to London - Will there be any rehearsal on Monday to which I could gain admission[?] -

Olive and Helen had their first experience of a great concert - Helen I have had to leave behind me exhausted with the unwonted excitement -

I must only add our kindest regards
Yours vy sincerely
C.V.Gorton[60]

After initially thinking that he would not be able to attend the Covent Garden festival, Canon Gorton now decided to take a few days off and stay with relatives in Stockwell in south London for the festival. He went to all the concerts with his sister May, who was a deaconess. In a letter to his wife the Canon described the first concert, which was *The Dream of Gerontius.*

It was a wonderful sight - King & Queen were there, just opposite me - and the whole world of fashion -
Mrs.Elgar waved to me from a box, and Elgar just put his head forward - in the interval I went up - Mrs.Elgar kindness itself & weeping with happiness[:] then Elgar came in, how simple & how affectionate - wondering himself from an outside point of view that the fine folk should come to hear such a subject - I am going to see them this afternoon & probably again tomorrow to meet the Dean of Westminster [*J Armitage Robinson, whom the Elgars had met and befriended when in Italy*] -
It was a wonderful rendering, far finer I think than the first at Manchester - chorus obtaining exquisite ppp - and orchestra superlative - Coates was simply admirable & of course F[frangcon] Davies...
I hope the invalids are better - they would like to have seen all the fine folk and the flash or rather blaze of diamonds from some boxes - I was more interested in Elgar & his wife than in King & Queen - and so too would they have been...

To commemorate the presence of the King and Queen at the performance of *The Apostles* on the Tuesday evening, the Elgars asked Jaeger if he could arrange to have Canon Gorton's book specially bound for presentation to Queen Alexandra. The binding (by Rivière's) was of white levant, with the Queen's monogram surmounted by a crown, and cost twenty-five shillings.[61] The gift was duly acknowledged, and the Elgars sent the letter on to Gorton.

60. EBML 2488
61. See Moore, 547-8

The Rectory, Morecambe
Good Friday [1 April 1904]

My dear Mrs.Elgar -

The very busy time of Holy Week has prevented me from answering
your kind letter and for thanking you for sending us 'the letter', of
which the family is very proud - But I am an awful radical, I am much
more proud that you and Dr.Elgar should say I had got a glimpse of
his mind than that all Kings and Queens should accept my small book
- But it was entirely like your goodness to send it -

How much the Apostles has been with me during this week -
interpreting the Gospels for each day - and opening out the unseen
behind the seen - the angels witnesses, and the unspeakable mysteries
music alone can suggest - And your husband's reward is not laurel
crowns, and press notices, but the gratitude of hearts whose devotion
he has quickened -

And I doubt not that Easter will bring him fresh visions for the future
- I am sure he will set forth the Triumph 'Thou art the King of Glory
O Christ'[*from the Te Deum*] - and the vision of the seer in Patmos[.]
The storms break on the islands - doubts and fears & tribulations but
'I was in the spirit on the Lord's day' - with the wondrous visions
which follow bidding him and us 'Fear not I am the Living one'
(R[evised] V[ersion]) [*Revelation chapter 1*]

And now to come down to practical things(?). What day may we hope
to see you? We look to your husband to conduct rehearsals on the
Friday - but we shall be delighted if he would come for the Wednesday
- Clarice[sic] we hope is coming - Would she not stay at the Rectory -

If only we have fine days can we not get a few days in the Lakes, the
week following -

My dear wife keeps fairly well, but how glad I shall be when the anxiety
is past -

With all Easter Greetings to you both
Yours vy sincerely
C.V.Gorton

Your husband must be weary of seeing his name in all papers -[62]

Alice's reply to this letter contained devastating news: they would
come for the first three days only, as Elgar had been invited to attend
the Royal Academy banquet on the Saturday evening.

62. EBML 2439

The Rectory, Morecambe
April 7 [1904]

My dear Dr.Elgar

Mrs.Elgar's letter comes like a bolt from the blue. It fills us with dismay - I cannot tell what we shall do if you are not with us on Saturday - We have the most phenomenal gathering of over 2000 performers for that day - and the attractive force is Dr.Elgar - a wish to sing or play before you - I enclose you a rough draft which shows the choirs concerned -

As a Latin exercise would put it - You being absent, it will be all up with the Morecambe Festival - The chief event is the Challenge Shield class on Saturday afternoon - and if some of the choirs knew you would not be here, neither would they -

I know what an important event the Academy Dinner is but still I am selfish enough to urge the claims of the many thousands here, and the bitter disappointment of keen lovers of music -

The press now has you on the brain, and in all directions your presence has been noted, it is a penalty you have to pay - and if we set on Hamlet without the Prince, we shall have a riot.

So of your extreme goodness reconsider the matter I pray - and resolve to stay over Sunday - I dare not say more, though I could in my anxiety fill sheets.

I have engaged your rooms (they have repapered them in your honour) at the Grand Hotel - also for Lady Mary Lygon -

With our kindest regards
Yours vy sincerely
C.V.Gorton[63]

The Elgar Festival had certainly brought the composer into prominence once more and, although most of the press comments were favourable, the anti-Elgar lobby was not slow to react. In *The Times* Fuller Maitland could not resist a sneer:

One may hesitate whether to rejoice or to condole with Dr Elgar on the fact that a three-night festival was held at Covent Garden in his exclusive honour. Such a compliment was never before paid to any English musician, and every means, some of them injudicious and rather comic, were taken to show that it was a unique occasion...Whether any ordinary human being can be expected, after such a festival, to maintain what may be called his personal

63. EBML 2467

equilibrium...may be doubted. In fact, all through Dr Elgar's career the strands of good and evil fortune have been interwoven with singular closeness. His practical isolation through his earlier life from the company of those who were worthy to be his fellows among the creative musicians was in some sort a misfortune, but it allowed his genius to pursue the course of its own development undisturbed. It is partly the reason, no doubt, why the pendulum has now swung perhaps a little too far in the other direction - a direction in which the composer's friends will see not a few dangers ahead, even if he escape the ordinary result of such a 'spoiling' as finds expression in unwieldy laurel-wreaths or the striking of medals.[64]

The weekly magazine *Musical News* conducted their own anti-Elgar campaign. In four successive issues beginning on 19 March they printed articles and other derogatory comment. Elgar was only one of a "distinguished group" of composers, the others being "less fortunate than he" in being denied an opportunity such as the recent Festival to show their worth. North-South tensions surfaced again: "The band and chorus were 'dumped down' on us from Manchester..." In fact Elgar's remarks from the previous year still rankled; in a lengthy article on 9 April entitled 'Choral Music in London', the arguments were re-opened with renewed vigour:

> Although it was pointed out at the time that the distinguished composer, who was deeply immersed in his work in the quietude of Malvern, could not be regarded as an authority on music in London...not a few unthinking and uninstructed persons accepted his curious assertions, and believed that London was a factor of very little account in the spread of music in our land..."

The article proceeded to deride provincial music-making and to highlight the large numbers of concerts in the capital. It concluded: "Such is musical London now, a very, very different place to what some of those who wrote about it, and are prejudiced or suffer from Provincial deceit, imagine it to be". But Elgar was not without his supporters. On 15 April Herbert Thompson gave a measured response in *The Yorkshire Post*:

> The present moment seems certainly somewhat inopportune for asserting the choral supremacy of the Metropolis, considering that on the very day when the current number of *Musical News* appeared, a chorus from Sheffield sang at the Queen's Hall a work of importance

---

64. An enterprising sculptor, Percival Hedley, had made and marketed busts and medals of the composer.

and difficulty in a fashion that roused the unmeasured enthusiasm of the whole of the 'sleepy London Press', and that its success, if exceptional, was not isolated, but was only one of a long series which choirs from Manchester, Leeds, Wolverhampton, and other Northern towns, have achieved before London audiences.

Discreetly enough, however, the writer of this article takes the line that 'in all this argument one need say little as to the merits of performances'. Quantity, indeed, rather than quality, seems to be his test, and he proceeds to number the achievements of Metropolitan choral societies during March...But in a matter of this kind it is idle to rely on statistics. Surely every one who has had an experience of choral singing in London as compared with choral singing in many northern centres must realise where the most vitality is to be found...

I must confess that patriotism in artistic matters is among the most meagre of my virtues, but it is impossible, from a sense of common justice, not to resent the unfair tone and unsound arguments used by this writer in *Musical News*, who talks of 'provincial conceit', and gives ample evidence of Metropolitan insularity. His favourite method seems to be to demonstrate the absurdity of things which Dr Elgar did not say. Because Dr Elgar spoke of a 'sleepy London Press', as taking so little cognisance of all that happens outside the Metropolis, it is assumed that he included the Metropolis and even its orchestras in this charge of 'sleepiness': because he asserted that the living centre of British music was 'somewhere further north', it is absurdly imagined that he designated Morecambe as that centre. We are told that none of the festivals can exist without a London orchestra, when Manchester supplied the bulk of the band employed at the last Birmingham Festival, and its recent inroad into Metropolitan preserves [*the Elgar Festival at Covent Garden*] is too fresh to require more than reference...Then it is said that festival principals 'have to be brought from London', a specious half-truth, since while they all gravitate to London as a convenient residential centre, nine-tenths of them hail from the Provinces, and the large majority from Wales and the Western Counties. These are, however, questions that are beside the mark, and I refer to them simply for the sake of indicating the kind of 'special pleading' that vitiates the article, which, coming after other essays whose aim seems to be to belittle Dr Elgar's achievements, leaves behind it an impression of spitefulness not altogether pleasant.

By the time Gorton got around to replying to *Musical News* he had heard to his great relief that the Elgars, no doubt influenced by the Canon's passionate pleading, had changed their minds and would miss their London engagement in order to be at Morecambe for the last two days of the festival.

The Rectory, Morecambe
April 12 [1904]

My dear Dr.Elgar -

I heard this morning from Dr.MacNaught - We cannot bring you down before the Thursday - though of course the longer you are here the better for us -

Can you not bring your bicycle and can we not get a ride in the May week in the Lakes[?] they are then in their glory -

I have written an answer to Musical News, which I only fear they will not print -

Yours gratefully
C.V.Gorton[65]

On 23 April *Musical News* printed Gorton's letter.

...When Dr Elgar wrote that famous sentence...we hardly concluded that he meant Morecambe as the hub of the musical universe. But if you do us too much honour, I venture to suggest that you do Dr Elgar too little. It will be found that Dr Elgar knows what he is talking about...

We deal in choral music - not with the larger choral bodies - but with the madrigal and part-song choirs, and if we accept the verdict of the judges, we achieve a degree of excellence hardly achieved elsewhere. But this is not the limit of our aim - we believe that this degree of excellence renders those who take part in the competitions singularly capable of achieving the highest ideals of choral singing - where not only the broadest, but the subtlest effects are demanded. He will find that these results are not obtained merely by 'ceaseless grind' at a few stock selections; the list that I enclose shows that we have drawn our music from as many as 124 composers - that in the fourteen years since the foundation of the Festival the same selection has not been given twice. He will find that we do not bring our orchestra from 'further south'. Our orchestra are home-grown, and year by year they achieve a more remarkable degree of efficiency. He will find that we have no guarantors - the only guarantee we possess is that the type of music which we offer will fill our hall with 6000 listeners, as keenly interested as the performers themselves. That we have no deficit, but that year by year we are enabled to aid those who unite in this educational movement. He will find that charity here is not a cloak for mediocrity, and that, alas! the profits do not go 'to the support of the poorer clergy'.

65. EBML 2466

This same issue commented on the Canon's letter, under the heading 'Musical Morecambe', following it with a paragraph entitled 'Attack and Defence'.

> There is another point to which we may refer, especially as it has already appeared in print, viz. that our article was an attack on Dr Elgar. Now let us say, in plain words, that this is ridiculous. Dr Elgar is a very distinguished composer, and, in our opinion, one of the brightest stars in the musical firmament at the present day; we defy anyone to point to any utterance in this paper contravening that estimate of his position...Dr Elgar is not likely, we imagine, to claim a special immunity from the criticism which must necessarily attach to any man in a prominent position, nor does he waste his time with suspicions of shadowy enemies lurking in his path. Injudicious friends may possibly do so, but we venture to say that such oversensitiveness on their part is but an ill compliment to the composer.

For the 1904 Morecambe Festival the number of competitors in the forty classes was well in excess of 4000. In his preface to the programme book, Canon Gorton was in no doubt about the debt he owed to Elgar's association with Morecambe.

> Dr Elgar is to be with us again.
> Much has happened in the world of music since our last Festival. Dr Elgar has received 'national recognition'. No festival, no programme occurs but his name recurs; he is 'observed of all observers'. But our choirs have needed no press notices to aid them to 'recognise' him; for years they have known him as one who writes music such as their hearts desire...And now to *The Dream of Gerontius* he has added *The Apostles*. What niche in the Temple of Fame this will occupy is not for me to suggest. But there is another Temple (into which the Kings of the earth bring their treasure) and in this every devout soul will be grateful to Dr Elgar for aid to their devotion...Thus to have helped others he will recognise as of more value than laurel wreaths and public recognitions.
> We are justly proud of Dr Elgar's presence, for he would not be with us except for his belief that our Festival is guided by aims, and accomplishes ends with which he is not unwilling to associate himself.

John Spencer Curwen's periodical, the monthly *Musical Herald* (possibly goaded by Arthur Johnstone's remarks the previous autumn) sent along its 'special representative'. He was duly impressed.

> As I walked along the breezy front at Morecambe, holding my hat on, I remarked to two of the judges 'how pleasant it would be if all our

work could be done here by the seaside'. The happy holiday feeling affects the whole tone of the proceedings at the Morecambe Musical Festival. Tongues are loosened. I venture to say that the people of Lancashire and Yorkshire utter twice as many words in a day as a Southerner...Providence has been bounteous to them. Their cheery chatter and fine independence, however, acted as an excellent tonic upon the spirits of the "Herald" representative. The best lesson is to mix with the defeated competitors. They are very free in their criticism of the judges, but there is not the least sign of rebellion...These people certainly have minds of their own, and their opinions are worth listening to. How fine is their artistic sense! Cultivated by listening to the best choirs that they can hear at every opportunity, the responsibility of the promoters is serious; they must feed the minds and ears of the people with the best music, and must encourage a high standard of performance by tempting the best choirs from a distance to compete with the local choirs. Morecambe is fortunate in having workers who carry out this high purpose. It is good fortune, too, to be situated in a district which has been thoroughly devoted to music for generations, and to be within reach of teeming populations who associate the seaside resort with their happiest days of the year....
In a phrase, the Morecambe Festival is a series of competitions by day, and a series of concerts by night. A word of praise should be given to the management...Here speeches (except the judges') are never heard, and never missed. Here the next choir is in its place ready to begin before the previous choir is off the platform.

The Festival began on Wednesday 27 April with the children's competitions. Granville Bantock had been expected to attend as one of the judges, but in his absence Henry Coward joined Elgar, McNaught and R H Wilson on the panel. Local anticipation of the event was tempered by the knowledge that, due to the continuing ill-health of Howson, the Morecambe Madrigal Society were not entering in the Challenge Shield class this year, although they were one of the four choirs chosen for the Festival Chorus.

The second day was devoted to the local competitions. Henry Coward was tremendously impressed by the standard, especially of the village choirs. "It is quite a delight to know that the gentler and more refined music is receiving attention in the villages of the district", he said, "and the fact reminds me of the remark of Dr Parry that music and sport very often go together. I give it as my deliberate opinion that the men and women who are smartest at music are generally smart at other things. Some long-haired people seem to get 'mooney' in their music, but they are exceptions. The smartest, sanest people are those who take music as their recreation".

As they had done in 1903, the Elgars travelled to Morecambe on the Thursday, leaving on the 10.21 train. They had a good journey to Lancaster but Alice was suffering from a heavy cold. It was raining hard when Canon Gorton met them at the station and escorted them to the Grand Hotel. Elgar was happier at the hotel as it was much nearer to the Winter Gardens: and life at the Rectory was hectic at this time as Mrs Gorton was in a nursing home in Heysham awaiting the birth of her baby.

The Grand Hotel on the seafront had only been open for three years, but the rooms the Elgars stayed in were repapered in honour of their visit. Elgar's friend Frank Schuster arrived later. He was a wealthy patron of music, and the inspiration behind the recent Elgar Festival at Covent Garden. After a meal the three of them went to the evening concert, which included C H Lloyd's choral ballad *Allen-a-Dale* sung by the local choirs under Dr McNaught: and a selection of part-songs by the Morecambe Madrigal Society, including the 'Lullaby' from Elgar's choral suite *From the Bavarian Highlands*. Many local dignitaries were present including the High Sheriff of Lancaster and the Bishop of Burnley.

Friday was a very busy day for Elgar. He was at the hall early to rehearse choirs and orchestra for the evening concert. The four choirs were Morecambe, Hanley, Blackpool, and Kendal, and the orchestra was from Nelson. In the competition based on the music to

The Grand Hotel, Morecambe

be performed, the Morecambe choir under their assistant conductor, Mr A Davies, won first prize. The spirit of the Festival was typified by the choir's response to their win: after a hurried consultation they announced that they were satisfied with the honour of their position, and they asked the other three choirs, who had rail and other expenses, to share the prize money in equal proportions.

After the rehearsal there was judging to be done in some of the open classes, so that Elgar did not get back to the hotel until 3 pm, and missed lunch. He also missed the Festival service at St Laurence's church, but was no doubt glad of the excuse.

The Festival concert began with Sullivan's overture *Di Ballo*, played by the Nelson Orchestra conducted by Mr Townsley. Next came the Bach double-chorus *Now shall the grace* conducted by McNaught. *Musical Herald* remarked: "It was more scientific than beautiful, and the hard work upon it kept the choirs from polishing up the other pieces".

Elgar conducting at the Morecambe Festival in 1904

Elgar now appeared on the stage. "His stepping on the conductor's stand was the signal for an outburst of cheering, which Dr Elgar could not mistake as a great and spontaneous welcome", the *Morecambe Times* wrote. The *Musical Times* commented: "The singing of the combined choirs was throughout of a high quality, but the standard of the orchestral playing showed a marked falling off from that of last year, probably in consequence of the more stringent regulations against professionalism. This was to some extent noticeable in all the orchestral music of the evening, but most of all in the *Song of Destiny*, where the extended harmonies peculiar to the Brahmsian scheme of orchestration gave so much trouble to the amateur instrumentalists that the result was far from satisfactory. In Elgar's *Wraith of Odin* they did considerably better, but were still scarcely equal to the occasion". *Musical Herald* thought that the orchestra was "highly creditable" considering it was amateur, but Arthur Johnstone in the *Manchester Guardian* suggested that a better orchestra might be procured for the principal concert in future. The evening ended with a recital by the Brodsky Quartet, who played quartets by Beethoven and Tchaikovsky.

After the concert choirs, orchestra and honoured guests were entertained to supper in the ballroom, with Canon Gorton presiding. It was the sort of formal occasion which Elgar hated. "E. was bored by Bishop's wife & escaped to the other table", Alice noted. In a short speech proposing the health of Dr Elgar and the other judges, Canon Gorton described his first meeting with Elgar at Birchwood. Elgar in reply said: "How I came here I don't know, but the puzzle is how I can ever get away, and I am not sure that I wish it. Although my name has been associated with those of Dr McNaught, Dr Coward and Mr Wilson as a judge, I ask you to bear in mind that I am not accustomed to act as judge at these sort of gatherings, although there are not many on the same level as Morecambe. I don't want it to be thought I am a judge. As a judge I am only an amateur" (laughter) "but I like to give my opinion and advice as far as possible. Here I will say one word: whilst in Morecambe I like to be a judge: in most other places 'further south' I should like to be executioner". The audience loved it.

Another speaker was Arthur Johnstone, who said that English people had commonsense in politics, commerce, and sport, but not one in fifty people had commonsense in art. Even when an Englishman admitted that a performance or a picture was inartistic he tolerated it. Morecambe, he said, was doing much to make people dissatisfied with inartistic things by raising the standard of performance, and by performing the best music that they could get.

The final Saturday was as busy as ever; the programme comprised female voice choirs (thirteen entries); full orchestra (three); string orchestra (three); open male voice choirs (fourteen); open mixed voice (thirteen); and Challenge Shield (twelve). The number of competitors on this day alone stood at over 2,100. In order to prevent congestion later in the day, the preliminary tests for the female voice choirs and smaller mixed voice choirs were held on the Central Pier.

The two orchestral competitions were very close. In the full orchestra class Nelson Congregational with 50 marks just beat Colne by one mark. Rochdale Philharmonic were one mark behind that. "It was remarkable that three such excellent orchestras should appear", said the *Musical Herald*.

Once again Elgar had gone to the hall early, and was the chief adjudicator in the string orchestra class, where the three entries were the same as for the full orchestra class. The test piece was the *Nocturne* (Op.40) by Dvořák. In announcing the result Elgar said: "As an old string player, I have listened with pleasure to the performances. Dvořák's piece, which I have known since it was first produced, is a very trying one, and the renderings have been of such general excellence that Dr McNaught and I have decided that the three prizes should be divided amongst the three competing orchestras. To make the amount more easily divisible, I have added a guinea". Each orchestra thus received four guineas, to the general approval of the audience.

Frank Schuster and Alice came in later, and the three of them lunched at the Midland Hotel. In the afternoon the male voice contest began, and the two pieces were from Elgar's *Greek Anthology* settings - 'It's oh! to be a wild wind' and 'Feasting I watch'. Alice noted in her diary: "Wonderful singing, heard the Greek Anthology part-songs - beautiful". Five of the fourteen choirs were chosen to go forward to the finals at the evening concert.

In the Challenge Shield class the twelve entries sang Vecchi's madrigal *Phillida, come tell to me* and Brahms's *Memories* (Op.104, no.3) for six-part choir, in Gorton's translation. The *Musical Herald* writer complained about the lack of simplicity in the singing of the madrigal, and spoke of the tendency of the choirs to "over-paint" it with too much unnecessary expression. The Brahms piece was marked 'Rather slowly', and most choirs took this to mean a metronome marking of crotchet = 30-40. "At such a rate pitch could not be maintained", commented *Musical Herald*, "and the chromatic character of the composition also affected the intonation". Of the four choirs chosen to contest the final in the evening, Southport had built up a six-point lead with 152 marks. The 1903 winners, Hanley, had performed indifferently for them, particularly in the Brahms, and were eleven points behind the leaders. The other two finalists were Nottingham and Blackpool.

The measures taken to reduce tension and congestion on the final day had worked splendidly, and the proceedings were much more leisurely than the previous year. Arthur Johnstone appeared to discern an extra dimension in the unruffled and orderly display:

> Apart from what it does as a purely musical institution, such a festival as this would seem to merit the attention of social reformers - that is to say of every sane and sensible person. It is a very striking revelation of music as a force of discipline - a discipline that is effective in spite of being mild and voluntarily undergone...Both competitors and listeners include persons of the roughest classes. They go in and out, appear at the proper time on the platform, disperse quietly, and make their way to the galleries to listen to other performances, with no mishap, display of bad manners, or serious friction of any kind. The demeanour of these uncertified minstrels, with their innumerable rivals and supporters, and the entire general character of the occasion is such as to suggest the immensely important social influence of art which brings people together in groups to do something decently and in order... This, which is not a matter of speculation but a fact of experience, merits far more attention than it has yet received from persons who are animated not so much by the special enthusiasm of music as by a general desire for the betterment of our multitudinous workers.

The afternoon session was over by six o'clock, and the Elgars were able to dine in good time and be back for the final concert. The Winter Gardens auditorium was filled long before the concert was due to start, and to pass the time the vast crowd sang hymns, of which *Lead, kindly light* was the favourite. "Such an immense choir, singing in harmony without a conductor, is seldom heard", said the *Musical Herald*. "Marvellous crowd & wonderful order", wrote Alice. "Much excitement".

The concert began with the combined orchestras playing the overture to *The Magic Flute*, and then Elgar conducted the combined string orchestras in Dvořák's *Nocturne*. The five finalists in the male voice class sang *The Young Musicians* by Küchen, a song which the audience loved. The first prize went to the formidable Southport

Vocal Union, who gained 111 marks with their richly resonant tone. Only one mark behind came the Habergham Church Glee Union, newcomers to the Festival. Mainly miners from a village on the outskirts of Burnley, they impressed the judges with their fine voices and keen energetic singing. Lancaster were third on 109, and the redoubtable Manchester Orpheus had to be content with fourth place, having lost pitch in the Küchen and with poor balance in their solo quartet.

The four finalists in the Challenge Shield - Southport, Nottingham, Hanley, and Blackpool - had to sing Parry's *There rolls the deep*, and 'On the Alm' from Elgar's choral suite *From the Bavarian Highlands*. There was a general improvement on the standard set in the afternoon: "these pieces brought out the best that was in the choirs", wrote the *Musical Herald*. Nottingham rose to the occasion, particularly in the Parry, and although Hanley scored highest in the Elgar, they could not make up the leeway. Southport, who led after the preliminary round, were disappointing: possibly the extra exertion of their tenors and basses in the earlier male voice competition had an effect: but in the final analysis Nottingham with 296 marks won from Southport on 295, with Hanley third on 294. Blackpool were well beaten with 288, the first occasion in eight years when they had failed to finish in the top three. There was some delay and confusion before the winners and marks were announced, but as Arthur Johnstone noted: "Dr McNaught once more justified his reputation as an indispensable member of the adjudicators' bench on such occasions. There was a moment...when the dragon of chaos was threatening to emerge from its cavern: but Dr McNaught, with his fine grasp of multifarious and bewildering detail, played a good Siegfried to the crowd's Fafner and the danger was averted".

In introducing McNaught and Coward to announce the winners, Gorton paid tribute to the judges and pointed out, to tumultuous audience applause, that Dr Elgar had denied himself the pleasure of attending the Royal Academy banquet that evening in order to be at Morecambe. The distribution of prizes by the Mayoress brought the Festival to a close. As the Elgars walked back to their hotel along the front with Mrs Gandy and her husband, they heard in the moonlight some of the choirs singing 'Feasting I watch' on the sands.

Despite a slight drop in receipts, the festival remained solvent: and artistically it had been another enormous success. Johnstone in the *Manchester Guardian* wrote: "This most important of all musical festivals associated with competitions has once more been carried through to a satisfactory conclusion...That Dr Elgar should on two successive occasions have been presiding genius of the Festival is a pretty handsome testimonial to the institution". *The Musical Times* was even more effusive: "Nowhere in the world probably can one witness a more imposing display of popular musical genius as an annual event".[66]

The following morning Canon Gorton preached his annual festival sermon:

> ...This event has come and gone. It must be obvious to all that as year by year it increases, it involves greater stress on the small executive...With all this cost in time and anxiety, ought I, as Rector, to concern myself with the movement? These are questions which I ask myself year by year. And as we are staggered by the success of it, still further I ask, what is to become of it? Financially it must prove of the utmost value to the town itself. It brings Morecambe into public notice which no other event could secure for it, it brings people from all parts of the kingdom, and in vast numbers. But I am not an advertising agent, and had we undertaken the work with this end in view, we should certainly have justly failed. Still if every person who comes leaves something behind, if those who come, return, then the executive would be the first to rejoice. But the sights and sounds on the Saturday prove more reassuring. The sight of the interested groups of singers on the pier or on the promenade in the pavilion, to see them enjoy the breezes, the view of mountains and sea, not a crowd idle, listless or noisy but keen, united and interested. To hear the vast audience unite while waiting in ballad or hymn, to listen when the town is quietening to a men's choir rendering *Feasting I watch*, to hear the station and the train echoing with music and song, these are signs of a good time coming, which is said to be the main music of humanity. But these are the outward and visible signs, how much to us is unseen? The gathering together of members of a village choir in a winter's night, the patience and skill of the conductor, the discipline of those taught, and the added purpose to life. But still greater the blessing where the need is greatest. Was there not a man and dog fight in Hanley? Contrast the power and shame of such a sight with the marvellously sweet tone of the Hanley choir. Contrast the common place of Nelson and Colne, the straggling, huddled houses, the stinted groups of tree and grass, with the employing of Mozart's overture. We cannot but feel that it is a good gift from God, a vast compensation for the toilers. We are not afraid to ask God's blessing on the workers for their work.

66. vol xlv, June 1904, 394

CHAPTER 6

THE CONDUCTORS' CONFERENCE

The Elgars did not hear the Canon's sermon. They went to Mass at 10.30 am and, according to Alice, found the music "trying". After they had lunched at the Rectory, Edward rested, while Alice went with some of the Gorton family to Heysham Towers to see Mrs Gorton. She was staying there for the duration of the Festival so as to avoid all the hustle and bustle at the Rectory. Frank Schuster joined the Elgars for dinner at the hotel, and later Howson and Gorton came and spent the evening with them.

On Monday morning Schuster and Elgar went with the Canon to the National School to hear the children.[67] Alice did not go as she was still suffering from a heavy cold. They left for home around midday.

[Manchester Diocesan Loan Fund notepaper]
May 4 1904

My dear Mrs. Elgar -

I am writing to you first on business - I enclose a cheque for 30 guineas - Will you kindly let me know the travelling expenses - and I will send further cheque - I hope you did not find the journey very trying - and that Dr.Elgar does not much regret the effort - It has been - well I need not say this, a great delight to us all, a great encouragement -

The worst of these efforts is the reaction, which I am feeling today - making it hard to return to every day life -

I hope now that your husband may get back to quiet, that he may fulfil his ministry according to the gift which is given him -

I am thankful to say that my wife has returned all the better for her rest & change -
With our united kindest regards
Yours vy sincerely
C.V.Gorton

As our accounts are audited may I ask for receipt -[68]

> 67. Elgar wrote in the school log book: "Heard with the same joy & pleasure as in 1903 the children sing. Edward Elgar".
> 68. EBML 2490

The following day Gorton sent another cheque, for when he went to the Grand Hotel to settle up he discovered to his horror that Elgar had paid his own bill before leaving.

[*S.Laurence Bazaar Morecambe notepaper*]
May 5 1904

My dear Dr.Elgar -

Fortunately I can find from Hotel what we are indebted to you for we certainly cannot permit you to incur this expense on our account - It was only a great disappointment that you could not stay at the Rectory - We are already concerning ourselves regarding next year -

What we should feel would be ideal, would be that your spirit should be moved within you to write for us, some short work for chorus & orchestra, and that we should be able to persuade Dr.Richter to conduct. His interest and recognition would prove invaluable - But you will think that I am never satisfied - you will know however that still more I desire that you should be undisturbed by the world's pettiness - and coarseness -

I hope Mrs.Elgar has quite recovered from her cold in these glorious spring days -

I remain
Yours vy sincerely
C.V.Gorton[69]

Craeg Lea, Wells Road, Malvern
May 5 1904

My dear Canon Gorton

Many thanks for your cheque, the desired receipt is with this note. My wife is laid up with severe cough & chill but is now better.

There is no claim against you for expenses.

In great haste
With kindest regards
Yours sincerely
Edward Elgar

My wife will write when she is better

69. EBML 2471

Meanwhile the tireless and enterprising Miss Wakefield had come up with a plan to co-ordinate the expanding competitive movement. She invited all interested parties to a meeting in London, and this of course included Elgar, with his experiences of Madresfield and Morecambe. However, on the day of the meeting (17 May) the Elgars were on their way to Cologne, where Fritz Steinbach was to conduct *The Apostles*. So Elgar replied to Mary Wakefield:

> We are leaving for the Lower Rhine Festival on Tuesday - the Apostles - or I should have been very glad indeed to have attended the meeting. You know that I greatly approve the general idea of the competitions which, properly conducted, can only be productive of good. I should like to see the whole of England covered, so that a child or, in fact, any singing person, could not escape when they move, as they often do, from one district to another.

The meeting of the festival representatives took place at 13 Belgrave Square, home of the Dowager Lady Beauchamp. There was a good attendance, though most of the large northern festivals, including Blackpool and Morecambe, were unrepresented. Lady Mary Lygon took the chair, and the meeting was addressed by many distinguished musicians. Henry Wood spoke very favourably of choral competitions, and admitted that in London choral work was "difficult". He went on: "Every one has his little world, which he thinks the most important, but London life is made up of things which are generally of very little importance". Other speakers included Arthur Somervell, W H Leslie, and Fuller Maitland; and topics included the impartiality of adjudicators, the possible compilation of a catalogue of suitable test pieces, the involvement of schools in children's competitions, the difficulties of financing a festival, and other matters. Not surprisingly, Miss Wakefield "spoke on most of the topics", as the *Musical Herald* remarked. It was decided to hold a similar meeting annually "to discuss topics likely to afford mutual help". The meeting then elected Lady Mary Lygon as chairman, Mary Wakefield and Dr McNaught (the latter was absent) as secretaries, and Leslie as treasurer. The "committee" was to consist of the secretaries of the various festivals, and the organisation was to be known as the Association of Musical Competition Festivals.

Canon Gorton was keen to have Elgar's views on the recent festival for inclusion in the report book, but they were not forthcoming before the Elgars left for Germany. However, Elgar sent a postcard from Cologne on 21 May to show he had not forgotten: "Apostles tomorrow. I will write as soon as we return. Yrs ever, Ed.Elgar".

Gorton was at this time anxious about matters nearer home, and was greatly relieved when his wife Ella was safely delivered of a baby daughter on 2 June - Elgar's forty-seventh birthday. The Elgars were naturally delighted, and Alice sent their congratulations.

[The Rectory, Morecambe]
June 15 1904

Dear Mrs Elgar,
Thank you so much for your kind good wishes to us both. I knew you would be glad to hear & also to know now that I am getting on well. I am up on the couch for an hour today. Our dear little daughter is also growing thriving & is very good! We have a request to make to you which is: may we be allowed to call her "Alice Elgar"? We hope you will not think this suggestion presuming - but if for any reason you object to the use of your name you will tell me. We felt that we should very much like it. in remembrance of the honour Dr Elgar has shown my husband in his friendship - & because of my own feeling for you.

With my love
Believe me, dear Mrs Elgar
Very sincerely yours
Ella Gorton[70]

The Rectory, Morecambe
June 15 [1904]

My dear Mrs.Elgar -
My wife has I find written to you regarding the name of our little girl -

The name Alice is marked in our own family with all that we would wish to perpetuate [*the Canon had an aunt and an older sister with this name*] -

The other name is a more serious point - and you will understand, I am sure, that I do not wish to presume on your husband's great kindness - strange I always consider it - But he has brought so much into our lives for the last two years - the child herself if I may so say, must have so much of the Dream & the Apostles in her being - that were she to have the name Alice Elgar it should prove an inspiration -

She was I believe born on Dr Elgar's birthday -

70. EBML 2493

I was ashamed to send such a scrawl - yesterday - but I did not wish to miss the post -

I expect you are in the middle of moving - We are looking forward to Dr.Elgar's promised visit - Could he possibly give us a Saturday towards the end of July - We should like to have plenty of time to notify the conductors -

My wife was sitting up a little today - and I hope before long to see her in the garden -

I had an interesting letter from Mr.Jaeger - who I am thankful to know was at the Lower Rhine Festival - and whose heart rejoiced at what he heard -

With our kindest regards
I remain
Yours vy sincerely
C.V.Gorton[71]

The request was gladly granted, and so the youngest Gorton child was christened Alice Elgar, and known thereafter to the family as 'Elgar'.

Elgar had returned from Germany at the end of May to a good deal of unfinished business, and it was a few days before he managed to write his report. Once again a portion of it was published in *The Musical Times*[72], but this time his letter was less controversial and more practical and helpful, though he could not resist a small jibe at the end of the second paragraph.

Malvern
6 June 1904

Dear Canon Gorton,

I am sorry that absence abroad has somewhat delayed my sending you any remarks on the Morecambe Festival; the same cause will necessitate their being quite short - a matter, however, for your congratulation rather than regret.

On looking over the letter I had the pleasure to send you a year ago. I find there is little to add to it - and nothing to revise - in connection with the gathering just concluded. The choral singing is of the same

71. EBML 2444
72. vol xlv, July 1904, 536

excellence, the orchestral playing as good as before, the general artistic feeling, the enthusiasm, and (not least) the goodwill are at the same high level as when I had the good fortune to become acquainted with your district, a district where you 'make music' yourselves first - and import it afterwards, thus happily reversing the procedure of places where they find it convenient to talk more and sing less.

I was glad to find my suggestion that a 'really noble piece of music, such as Brahms' "Song of Destiny"', should have been followed, and that the cantata found a place in the programme as the chief piece for the Combined Choirs. The choral portion was admirably sung, and it gave me great pleasure to direct the performance. The orchestral part of the work proved, as all modern works must do, a little too exacting for the amateur orchestra, but all three of the competing orchestras must be credited with really excellent performances of the overture to "The Magic Flute" and Dvořák's "Nocturne" for strings.

In the unaccompanied choral singing, there is still a tendency (more noticeable in the Male-voice Choirs than in the Mixed-voice Choruses) to exaggerate the expression marks, and I hold this to be as great a fault as omitting expression altogether. Looking to the fact that there were many discrepancies in the tempi adopted by the various conductors in those pieces where no metronome mark was printed, it would be well in future to have the exact tempo indicated before the music is issued for rehearsal.

During the Festival the time at the disposal of the adjudicators is so short that only the merest criticism is possible, and a great deal they would like to say is necessarily omitted. My sympathies are very frequently with the losing side, and, much as one would wish to enumerate the good points, the exigencies of competition somewhat restrict adjudicators to a recital of the errors which debar competitors from the first place. I look forward, therefore, to the gathering to be held in Morecambe shortly, when I hope to meet all the conductors, successful and unsuccessful, whom I have only seen for a moment under the public eye and at the distance between the 'bad eminence' of the judges' box and the platform, and I hope to have the pleasure to make the personal acquaintance of these gentlemen to whom we owe so much artistic progress and pleasure, and to whom is due the main credit for the wonderful spread of music 'somewhere further north'.

Yours sincerely,
Edward Elgar.[73]

---

73. From the Report Book of the 1904 Morecambe Festival (EBM 1076).

During the festival in April the composer had intimated his willingness to attend a meeting of conductors, and now this public statement had confirmed it. The only problem was to fix on a date, for not only was Elgar's growing popularity making increasing demands on his time, but he and Alice had decided to move from Malvern to Hereford. They had found a house called Plas Gwyn on the edge of the city, and would be moving at the beginning of July.

The conductors normally met in July before the real holiday season was under way, and Gorton had originally proffered the 23rd. In his letter of 15 June he now asked Elgar to confirm this so that the conductors could be notified in plenty of time.

Then, on 22 June, Elgar heard that he was to be made a knight, in the same honours list that Alfred Harmsworth, the newspaper proprietor, was created Lord Northcliffe.

> The Rectory, Morecambe
> June 24 [1904]
>
> Dear Lady Elgar
>
> This is the best part of it - for it is the prize at the tournament that the good knight places at his lady's feet - otherwise I prefer then Dr.Elgar, but I suppose your husband felt it would not be gracious to refuse -
>
> It is moreover a recognition which music claims - but the Daily Mail a baron, and the Apostles a knight seems so wholly absurd - From Alice Elgar upwards and downwards the family send hearty congratulations - What shoals of letters you will receive[!] -
>
> You will be sorry to hear that we have been passing through an anxious time - Our two girls went to their grandmothers, and while away Helen was taken ill, and last Tuesday was operated on for appendicitis - I am thankful to say all has gone well - She has been much aided by her calm courage. But you can well imagine how trying to my wife, who could not be with her -
>
> Can you get from your husband (Sir Edward Elgar, I write it to see that it looks very well[)], the promised date in July or August if need be for meeting with conductors -
>
> With kindest regards to you both
> Yours vy sincerely
> C.V.Gorton[74]

74. EBML 5273

Elgar wired his confirmation of the original date, and this enabled Gorton to send the following circular to the festival conductors:

> The annual meeting of conductors will be held at the Grand Hotel, Morecambe on Saturday July 23rd at 1.30 pm.
>
> It is our singular privilege to announce the fact that Sir Edward Elgar suggests that he would wish to attend this meeting. He feels that the conductors of these choirs are doing a great work, and that in this work they deserve all encouragement and help. He is coming from Hereford to express his personal sympathy - to discuss with them in a friendly manner their difficulties, and to give them his advice.
>
> It is a singular thing that this great musician, who takes so unwilling a part in public functions, should honour us in so marked a manner.

After the investiture by King Edward VII on 5 July, the Elgars returned to their new home, and the following day Alice wrote to Canon Gorton:

> Plas Gwyn, Hereford
> 6 July 1904
>
> Dear Canon Gorton
>
> We were much concerned to hear of your Helen's illness, & of the anxiety you & Mrs.Gorton must have gone through & so sorry to think of her sufferings, it must have seemed most *heartless* of us not to have written but I am sure you know it was not that, but there really has been no moment of time in any corner to write in or material to write with! Now though there is still much to do, my writing table is approachable & I want to say how glad we are of the good accounts & hope now she will soon regain strength.
>
> We were in London yesterday. Edward went to the Investiture & had some charming words of welcome from the King on the occasion - He is looking forward to being with you on the 23rd, but will let you hear all details himself. So far, we simply love this house &c, & I do hope & pray it may be a prosperous move. The quiet & more space is most delicious.
>
> With love to Mrs.Gorton
> Yrs.sincy
> C.A.Elgar
>
> We hear wonderful accounts of the Apostles in York Minster: it must have been most beautiful.

Plas Gwyn, Hereford
July 7 1904

My dear Canon Gorton

I have had to fly up to town, & the hurry of moving & settling the house have made writing more difficult than usual.

I wired about the date of meeting & expect to hear that you have fixed on your own suggestion, the 23rd of July.

I am so glad to hear that your daughter is better & recovering: it must have been an awful time for you & her with Mrs.Gorton ill also.

As to Professor Knight[75]: I am sorry I did not meet him in Malvern: now we are fixed here I fear it is too far from Malvern for him to come; at any rate we shall not be fit to receive anyone for a long time to come: later on I will write to him. I think he knows some friends in Malvern.

With kindest regards
Yours always sincerely
Edward Elgar

The Rectory, Morecambe
[n.d., c.9 July 1904]

My dear Sir Edward -
Many thanks to you both for your kind enquiries about Helen - I hope that in about a week's time I may be able to bring her home, all has gone well - I enclose a copy of the circular which I have sent out -

I hope you will be able to come on the Friday - and is there no chance of our getting Monday in the Lakes[?] -

If Lady Elgar should come, you know it will greatly add to our pleasure and of course we have rooms at your disposal in the Rectory -

I am sitting with the Apostles and Gerontius - seeking for help on sermon on Beatitudes - Blessed are the pure in heart [*Matthew* 5:8] - Of course the one work throws a light on the other and the Beatitudes of the Apostles finds its explanation in the Beatific vision of Gerontius and the pain of the soul in the Divine Presence -

---

75. William Angus Knight (1836-1916), Professor of Moral Philosophy, University of St Andrew's 1976-1902. Retired to Malvern, then later to Keswick. An authority on Wordsworth, and on the Lake District.

But I get no help, except to realise my helplessness as I recall your message & revelation and am haunted with that wonderful recitative in the Wayside -

That 'seeing God' how much it means on earth - and how hopeless and earthy art becomes which ignores this fundamental principle -

We are living in a perpetual glory of sunshine, I only hope it and the roses may last till you come -

With our kindest regards
Yours sincerely
C.V.Gorton[76]

On 16 July, three months after its attack on Elgar and Morecambe, *Musical News* carried a leading article entitled 'Musical Competitions and their value', which, while recognising the dangers inherent in competition, acknowledged it as a force for good in the musical and social life of the nation:

> ...Students of events cannot have failed to have noticed the extraordinary hold that musical competitions are obtaining throughout the country. Of course Wales with its historic Eisteddfods has for long enjoyed this species of musical pastime, but it is only of comparatively recent years that the example thus set has been followed to any extent by England. From the parts contiguous to the Principality the movement has spread eastwards and northwards...It is gradually making its way southwards, though slowly, and even in the metropolis there are to be found examples of competitions organised by more or less important bodies...

> The great number of societies which compete in the various festivals that are held and the interest they display point to a real want which is being thereby satisfied. Many of those who take part therein belong to the working classes, and it is surely a healthy and encouraging sign of the times that the pure and elevating character of music should have a more potent attraction for them than the streets and the beer-shop. Those who have been in our great manufacturing towns know that British commercial prosperity has been purchased with a heavy price - a price paid not in mere flesh and blood, but in mind, soul, and those qualities which raise man above the animal. There is, without doubt, cause for thankfulness that music, as one of the agencies for good, is helping to brighten the daily life and to elevate the thoughts of those whose days are spent in toil amid sordid and depressing surroundings.

76. EBML 2440

Canon Gorton hoped to use the weekend of Elgar's visit to persuade him to commit himself to the 1905 festival. The situation had changed enormously from the time two years earlier when Elgar had first agreed to come. The Canon was wise enough to realise that Sir Edward Elgar, the head of his profession in England, would need some real incentive to attend, despite his close friendship with Gorton and his sympathy with the festival and its aims. From the outset Elgar had made clear to Gorton his reluctance to act as an adjudicator: but he may be more easily persuaded to conduct a large-scale choral work, possibly one commissioned by Morecambe, and given its first performance at the festival.

On 18 July, the Monday before the conference, the Morecambe executive met and invited Henry Coward to the meeting. The proposal put to the committee was that a festival choir of 250 to 300 voices be formed from Morecambe, Lancaster, Preston (and possibly Southport) to perform a new work to be written by Elgar. The composer had already told Gorton that he was considering a setting of Arthur O'Shaughnessy's ode *The Music Makers*, but the Canon did not refer to this by name. However, if Elgar was unable to produce a novelty in time, then the work given would be *King Olaf*, an extract of which 'The Wraith of Odin', had been performed at the previous festival concert. Henry Coward was engaged to train the choir, and if Elgar was unable to be present, would conduct. Coward was immensely impressed with Howson: "a gifted man", he wrote in his diary.

Gorton had hoped that both the Elgars would go to Morecambe for the conference, but there was still a good deal to be done at Plas Gwyn, and in the end only Edward went, leaving on the Friday afternoon. His presence at the conference had aroused the interest Gorton had hoped for, and seventy-two conductors were present, from places as far apart as Carlisle in the north and Nottingham in the south. Most were from Lancashire and Cumbria, but there was also a significant number from Yorkshire. McNaught had been invited too, but was unable to be present.

The conference was held in the Grand Hotel. Gorton, as chairman of the executive, presided, and after welcoming the conductors, thanked Elgar for his kindness in attending the meeting, saying that in him lay the great future hope for the festival. They remembered how he left the great function in London to be present at the Festival, and how he left the hundreds for the thousands. (Applause). The Canon then referred to Elgar's recent knighthood. He rejoiced that the country had acknowledged the debt they owed to Sir Edward, who had fought a good fight for music and had received his reward in being honoured by the King. "I will not ask for a resolution to be proposed and seconded", Gorton said, "but I hope, Sir Edward, you will take it as a tribute of our thankfulness that we are proud indeed that your great services have been acknowledged by the whole country". (Applause).

There was some initial business to be settled, mainly regarding the dates of the 1905 Festival. Some time in June had been suggested, in order to attract people to the seaside, but the general feeling was to agree a date which would suit choirs and orchestras rather than think of the pecuniary interest. They eventually agreed on 17-20 May: this was a good deal later than usual, but Easter was late in 1905. The provisional arrangements regarding the Festival Chorus and the work by Elgar were then announced. Some discussion about local classes followed, after which Gorton introduced Elgar. The following is the account of the speech as reported in the *Morecambe Visitor*.

> Sir Edward Elgar, who was warmly received, acknowledged their cordial reception and appreciated the kind remarks which Canon Gorton had made concerning what he would call 'the new state of things'. It was a pleasure to see so many of his friends and musicians greet in such a pleasant fashion the honour which had recently been conferred upon him by the King. (Applause). But he would always remain what he always was - the worker. (Hear, hear). After stating that he was not a professional judge, but an amateur judge, he said he had expressed a desire to attend that gathering in order to meet the conductors face to face, to show them that he was not an ogre or anything very desperate, but a musician like themselves. One of them had rather staggered him that afternoon by asking if he had had any experience in amateur orchestras. 'Well', said Sir Edward, 'I think so, considering that I started life as a second violin player and conducted an amateur orchestra for many years'. Some of them seemed to think he had come to that gathering to be extremely rude: to look down upon their efforts and be very sarcastic. Nothing of the kind. If one's judgment was worth anything one must have been brought up in the things one was judging. He had taught an amateur choir - very badly, no doubt, for they sang very well in spite of him. (Laughter). The reason why he had taken so much more interest in the Morecambe Festival than any other he had been connected with was because the commercial side did not exist - at any rate if it did exist it was kept very decently out of sight, and the artistic was on the top and everything was done to keep it there.
> After briefly referring to a letter he had sent at the close of the festival, Sir Edward said he would like to say something respecting the

'individual conducting', or the demeanour of a conductor before the audience and choir. It seemed to him there was room, he would not say for improvement, but for alteration - (laughter) - in a great many cases. Take the greatest conductor in England, Dr Richter. Dr Richter conducted an orchestra of artists, and consequently he had only to give them a lead, explain a piece to them, and they followed him; and you saw in his case absolute dignity in gesticulation, no exuberance of gesture, or anything of that sort. The result that he attained was what all conductors should aim at - the absolute purity of a rendering without any (he would use the word) humbug. 'In playing in an orchestra or singing in a choir you soon find your level', said Sir Edward, 'but a conductor is allowed to do pretty much as he likes, and some people seem to think the more he jumps about and exerts himself, the more the public are impressed'. (Laughter). It seemed to him that there was no school for conducting. It was a thing that could not be taught, but the man who arrived at the greatest result with the simplest methods must be the artist. He had known instances where the simpler the music was, the wilder the conductor became, 'although personally', added Sir Edward smilingly, 'I cannot see the relation between the two'. Of course, in judging, the judges went only by what they heard; they did not see the singers and conductors,[77] and judged simply by the result. He would really like to see a little more dignity and restraint, and a little more usefulness in the conductor, for a great deal that was done by conductors was of no use whatever. There was, he knew, a great difference in choirs. Many of the members were not artists, and in the early stages of training a good deal was required to keep them in order, but for all that he wished that conductors would avoid exaggeration and study how to get the best results with the least possible exertion. The best conductors were those who tried to make the position of conductor a little more dignified to look at. And here Sir Edward related an amusing story, in which a clergyman friend of his - an enthusiastic amateur - had decided to give a performance of *The Creation* in the church. Along with others, Sir Edward attended the rehearsal in the chancel, when his friend, who was conductor, said, just before the start, 'Now don't any of you chaps look at me' - (laughter) - 'because it is of no use if you do'. When the chorus met it was found out that the conductor had taught the choir that on a semibreve he would beat one down, at a minim two, crotchet four, and for a semiquaver sixteen beats down. (Loud laughter). The conductor no doubt was absolutely well intentioned, but he had no practical skill in conducting.

77. Elgar may have been misreported. Certainly the judges at Morecambe were able to see the performers (though some argued that they should be screened off). It seems that Elgar meant that the judges should not be influenced by the appearance of choir and conductor, but should mark solely according to the sound produced.

Again, the conductors in many cases had to deal with persons who had not much literary culture, and in that case the singer was apt to see only the mere surface of the words he used; he did not discern their meaning. As illustrating his meaning he said that for instance in Bavaria there was seen on every roadside a crudely carved crucifix indicating that the uncultured peasant had no sense but of the mere physical suffering of the Saviour. It was a painful representation with no symptom of the Divine in it. Travelling further, the same subject is seen where the people were educated, but instead of the crudeness one saw the Divine light showing through the whole subject. 'That is what is possible to do in music', said Sir Edward. Expression made all the difference, and it was their mission as conductors and as educated men to bring home to their choirs something more than the mere fact that it was music they were singing; it was theirs, in short, as someone had said, to make romance into reality and to give their musical realities a great deal of romance. (Cheers). He wished them to aim more and more at the cultured and refined in music. By persistent effort they would no doubt get more of that sort of expression into their singing to which he had referred. He was not complaining of what he had heard, and he wished his hearers to remember he was not speaking now from his experiences at Morecambe, for the singing there he had praised, and he stuck to what he had said, but behind the mere rendering of music it seemed to him that there was a great deal to be done, his idea not merely to understand a syllable but the general rounded idea of the whole thing.

The speech was well received by the audience, and Elgar sat down. A time of open discussion followed, and one of the most hotly debated issues was the strength of choirs in the Challenge Shield class. A recommendation sought to increase numbers from 30-50 up to 50-80. Howson maintained that the richness of effect and massive climaxes which they were striving for could not be obtained with fifty voices. Mr Whittaker of the Blackpool Choir agreed, but Mr Tattersall from Southport argued that eighty would be more like a choral society, and other conductors from smaller towns supported him. In the end, it was agreed to raise the maximum to sixty for the following year, and then possibly by stages up to eighty.

When discussing the choice of music, Mr Blacow of Salford suggested that more tuneful music should be given, something people could read without being too abstruse, and something that would be of service afterwards. For instance, last year some of his choir had suggested that he should either burn or lose the copies of the music of Brahms's *Dirge of Darthula*. There was a general outcry against this, and Elgar sprang up and retorted, "You had better by half burn your choir!", to loud laughter and applause.

Further discussion raised the issue of whether the male alto could be introduced; and Arthur Johnstone's suggestion of importing an orchestra. Gorton asked Elgar to comment on these and other issues raised. Elgar said that when he first came to the Morecambe Festival he was surprised to see three orchestras and was more surprised when he heard them. The question of the importation of orchestras aimed at the root of local improvement. He preferred to see the amateur orchestra used as far as possible, especially when they had the opportunity now and then of hearing such an orchestra as Hallé's as an exemplar. Of course, not all districts were circumstanced the same.

Concerning the male alto question, Elgar said it made him wonder how old he was. He began to think he had gone back forty years. Happily the cathedrals had done much to preserve the male alto, and there it flourished. He did not pretend to have written anything for male voices, though many had, but they were educated in Germany. For the last twenty or thirty years there had been no music written for male alto, and it had dwindled just in the same manner as language would if there were no literature or poetry attached to it. In cathedral music the male alto had been considered, but in the music of everyday life it was not. The trouble began when the English composers ceased to write for the male alto. If, however, the English composers could be persuaded to write for it it would still go. At present the thing was quite unsatisfactory, and would have to settle itself by the survival of the fittest. The district that had alto voices swore by them, and the districts that possessed the tenor voice thought there was nothing so fine as tenor, and some who had neither liked to hear both.

As to the enlarging of the choirs, Elgar said that the great bulk of part-songs was in four parts, but there were six, seven and eight parts, and they could go up to forty parts. He supposed the practical ideal was in four parts, but it would never do for such an artistic institution as the Morecambe Musical Festival to shut their eyes to eight parts. The limit should be increased by five or ten members each year until they got to eighty voices. You could get a better, broader and more emotional effect out of eighty voices than you could out of fifty, however finished the fifty might be. (Applause). He was sorry he had interfered about *The Dirge of Darthula*, but it had been accidental. (Laughter). The rhythm, he admitted, was not obvious, but was rather trying to young people. Something should be done to make young people understand the artistic and varying beauty of Brahms compared with the easy sort of jingle they could rattle through. That was where educated expression ought to be cultivated. If conductors explained to their choirs the reasonableness of its unrhythmical quality their singers would come to appreciate the piece very highly. Elgar concluded by thanking them for their very patient hearing, their kindly interest in his remarks, and expressed the pleasure he had derived from the discussion.

He stayed with the Gortons over Sunday and returned to Hereford early on Monday to find Alice still putting the new house straight. She wrote to Gorton immediately, confirming Edward's safe arrival. Despite the relaxed atmosphere and the badinage of the conductors' meeting, Elgar had begun to share his deep personal misgivings and doubts with the Canon.

The Rectory, Morecambe
July 26 [1904]

My dear Lady Elgar

It was very kind of you to write - Sir Edward was never meant to be knocked about in a train - and I was anxious to know that he suffered as little as possible - It really took him to Sunday to recover [from] - his journey here -

I hope he realised that he did not make the sacrifice in vain - for he gave a very great deal of pleasure to a great number of people, he would give their lives a lift - I send you a local report, which is fairly correct - They were all charmed with his simplicity and touched by his sympathy -

I hope now in his new house that he will be disturbed as little as is possible - and have quiet to gather for others some treasures from that unseen world - He speaks sometimes as if people did not care - all those who have not bowed the knee to Baal care, and there are very many thousands such -

We are not without hope that we may be entrusted with Makers of Music. I think he will not object to my seeing Richter & saying *if* Sir E Elgar - gives us this work will you come & bring orchestra and conduct -

It is not reasonable to expect your husband next year - but without him we feel like a ship adrift - I enclose a cheque for railway ticket, which we cannot think of not sending -

Alice Elgar thrives, & Helen is able to spend most of the day in the garden -

I need not tell you how much the visit meant to us - as for Mr Howson he is really better than he has been for months and chiefly owing to the stimulus he has received -

With our kindest regards
Yours vy sincerely
C.V.Gorton[78]

Elgar's comments at Morecambe were again widely reported in the musical press, and he was taken to task by some of the critics. *Musical Standard*, 30 July:

> ...He would like - though he does not actually say so - conductors to be as quiet as time-beaters but to get the finest possible results. He mentions Dr Hans Richter: he might also have mentioned Arthur Nikisch. And of course there are other great conductors who are quiet. But, to speak here of the living, are there not some great ones who are not quiet? It is no use laying down the law. As natural is it for one conductor to be demonstrative as it is for another not to be. Of course, occasionally there may be some 'humbug' on the part of totally insignificant conductors, but it is well to remember that different natures have different ways of doing things. Sir Edward does not convince us there is only one way. Let him think again of the results achieved by some non-quiet (yet perfectly sincere) conductors.

The *Sheffield Daily Telegraph* for 29 July endorsed Elgar's views on choir training and the behaviour of conductors, but the writer continued:

> ...when the question of the male alto voice arose, he was on less secure ground...Sir Edward suggested that the alto voice was dying out...In this, [he] showed himself to be strangely ignorant of the facts. Music with alto lead is still extensively written, and probably more glee and part-song music for that particular voice has been published during the past thirty years than during any previous period of the same length...The large bulk of it can only be sung by the cultivated alto voice, and if as seems to be the policy at Morecambe, the voice is to be discouraged in secular music, its gradual extinction will follow...

The move to Hereford had had a depressing rather than inspiring effect on Elgar. On 15 August he wrote to Hans Richter: "Work has not yet commenced here and I sometimes wonder if I shall ever invent any more music; we hope, however, that in time I may again take a pen in hand with the old zest, but at present too many worries seem to oppress me and nothing comes, musically, to relieve them".[79]

78. EBML 2445
79. Moore, *Edward Elgar: Letters of a Lifetime* (Clarendon, 1990), 154

CHAPTER 7

THE 1905 FESTIVAL

The 1904 Blackpool Festival was held on 5-8 October. Since its rather over-ambitious inauguration in 1901, it had successfully switched to the autumn and was a mixture of competitions and concerts broadly similar to Morecambe. Like its neighbour, Blackpool had the benefit of a magnificent hall in the Tower which was considered by such as Richter and Paderewski to be the finest concert hall in the country.

The Morecambe Madrigal Society had been bitterly disappointed at being unable to take part in their own festival, but their appearance at Blackpool that year proved a considerable compensation. Under their assistant conductor Mr Davies they won first prize in the chief competition, the Challenge Shield class where one of the tests was 'The Challenge of Thor' from Elgar's *King Olaf.* They also won first prize for sight-reading, and the Novello award for the highest combined marks. They were also second in the female voice class, just one mark behind the winners. It was an immensely gratifying occasion for Charles Gorton, who was there to award the prizes. He also gave a speech in which he considered the aims of the competitive movement, and the future prospects particularly in the area of orchestral music. The occasion found Gorton in his most lyrical and prophetic mood.

> ...What then is our aim? First and foremost, music and education. This is a big school. We would recover our character as a musical people. We would trust our choirs and our audiences to love the highest when they hear it, to stimulate choirs to do their best - for art is the people's best. But we are not only creating performers, we are creating audiences. A man enters here who is well satisfied if he knows when a choir ends not less than a note down. But he soon perceives other points of excellence. He soon becomes a critic...and if the judge coincides with his opinion he thinks the judge a very clever fellow. His musical horizon is widened. He not only contrasts choirs, but also composers. He knew before *Three Blind Mice,* and has sung in *Oh who will o'er the Downs,* but now the early English Madrigals, Brahms, Cornelius, Berlioz, are names which slip off his tongue. Then those who sing, what do they get? Perhaps the prize, perhaps not. But

they have the evenings of practice, friendships based in a common interest, and instead of talking about how someone else kicked or didn't kick a piece of leather, they discuss this lead, and that harmony, and this melody. They have a common possession...

We are making an advance, the whole line is advancing, but not at the same pace. We are making our northern folk a people who can sing. We want also a people who can play. The instrumentalists start later, and theirs is a more arduous task, demands more time, entails great expense. It is vital that all aids should be given them. What is the present condition of things? A local choral society prepares a work, and then comes the question what about the orchestra. A very small orchestra is got together, a contingent is got from Manchester or London. It is putting a piece of new cloth in an old garment. What is the result? The listeners shiver, and the conductor perspires. Again and again the choice of music is limited by the fatal question 'What about the orchestra?' Again, it is because the players are so few that the demand for chamber music is so small.

The extract from *King Olaf* which the Canon heard prompted him to remind Elgar of the performance of the complete work at the next Morecambe meeting.

The Rectory, Morecambe
Oct 12 [1904]

My dear Sir Edward -

I need not say that we are anxious to know as soon as you can let us, what your movements will be in May - May 19th & 20th are the two days, when we should welcome you both - Everyone wants King Olaf - it will secure the success of our new Festival Choir under Coward's training -

But if you will conduct & judge in open choirs & orchestras with McNaught & Gr[anville] Bantock, this is what we need - Sir Hubert Parry will most likely be coming - he wishes to come, but his movements are not quite certain -

Is there anything definite about America as yet[?] -

I was sorry not to be able to get over to Leeds [*for the Festival*] - there was but little time obviously for you to get away - and you like an old bottle of port travel badly -

I hope these glorious autumn days are bringing you many things[.] I keep on wondering about the Apostles - Will you give illustrations on their Gospels (though there is but one)[?] Still there must have been the personality of the individual - The Gospel according to S.Peter - S.John - S.Thomas (see logia) [-] S.Paul - S.James - eg.S.Paul 'to give the light of the knowledge of the glory of God *in the face of Jesus &c'[2 Corinthians 4:6]* The subject is so vast, and the difficulty must be the links -

May the Spirit of wisdom & understanding be with you -
With all kindest regards
Yours sincerely
C.V.Gorton -

As to orchestra for King Olaf Coward will bring leaders from Sheffield - We ought to have chorus of 350 - 'I am the God Thor' will make people sit up! [80]

The musical world was shocked when on 16 December 1904 Arthur Johnstone died from complications following appendicitis. He was forty-three. That same day his widow wrote from her home in Victoria Park in Manchester:

My dear Sir Edward Elgar,

I want you to know that my beloved husband, in one of the clear moments in the last night but one of his life, wrote the word "Elgar" on a scrap of paper & gave it to the nurse, then seemed satisfied that something important had been done. I imagine that he wanted you to know at once that he was dangerously ill - you will know I expect by now that the end came at six o'clock this morning.

I should like you to know that you were one of the last in his thoughts. The funeral is at 2.30 at the Manchester Crematorium on Monday -

I remain, dear Sir Edward Elgar,
Yours very sincerely,
Lucy Johnstone.

Plas Gwyn, Hereford
Dec 28. 1904

Dear Mrs. Johnstone:

I have been absent from England & a vast accumulation of matters has prevented my writing earlier.

I cannot tell you how deeply I feel the loss we have all experienced. It may seem impertinent to appear to share in a sorrow which is really your own, but your dear husband was so much to us musicians that I ask you to forgive me if I put myself forward as one sorrowing more than he can express.

80. EBML 2443

Our deepest sympathies are with you & I thank you especially for writing to me the very touching, & to me priceless, words describing the writing of my name so near the end.

My wife joins me in best wishes & again with deepest sympathy.

Believe me
Very sincerely yours
Edward Elgar.

That same day Elgar wrote to Jaeger, describing Johnstone as "...one of the best fellows & *the* best critic we had".[81]

Canon Gorton was called upon to conduct Johnstone's funeral, less than six months after officiating at his wedding. In the introduction to a memorial volume of his writings, published the following year, Gorton wrote:

> ...He held a high view of his office, and would make a sacrifice of self rather than a sacrifice of truth. It is difficult to calculate the extent of your loss. Musicians succeed musicians; they being dead may yet speak. But the critic's words are ephemeral; they remain in the files of the newspapers. For musicians there are schools; but what school is there for critics? In music we need guides, men with a wide horizon, a general culture, men unfettered by musical faction, with definite ideals, with command of the English tongue, of courage and of true instinct. Such an one, I take it, was Mr Arthur Johnstone. Who will fill his place?...
>
> The debt we owe to him was not merely because he was a critic keen to discern the good, not merely because he proved a fearless champion. He became a friend always ready to discuss methods of development, and to place his exact and wide knowledge at our disposal, and after we had formed our plans it was a great gain to Mr Howson and myself to test their wisdom by his opinion.[82]

In his Birmingham lecture on the subject of critics, given on 6 December 1905, Elgar said:

> I do not agree with all the views held by the late Arthur Johnstone, and I have never read a word of his criticism on my own works; but referring only to his own writings on the classics and large works produced in Manchester, I should place his very high. His training at Cologne Conservatorium gave him great distinction and his

81. Moore, 603
82. Johnstone, xci-ii, lxxxvii

knowledge of things outside music - things and forces which go to make human beings of men - assisted his judgment in literature, art and music in a wonderful way.[83]

Meanwhile the North-South controversy which Elgar had stirred up the previous year rumbled on. Vernon Blackburn, who had been so offended by Elgar's comments then, was now honest enough to admit the truth of those remarks. Writing in the *Pall Mall Gazette* for 24 December 1904 Blackburn said:

> ...We have before this referred to a certain speech of Sir Edward Elgar in which he stated that if you wanted to find something genuine and real in English music, it is somewhere to the North that we must go. At first such a statement rather alarmed us, remembering our numerous halls and all the great foreign artists who come over to London to bow to especially critical audiences. But, by degrees, we have entertained a growing conviction that, after all, Sir Edward Elgar is in the right. When you come to think of the whole matter, London, in fact, has no cohesion in the cause of art; and though the greatest artists come here to play...the fact is that there is no continuous sense of music in a metropolis which has been described in this column as a congeries of villages.

The new year saw Canon Gorton in typically forthright mood in his assessment of the economic situation. In his parish magazine he wrote:

> May the New Year mark an advance in our parish - a firmer hold on truth, a deepening of spiritual life, a more living unity among the faithful, and a quickening sense of our need to help others in the world...If the present distress is the outcome of the fact that we are paying in cash what we have already paid in blood for the Boer War, it serves one good purpose in bringing home the horrors of war - in enabling us to realise that war is the setting back of the clock, and the leading us to strive towards the Christian message 'Peace on earth, goodwill towards men'.

Gorton's goodwill did not extend as far as Madame Sadler Fogg, the soloist whom Johnstone had criticised so heavily a few years before. She had approached Elgar with the hope of being given the solo soprano part in *King Olaf* at Morecambe.

---

83. Young (1968), 183-5

The Rectory, Morecambe
Jan 16 [1905]

My dear Sir Edward -
Parsons for begging are not in it with professional lady singers - I hear that Madame Sadler Fogg - otherwise Mrs.Fogg - has suggested invading your quiet with her voice - Please do not be bothered with her - She is not good enough - and Coward will submit to you the names of the vocalists - I wish I could invade you, but I am kept incessantly at work - and have not left the parish of which I am getting tired for months -

We are anxiously awaiting your movements at Birmingham, when with a free hand you will doubtless do much -

A friend of mine A. Marriott secretary of Oxford University Extension writes to me asking if I can press the claims of Oxford - but Oxford comes in shamefully late in the day - and finds you out after everyone else - and I can urge nothing -

I hope the Apostles is developing happily in your hands - but of this I may hear something next May to which we are already looking forward -

With our kindest regards to you all
Yours sincerely
C.V.Gorton[84]

The rehearsals for *King Olaf* started early in the new year, and Henry Coward began to travel from Sheffield to the various venues in Lancashire. He was in Lancaster on 25 January and in Morecambe on 15 February. Coward was no stranger to *King Olaf*, having trained the chorus for the work when it was performed at the Sheffield Festival in 1899. An enthusiastic and grateful composer had given Jaeger his reaction to a rehearsal he had taken at Sheffield on 19 July 1899:

> ...I went to Sheffield & heard that Chorus & was lifted into the seventh paradise: never you complain of my choral effects again - they're grand & mighty when properly sung & by Heaven I've never, never heard *anything* like that chorus - you *must* hear Olaf at the Festl. - Coward must be a genius to get the dramatic force & perception:- it is simply marvellous & colossal [85]...

84. EBML 2482
85. Moore, 132

He told F G Edwards that "...for fire, intelligence, dramatic force they are electrical [86]..." Ten days after that he was still excited by their performance, especially when compared with the local singers: "Oh! that Sheffield Chorus - I had to go & rehearse the combined 3 Choirs yesterday - & - well I 'got cross' & pizenous - a weary crew [87]..."

Coward always ensured that his chorus made a strong impression from the outset. In *King Olaf* the singers soon had opportunity to prove their worth in the chorus 'The Challenge of Thor'. At the final rehearsal for the performance of the work at the Sheffield Festival, Coward sat in the balcony with "a select few", including William McNaught, and later described the effect his "expression attack" had on the doctor:

> When the chorus sang the first bar, with its test of attack in the staccato notes, he gave a slight start and looked at his score. The second bar seemed to impress him still more. At the third and fourth bars he seemed to quiver. At the words 'I am the Thunderer' he gave the book a bang with his closed fist, passed his fingers through his hair, turned to his colleagues and said, 'Well! This beats all I have ever heard' [88]

The performance on 11 October 1899 was widely acclaimed although the orchestra was far from perfect.[89]

Henry Coward[90] was an amazing man, the greatest English choral trainer of his time, and possibly the greatest ever. Yet he came from a humble background and was self-educated. He became a master cutler, then a teacher, and eventually a doctor of music. He founded the Sheffield Musical Union and, with this and other Yorkshire choirs,

86. Moore, 131 [20 July 1899]
87. Moore, 135. A T Shaw, the first chairman of the Elgar Society, found the same difference between choirs from the North and South when he moved to Malvern from Lancashire in 1922: "I found myself thinking that the festival chorus could not stand comparison with the fine competition choirs I had heard at Morecambe singing as though their lives depended on it" (*1978 Three Choirs Festival Book*, 30)
88. *The Musical Times*, vol xli, July 1900, 450
89. See Hodgkins, Geoffrey, "'Oh! That Sheffield Chorus'" in *Elgar Society Journal*, vol 11, no 3 (1999), 180-87
90. See a contemporary biography, *Dr Henry Coward* by John Rodgers (Bodley Head, 1911); also 'Henry Coward' by Gareth H Lewis in *Elgar Society Journal*, vol 2, no 6 (1982), 10-13; and vol 3, no 1 (1983), 11-18

established a standard of choral singing without equal in the country, as Elgar found. A man of great personal magnetism, he inspired singers with his dedicated and uncompromising attitude, although he could be a martinet if the need arose. It was therefore a wise decision of the Morecambe executive to engage Coward to conduct the rehearsals. Obviously no matter how skilled Howson and other conductors were in preparing choirs in part-songs and other small scale pieces, a work as dramatic and complex as *King Olaf* needed a completely different approach and technique. His biographer wrote of him:

> Dr Coward is seen at his best when appearing before a strange chorus for the first time. The newness of his method, together with the eccentricity of his mannerisms, occasions mingled wonder and amusement.[91]

This was certainly true of the Lancashire singers; and after the first Morecambe rehearsal on 15 February Gorton wrote an article for *Musical World* entitled 'Nuces Cowardienses: how Dr Coward trains a choir'.[92] Referring to the *fff* at the words "the blows of my hammer ring in the earthquake" in 'The Challenge of Thor', Coward said, "You sang that as loud as you could, now when you have sung as loud as you can, remember I want it just twice as loud. Open your chests, throw back your shoulders, back with your heads, and then with 300 voices lift the roof". He was equally insistent on accuracy in the quieter passages. "We don't call it a *pianissimo* at Sheffield unless, when 300 are all singing, I can hear the clock tick".

It was clear that the forthcoming Festival concert, with *King Olaf* and *Blest Pair of Sirens* conducted by their respective composers, was to be a momentous occasion, and Gorton intended to increase his audience's enjoyment and understanding of the Elgar work by writing an explanation of the libretto. He realised that the majority of listeners would be completely unfamiliar with the world of the Icelandic sagas.

The Rectory, Morecambe
[n.d., c.20 February 1905]

Dear Lady Elgar -

We are full of King Olaf which reveals more and more each time we hear it - I send you an account of Dr. Coward rehearsing - I think Sir

91. Rodgers, *op cit.*, 51
92. *Musical World* 25 February 1905, 135-6; reprinted in *Elgar Society Journal* vol 6, no 6 (1990), 12-3.

Edward would forgive him his irritating method of speech if he saw him at work - He really picks out some excellent things and has a soul which appreciates beautiful music -

I shall wish to write something for our Festival Book on King Olaf -

The Libretto is admirable, Longfellow at his very best - Even what your husband omitted, cries out for his interpretation[.] Who is Acworth? He has done his work excellently -

Have you among your records any article which in any way satisfies you with regard to the work -If so would you kindly send it to me[?] - There is something refreshing in the vision of King Olaf 'onward sweeping, preaching the Gospel with the sword'[.] I am but at the beginning of understanding it, and it has been yours for many years - so please give me your help -

You know there is very much I should like to hear - first and foremost what progress is being made with the Apostles - and then what the Professor is going to develop at Birmingham -

Alice Elgar thrives, but I am very anxious about the shape of her *nose* - but as it is said God makes our *noses* and we make our *mouths*[,] I must be content -

With all kindest regards
Yours very sincerely
C.V.Gorton[93]

Elgar was quite busy during the early weeks of 1905. He completed a new work, the *Introduction & Allegro* for string orchestra, on 13 February, and was compiling a libretto from the Bible on the subject of faith for his friend Ivor Atkins, who had been commissioned to write a choral work for the 1905 Three Choirs Festival. Elgar sent the words of the *Hymn of Faith* to Atkins on 21 February, and also sent a copy to Gorton.

Morecambe
Mar 2 [1905]

My dear Sir Edward -

You are truly a wonderful man to supply one man with his orchestration [*"Emmaus" by Herbert Brewer in 1901*] another with his Libretto - The latter interests me much more especially in contrast to the spirit of the age - The motive of the whole would seem to be met rather by [the] verse - 'When the Son of Man cometh shall He find faith on the earth' [*Luke 18:8*]

93. EBML 2478

One is sorry to miss 'he that *wavereth* is like a *wave* of the sea ['
James 1:6] - though there is no play upon the words in the Greek, and
'*surge of the sea*' [*Revised Version*] sings better, though it represents
not feebleness but strength - May the setting be worthy of the words -
& subject.

I was of course greatly interested in your notes on King Olaf - I had 2
hours read yesterday of Laing's Book on the Sagas[.] What subjects it
opens up, and the introduction throws much light on your fascinating
picture - What startled me most was to find that Olaf was as late as
950 to 1000 - the breezy heathen that he was - the odd servant of the
Christ - But how much more real he is than the blameless Arthur and
much more concerned with us than that visionary being - I hope in
time you will lead others back to this quarry from which we were
digged -

Please excuse this horrid paper - I wish they would make me a
Bishop, I would have a type-writer - but not a motor car -

With all affectionate & grateful greetings
Yours
C.V.Gorton[94]

Elgar had also responded to Gorton's request for some notes on King
Olaf, and from Frank Schuster's London home on 3 March he sent
an illustration for the Canon to consider using:

at 22 Old Queen St, Westminster
for some time
3/3/05

> With
> SIR EDWARD ELGAR'S
> compliments

for the sake of the title page - rather a good presentment of K Olaf's
boat! red cloak & all.

Thanks for your letter
just off to town

Yrs ever
Ed.Elgar

Overshadowing all else at this time was the forthcoming inaugural
lecture at Birmingham University on 16 March. Elgar had chosen the
title 'A Future for English Music', and he addressed his distinguished

94. EBML 2480

audience in the same forthright uncompromising tone as he had used in the notorious "somewhere further north" letter. He criticised contemporary English music as being commonplace and imitative. The future he wanted to see was, he said, "something that shall grow out of our own soil, something broad, noble, chivalrous, healthy and above all, an out-of-door sort of spirit" [95]: he could well have said the sort of spirit prevailing at the Morecambe Festival.

The lecture was greeted with outrage and opposition. Once again Elgar in speaking his mind had only echoed what many critics had been saying already, but some observers felt that Elgar would have been better advised to keep his opinions to himself. Ivor Atkins was sitting next to Dr Sinclair, organist of Hereford Cathedral, and later wrote:

> ...It was stirring enough, and as Elgar lashed out fiercely at musicians and critics alike, we both fidgeted in our seats, becoming more and more anxious as the lecture proceeded about the effect of his words in the musical world at large...[96]

Elgar was unwell immediately afterwards and Gorton wrote in his usual supportive and sympathetic vein. He had wondered whether the 'Beatitudes' motif from *The Apostles* could be adapted slightly into an Anglican chant for his church choir to sing. Towards the end of the month he received the following reply from Alice.

Plas Gwyn, Hereford
25 March 1905

My dear Canon Gorton

Very many thanks for your note & kind enquiries &c for Edward. I trust he is *somewhat* better, but still very far from well & it is very sad to see him so wretchedly.

He asks me to say he is *much* touched by your wishing to sing his Wayside & he has carried out a little arrangement as you will see -

He has no objection at all, but you must not print it as the publishers naturally wd. not like it.

It is *very* sweet to think of yr. delightful singers doing it, I think I can hear them.

95. Young (1968), 57
96. Atkins, 133

I trust that I shall be able to send you good accounts soon -

With our love to you all
Believe me
Very sincerely yours
C.Alice Elgar

The Rectory, Morecambe
Mar 27 [1905]

My dear Sir Edward -

I am much concerned to get Lady Elgar's letter with so poor an account of you. Dear man, you must have peace & quiet, and rest - I earnestly trust you are getting this now, and that these soft spring days in your lovely land are resting you -

I had a good day yesterday as I was preaching in Carlisle cathedral, and the organist gave me the Angel's song from the Dream, and much else - it was hard to think of getting so much delight and calm from you, and you yourself not feeling fit - I need not say how grateful we all are for the Beatitude[:] it will help us all much -

If Lady Elgar would send me a post card during the week to say how you are I shall be grateful -

Yours vy sincerely
C.V.Gorton[97]

Three weeks later Gorton completed his article on *King Olaf*.

The Rectory, Morecambe
April 19 [1905]

My dear Sir Edward -

I sent you by this post my exposition of your King Olaf - Would that I could come to read it to you - I would on Easter Monday, if I have missed what was in your mind - It is a fascinating subject - and I feel ashamed of my previous ignorance - If you wish me to come, and if by coming I can turn out anything which would prove of permanent value when King Olaf is given please let me know as soon as possible.

It is written in my best hand and is therefore I fear horrible to read - but perhaps Lady Elgar will have pity on me, and master it first and then read it through to you, and add at side, points omitted

97. EBML 2477

If I had the knowledge I should have liked to draw out the difference between your treatment of the Norse tales - & Wagner's - With you it is history[,] with Wagner myth - Can you give me any guidance[?] -

I was glad to see that you were able to conduct at Leeds [*The Dream of Gerontius* and *The Apostles*] for I concluded you were better -

I want to enlist your sympathies with Coward - He is a wonderful man - no education other than self tuition since the age of 8 - and first an expert maker of knives & forks - He was speaking to me last week of his own compositions - He told me that in Sheffield they always filled a house 'but Elgar has knocked the conceit [out] of me, since I conducted Gerontius I have not written a bar' -

With our united love to you all
Ever yours sincerely
C.V.Gorton[98]

Alice's reply contained Thomas Carlyle's essay 'The Early Kings of Norway', which had appeared in *Fraser's Magazine* for January and March 1875; and a typed copy of an old Danish balled 'Sir Morten of Fogelsang', which had been translated by Alexander Prior in 1860.

Plas Gwyn, Hereford
Saturday [22 April 1905]

Dear Canon Gorton

May I first say *how* interesting & delightful I think yr description is, what a happy audience to be so helped -

I have always been *crazed* about Scandinn. mythology -

I enclose Carlyle as E. wished & a copy of Sir Morton [sic] wh. explains it all - forgive bad typing done in haste.

E. is better but not well as we cd. wish yet -

We shall be so pleased to see you all again. 17th.18th.19th,20th. are the dates are they not?

With love to you all
Yrs.sincy
C.A.Elgar

The Canon's booklet contained his introduction to the work and some explanatory notes: and the complete libretto. It was printed at the Beaver Press at Laleham near Staines, which was owned by Noel

98. EBML 2481

Rawnsley, the son of Gorton's great friend Canon H D Rawnsley.[99]
Gorton explained his reasons for writing the booklet:

> We know much about the Norman Duke, of King Harold, still more of
> King Arthur and his Table Round, still more of the heroes of Greece
> and Rome...

> These Celts and Romans and Greeks are foreign folk, not my kith and
> kin, and when I listen they speak in a foreign tongue...I may sing of
> the 'Hardy Norsemen' but except that their home of yore was 'on the
> waves' I may well know but little. Yet they were cousins of the Angles
> and Saxons, - we in them conquered Britain. Their gods occur in our
> names for each day, they too named most of our towns, their blood is
> the best in our veins, to them we owe our instincts of freedom and the
> sovereignty of the seas.

After his comments on the libretto, Gorton concluded:

> It is not for me to deal with the manner in which this story has been
> beaten out into song by Sir Edward Elgar. But I am certain of this, if
> we are to comprehend to the full the music, if it is to mean for us
> somewhat of what it means for the music maker, it must be by effort.
> It is not incumbent on Poet or Musician to explain; to repeat the
> obvious, this is the occupation for the 'man in the street'. The Poet
> and Musician alike are not so much heard, as *overheard*. It is the
> faculty given them to breathe the spirit of the age in which they enter
> - this is their dramatic power. They speak from the summit, and if we
> would overhear what they say, we must do some climbing. What has
> cost them pains must cost us pains....

> Those of us at least who are at pains will listen and be assured that
> the gift of the Musician is not one only of the craftsman, but that it is
> a gift from above, -

> > 'That God at the fountains
> > Far off has been raining'.

Henry Coward was supervising the rehearsals with his customary
thoroughness. He was in Morecambe on 5 May, Lancaster on the
12th (at which the Kendal contingent was also present), and
Southport on the 13th. The chorus numbered 268 with 100 from
Morecambe, 106 from Lancaster, forty-six from Southport, and
sixteen from Kendal. They all came together for the first time under
Coward at the Winter Gardens on 15 May, two days before the

99. A copy of Gorton's book can be found at the Elgar Birthplace.
    Rawnsley was one of the founders and the first secretary of the
    National Trust, and a great expert on the Lake District. He was later a
    chaplain to King George V.

Festival began. "Fine rehearsal; gives great promise", Coward wrote in his diary. Havergal Brian wrote his impressions of the great Sheffield conductor thirty-three years later:

> ...Coward always was a character, and I recall him now gesticulating before the chorus, at a rehearsal, to show how Viking roysterers probably behaved at their carousals.[100]

By this time Coward had been asked to conduct *Blest Pair of Sirens*; its composer, Sir Hubert Parry, was ill and wrote to Gorton:

> ...I most faithfully kept the date open, but the fates are too strong for me, and the serious strain of the last six months has brought about a sudden collapse. I am at present in the doctor's hands, and he says it is utterly and entirely out of the question for me to think of going to Morecambe. I am sorry to disappoint anyone, and would not if there were any chance of getting through with it; but it would be physically impossible.

At the last moment the Morecambe executive obtained the services of Frederick Corder to assist Elgar, McNaught, and Sinclair in the judging.

Writing in the Preface to the programme book, Charles Gorton commented on the recent death of Arthur Johnstone:

> ...We shall greatly miss his stimulating presence. May we at least not ... the high standard which he was the first to demand from us. ... me of the results for which he so strenuously and ... red.
>
> ... w attention to the fact that, in the fifteen years of ... hey had featured 359 separate pieces by 140 ... o piece had ever been repeated. The *Musical* ... ressed by the choice of music:
>
> ... nposers whose music has been used for test pieces ... ncement of this Festival in 1891 there is evidence of ... desire to favour the works of the great masters, and ... most important that the classic schools should figure ... competitions, for so long as the State refuses to ... igher claims of music in this country, these functions ... stimulating agency for the betterment of the art, ... ng artisans who have not the privilege of attending or ... he greater provincial Festivals.[101]

Musical Opinion, March 1938, 491
27 May 1905

ERRATA

Page 92, footnote, line 2: for '1976' read '1876'
Page 113, line 17: for 'balled' read 'ballad'
Page 132, line 19: for 'us' read 'up'

The Festival began on 17 May in familiar fashion with the Children's Day. A new class for violin solo had been introduced. The Elgars travelled to Morecambe on this first day, and once again stayed at the Grand Hotel. They attended the evening concert, when the combined choirs gave the first performance of a cantata entitled *The Lobster's Garden Party, or The Selfish Shellfish*, which Sir Frederick Bridge had composed for the Festival. Mrs Olga Wood sang songs by Grieg and Schumann, accompanied by her husband.

Elgar was adjudicating at the local competitions all day on the Thursday. One of the pieces for choirs was 'Aspiration' from the *Bavarian Highlands* suite. He and Alice lunched at the Rectory with the Gortons. For once the weather at Morecambe was agreeable: "Lovely day & views", wrote Alice. And as the *Lancashire Daily Post* pointed out the following day:

> The glorious weather so far has had a somewhat detrimental effect on the attendance, some preferring the fresh air and unaccustomed sunshine to the mustiness and gloom of the Winter Gardens.

The highlight at the evening concert was a recital by the contralto Muriel Foster of some nineteen songs given, the *Post* reported, "in a most artistic manner". The programme contained *The Shepherd's Song* by Elgar.

Friday was another "lovely day", with a "beautiful view of the mountains", Alice wrote. The festival for church choirs was held at St Laurence's church in the afternoon, but the chief interest that day centred on the Winter Gardens where the rehearsals were taking place for the evening concert. Gorton, Howson, Elgar, and the other judges were all present. Henry Coward had arrived from Retford where he had adjudicated the day before. He took the morning rehearsal, concentrating on *Blest Pair of Sirens*, and the choral sections of *King Olaf*. The effect of Coward's training was obvious: Sinclair told him the singing was a revelation to him, and added: "You have taught me much". To save the choir's voices, Coward was going to stop after 'The Wraith of Odin', as there were no more difficulties, but Elgar shouted out, "Will you finish it for us?" and so they did. Edward went for lunch to the Midland Hotel with James Gandy, while Alice went to the Rectory.

The Nelson orchestra, which had been selected to accompany, was augmented by professionals from the Hallé and Sheffield Municipal orchestras. Gorton had realised that the amateurs would be found wanting in *King Olaf*; but even with professional help there were problems. At the afternoon rehearsal, conducted by Elgar, Alice found the orchestra "*very* trying".

The great hall was packed for the evening concert, of which *King Olaf* (which takes an hour and a half in performance) comprised the first half. "The appearance on the platform of the principal vocalists was the signal for an outburst of applause, which culminated in the enthusiastic reception accorded to Sir Edward Elgar", reported the *Visitor*. It was generally agreed that what followed was an outstanding performance of Elgar's cantata. "From the quiet, forceful opening right through the conflict between Thor and Olaf, the weird picture of the latter's death to the tranquil close, the audience were held spellbound", said the *Post*. The three soloists were Emily Squire, John Coates, and Charles Knowles: "all were heard to great advantage and rendered most efficient service", according to the *Visitor*. However there were some reservations about Miss Squire: the *Manchester Guardian* thought that she was "...not particularly strong on the high notes abounding in her part", while the *Musical World* added: "Mme Emily Squire was much overweighted, the music being beyond her range and too high: to do one's best under such circumstances does not always argue a satisfactory result". John Coates' singing met with universal approval: Alice thought he was "magnificent". Charles Knowles had sung the bass part in the 1899 Sheffield performance, when Elgar had described him as "frightened" [102]: but he too came in for praise. "[He] has much improved and made a very good impression", said the *Musical World*.

The chorus gave a performance which amply justified all the work Coward had done with them. The *Visitor* said: "The choir realised the possibilities of the music and sang in a manner truly magnificent". They sang "with an alertness and intelligence which spoke volumes for the genius of Dr Coward as a chorus master". The *Musical Times* agreed: "The chorus singing...was a triumphant exhibition of Dr Coward's skill as a trainer. It was not merely that the music was perfectly correctly performed, that the words, vowels, and consonants were all clearly defined, and that the rhythm and attack were as perfect as one could imagine, but over and above this there was the intensity and convincingness of the expression".[103] The *Post* endorsed this: "The voices were full of freshness and resonance, and there was nothing mechanical in their work".

102.   Letter to Jaeger 11 October 1899 (Moore, 142)
103.   vol xlvi, June 1905, 396

"Splendid chorus in evening...orch. rather better", wrote Alice. Press reports on the performance of the orchestra vary. The *Morecambe Visitor* said: "It would be too much to say that the orchestra quite realised all the opportunities afforded by the masterly orchestration with which the composer has dowered this work, but its performance was still a very fine one". The *Post* was full of praise for the players' enthusiasm: "The orchestra threw full zest into their work and did nobly". The *Sheffield Daily Independent* was quite unequivocal: "The score had no terrors for the bandsmen...Their playing lacked the suspicion of anything that could justly provoke the animadversions of any one of the crowd of critics".

However, there were dissenting voices. The *Musical Times* said: "The band, although containing many excellent players, did not always adequately support the singers".[104] *Musical Standard* commented: "Occasionally the orchestra was wanting in clearness and precision, but worked with commendable earnestness and goodwill". "The attack, principally in the second woodwind, parts of the brass, was uncertain; the incompleteness of the orchestra also affected the colouring, chiefly because of the want of a second harp and the organ", said the *Musical World*. The *Lancaster Guardian* agreed that "...at some points the orchestra were very ragged, and the brass, especially the trombones, were not always in tune".

But Elgar was in his element, as he had been two years earlier when conducting *The Banner of St George*. An appreciative audience, plus performers willing to give their all on his behalf, brought the best out of him. "Sir Edward swayed band and chorus with the greatest of ease, now smiling his passing appreciation, now knitting his brows as an obstacle came along", wrote the *Post* reporter. After the chorus 'A Little Bird in the Air' there was prolonged applause, and Elgar had to bow several times. At the end of the work there was, according to the *Sheffield Daily Independent*, "a demonstration which will not soon be forgotten". Elgar's self-effacement in the face of this ovation was not lost on the *Visitor*'s critic: "Without a trace of affectation, Sir Edward is the most modest of men, and the manner in which he, an intellectual giant in the land, hastened off the stage, must have touched a tender chord in the hearts of those near enough to see the details of this little episode". After Elgar had been recalled several times there were vociferous and persistent calls for "Coward", and later for "Gorton". The former appeared on the stage to acknowledge his acclaim: for the latter the performance was sufficient reward.

104.   ibid.

Possibly the degree of preparation given to *King Olaf* had its effect on the rest of the programme, which must in any case have been something of an anticlimax. The *Manchester Guardian* reported that in *Blest Pair of Sirens* "...the reading was somewhat erratic, with a consequent loss of dignity in the more massive sections". The rest of the second part consisted of Weber's overture to *Der Freischütz*, and a work for each of the three soloists. John Coates sang Lohengrin's 'Narration'; Charles Knowles sang 'The Song of Hiawatha' by Coleridge-Taylor; and Emily Squire took the solo in Bishop's chorus *Now tramp o'er moss and fell*.

Coward wrote in his diary: "Concert a brilliant success. Sir Edward and Lady Elgar most glowing in praise of what they had heard". The concert was followed by supper for those involved.

There was little chance to recuperate from the excitement, as the final day was as crowded as ever. "E. to Hall early", wrote Alice. The proceedings began at 10.15 and there were 2480 people competing on that day - six orchestras and around seventy choirs. Once again some of the preliminary tests took place on the Central Pier. Ten choirs entered the female voice class, won by Colne Co-operative Society. In the smaller mixed voice class the prize went to the Isle of Man Choir, competing for the first time. There were twelve entries in this class.

The Colne orchestra took advantage of Nelson's preoccupation with the concert of the previous evening to win both the string and full orchestra classes. In the former they won by one mark from the Lancaster Orchestra, with Nelson third; the same order as in the full orchestra class.

Following the discussion at the conductors' conference about the male alto, it had been decided to have two classes for male voice choirs. The first was for choruses of 16-30 voices; the other was for larger choirs of 24-40 singers. Habergham Glee Union won the first group, and Manchester Orpheus the second. Only four choirs entered this larger and more demanding competition, for which there were four test pieces (two in the afternoon, and another two in the evening, as in the Challenge Shield): *The Song of the Spirits* by Schubert; *Love* by Richard Strauss; *Boot and Saddle* by Bantock; and *A Franklyn's Dogge* by Mackenzie. This last came in for some censure from the *Manchester Guardian* critic:

> ...Whilst sympathising with the desire to provide something of a lighter order, we doubt the wisdom of the inclusion of *The Franklyn's Dogge* in this male-voice section. We are accustomed to associate items of this type with a desire to tickle the musical palate of the

unthinking multitude, but not with such a serious educational movement as the Morecambe Festival.

The programme was well behind schedule by the beginning of the afternoon: the Challenge Shield was due to begin at 1.15 but it was after two before it started. Despite the fears expressed at the conductors' conference over the increased number of singers permitted, no less than fourteen choirs entered, The first test piece was an eight-part song of extreme difficulty: a setting by Peter Cornelius of Heine's poem *Der Tod, das ist die kühle Nacht*. It was translated by Gorton and published under the title 'O Death, thou art the tranquil night'. Dissonances abound, and there are several difficult key changes - for instance, at one point G minor, B minor, D major, C minor, G minor, Bb minor, all within thirty bars. The second section begins with a tenor solo, and the final pages need expressive and controlled *pianissimo* singing. McNaught gave his opinion that he knew nothing more difficult. Gorton put it more discreetly in the programme book: "When it has been sung fourteen times, [it] will still for many doubtless contain beauties unrevealed".

The *Manchester Guardian* critic loved it:

> ...In the choral work of Cornelius we find the intimate expression of his deepest wells of feeling and gain an insight into his wonderfully poetic and musical nature. Words and music, in the hands of this creative genius, are blended into one harmonious whole...Until quite recently...his part-songs for mixed and male voices have been neglected here and in Germany in the most unaccountable manner; and yet what glorious things he has accomplished in this domain of music - veritable pearls of great price in our choral literature!

Musical World saw it as part of a continuing process of choral improvement - the very thing Gorton and Howson were aiming for:

> Such music [Brahms' part-songs] was far beyond the powers of the ordinary vocal society, but its being selected from time to time has made its performance compulsory. The difficulties which have taxed the conductors to discover a true interpretation have at the same time improved the abilities of the singers, until the music, which at first seemed only difficult and incomprehensible, has become understood, its beauties thoroughly appreciated, and the singers have come to be satisfied only with what is best in music. The efficiency now is such that Brahms has become intimate, and in Peter Cornelius has been reached the extreme of difficulty in these competitions.

The *Lancashire Daily Post* opined:

It possesses great distinction, though its beauties are of a sombre character, and its strange chords had an impressively weird effect. As a test it presented unusual difficulties to the singers. Its constant iteration did not produce a very heartening effect on the audience, though the mournful atmosphere was in a measure lightened by the lively madrigal which preceded it.

The song referred to was the other test piece in the afternoon, a five-part madrigal by Thomas Tomkins, *Fusca, in thy starry eyes*.

The first six choirs were greeted politely, but did little more than emphasise the problems of performing the Cornelius. Hanley were seventh to sing, and the *Staffordshire Sentinel* reported that "...it was transparent that the audience were expecting something exceptional from the Hanley choir. At all events it was noticeable that no sooner had Mr James stepped on to the platform than he was received in a way which was hitherto observable by its absence". Nor did the Potteries choir disappoint the expectations of the audience. "The first phrase of the madrigal was sufficient to demonstrate the superiority of the vocal quality and perfect combination over any of the choirs so far heard", said the *Sentinel* proudly. In the Cornelius they did even better. "The reading of the second piece was a triumph in regard to feeling and expression. It was one of the most soulful renderings of a majestic conception that one has had the pleasure to listen to at any time. It was pretty generally realised...that the choir which would beat that had to accomplish the practically impossible".

McNaught later described the reaction of the four judges, in what was "one of the most extraordinary moments of my life...I was in the box, along with Sir Edward Elgar, Dr Sinclair and Frederick Corder. Never in my experience had I heard such fine choral singing. When that choir began to sing all the adjudicators were at attention. There was no talking in the box. I myself was registering the marks, or trying to do so. After it was over I said to Elgar, 'What do you think of that?' Elgar replied, 'I don't know. I know it is the finest singing I have heard in my life'. I turned to Corder and said, 'What is your view?' Tears were running down his cheek, and he could not reply. Sinclair had nothing to say. I will never forget that moment, for it left an enormous impression upon my mind, as I know it did upon the minds of the others with me in the box".

The chief threats to Hanley were four of the last five choirs to sing - Southport, Morecambe, Blackpool, and Nottingham. Blackpool sang the madrigal beautifully, and the judges selected Hanley, Morecambe and Nottingham to join them in the final.

"*Wonderful* singing", wrote Alice. "Judges very late, hurried dinner & back to hall". The concert began with the finals of the full orchestra and male voice classes, and it was gone nine o'clock before the final round of the Challenge Shield was able to get under way. "The test pieces in the evening were of slighter character, but none the less exacting", wrote the *Manchester Guardian*. They were *Night Whispers* by the Swiss composer Möllendorf; and Parry's *Tell me, O love*. The *Manchester Guardian* said:

> The singing of Hanley, Blackpool, and Morecambe (the result being in this order) was simply marvellous. At no previous festival has such a uniformly high standard been maintained by the first three choirs, for each attained the distinction of full marks in one or more of the four test pieces, and none obtained fewer marks than 76 out of a maximum of 80.

Hanley in fact totalled 316, including 80 each for the Cornelius and the Möllendorf, and 78 each for the English songs. Blackpool scored the maximum for the madrigal, and finished second on 311, one more mark than Morecambe, who were awarded full marks for the Parry. It was the last time Robert Howson was to hear his beloved choir.

The high standards of singing now being achieved by the best choirs was making judging difficult, as the *Manchester Guardian* commented:

> At such competitions as this varying degrees of executive ability are usually sufficient to enable the judges to discriminate, but in the finals for the Challenge Shield and male-voice classes there is no such marked disparity, all displaying those finer qualities which are inseparable from singing of the highest excellence, so that the contest resolves itself into a question of coincidence between the several choir conductors' conceptions and interpretation of the music and those of the adjudicators. The conductor whose reading coincides with their ideas gains the first prize, but it does not follow that the second choir was one whit inferior to its rival in the matter of artistic interpretation.

Before Dr McNaught announced the winners, and Alice Elgar presented the prizes, Canon Gorton gave a speech of thanks to all concerned, and then invited Elgar to address the gathering. His speech was reported in full by the *Morecambe Visitor*.

> Rising amid loud and prolonged cheering, Sir Edward said he was going to say that that was the proudest moment of his life - but it wasn't. (Laughter). He had hoped at the Festival this year to have welcomed and introduced to them his old friend Sir Hubert Parry, but

unfortunately illness prevented him attending. However, he hoped that that great honour and pleasure was only deferred until next year. (Applause). Therefore the culmination of the Festival was not yet: Sir Hubert's genial presence and real English feeling would do them good and set them all going again. It had always been a pleasure to come to Morecambe to see and hear the wholesome sort of effect which music had in Morecambe and the surrounding districts. It was rather hard work being surrounded by 6000 people all ready and willing to take up the extremely heavy duties of judge - and the very small emoluments attached to it (laughter) - without the slightest hesitation, and it was so very hard to occupy their time by telling them that which they knew already. Looking back over the past, he thought a vast work had been accomplished at Morecambe in being able to get together such a splendid chorus as the one which the previous night had sung *King Olaf*. (Applause). Of course for the actual singing and finish of their performance they had to thank Dr Coward (Applause). Dr Coward loaded the gun and he (Sir Edward) came and let it off. (Laughter). If it missed the mark then it was Dr Coward's fault and not his. There had been called into being a splendid chorus which was a credit to any part of England (Applause). Two years ago he had either said, or wrote them first and said them afterwards, some words which had been quoted and misquoted, and generally used for newspaper paragraphs, to the effect that the living centre of music was not in London, but 'somewhere further north'. Of course they had not so much music here as in London, where the great teaching centres must be - and in this connection they were proud to welcome Professor Corder - but what he meant, and what was perfectly well understood by honest people (hear, hear) was that the spirit of music among the people was stronger in the north than it was in the south (Applause). Southerners knew it was true, but they did not like to be told so (laughter and applause). And now the opinion was settling in people's minds that somewhere above the centre of England there was an enthusiasm amongst the people, and music was spreading amongst them in a way in which it was not in the south. 'You are making your own music among yourselves, and not importing it', said Sir Edward.

He thanked them sincerely for the warm reception they had given him and extended thanks to the chorus and orchestra for having done so well on the Friday night. He could only say go on in the way they were doing. They did not come for the mere winning of prizes, they came there for criticism, and he was sorry that the vocabulary of the judges was sometimes less limited than the vocabulary of the candidates (laughter). At one place some time ago, where he had the honour to look on - not as a judge - a disappointed candidate told him, in strict confidence, that the adjudicator was a - 'well, you can guess', added Sir Edward, with a smile. 'In strict confidence the same candidate told another judge that I was another', continued Sir Edward, amidst great laughter. He had thought only that evening that if another noun of the same kind could be found for his friends Dr McNaught, Dr Sinclair and Dr Corder, they would have at Morecambe what Dr McNaught is always asking for, 'a particularly good blend' (renewed laughter). One serious word: they had now got something which they had not fifteen years ago, the high and holy gift of music. He was not going to preach a sermon, but he begged them to always keep the artistic side in front, and not to let the mere winning of prizes run away with it (Applause). Sometimes choirs thought how much they were going to knock the other choir about and not of interpreting the spirit of the composer. 'I simply say', concluded Sir Edward, 'let us at Morecambe - for I consider I am now one of yourselves' (loud applause) - always keep the artistic side at the top and we shall go higher and higher'.

Elgar's reference to the earlier controversy was picked up by some of the press. In an article entitled 'The South and the North', *Musical World* referred to the phrase "you are making your own music, and not importing it", and said:

> This is a most important observation, and one it would be well to lay hold of, whether it applies to London or not. In London we have our competitions, it is true: but they cannot be reckoned in any way, as yet, essential to the community, like those in (say) Blackpool, Morecambe, Kendal, and other places...The conditions existing in the metropolis are necessarily very different from those in such towns as Sheffield, Manchester, Leeds, and Hanley: but a place that only 'hears' and does not seek to 'express' cannot claim the title 'musical', and so far was Sir Edward Elgar justified in locating the centre somewhere farther north.

The magazine *Truth* agreed:

> Unabashed by the outcry which his former utterances on the subject excited, Sir Edward Elgar has been developing again at Morecambe his favourite theory that in the matter of musical culture the sleepy south lags far behind the vigorous districts of the North, and really, taking his words in the sense in which they are doubtless meant, there would seem to be not a little warrant for the assertion. After all, the musical culture of a locality is truly indicated less by a multiplicity of concerts, given for the most part, in the case of London, by foreign visitants (and for the most part, also, not very adequately supported), than in active music-making of the right kind by the people themselves: and accepting this as the right test, there can be little doubt that Sir Edward Elgar's judgment is just.

One of the most eminent London critics, Joseph Bennett of the *Daily Telegraph* admitted:

> Concerning the choirs which make pretence to stand for the culture of choral music in London as a whole, a metropolitan critic must speak, if not with shame, at least with some confusion of face. We have fallen back from the point at which we stood less than half a century ago. The great cities of the provinces, with many a small one, are so far infinitely better off than the mother of them all, and there appears no sign of change.

In commenting on this, *Musical World* once again drew attention to north-south differences:

> Nowhere is this difference between the Metropolitan and the provinces more perceptible than in Lancashire and Yorkshire, where choral singing has reached a standard of excellence little dreamed of in London and the south. Among those works rendered during the past season, Sir Edward Elgar takes first place.

There had been nine performances of *The Dream of Gerontius*, three of *The Apostles*; and *King Olaf* at Morecambe. The article continued:

> Most of these choirs have, so to speak, been brought up on Handel's music, so that big fugal choruses have no terrors for them; but Elgar's music, with its strong emotional force and element of mysticism, is of a very different calibre, and it speaks volumes for the instinct and training of the northern chorus singers that they should, in almost every case, have so fully grasped the spirit of these works.

On Sunday morning, 21 May, Elgar went to church but Alice was "badsley cold in bed". In the afternoon Gorton took them to see Howson, and in the evening Elgar, Sinclair, and John Coates had supper at the Rectory. Coates was staying on at Morecambe, and he and Gorton had hoped to persuade Elgar to go climbing with them in the Lake District. But the composer wanted to return home, and he and Alice left at 12.30 on Monday. It was a "long cold journey" and they had to wait for an hour and a quarter at Crewe.

Alice wrote to Jaeger, who was now at Davos in Switzerland in an attempt to cure his tuberculosis:

> We had a nice time at Morecambe, the Fest. was more wonderful than ever, & the singing more truly unimaginably beautiful. It is of no use trying to describe it, it must be heard. It wd. have done you good to have heard 'King Olaf' with such a chorus[105]

And Elgar himself confirmed a week later: "Morecambe was a real joy: such singing & such real *art* feeling".[106]

105. Moore, 617 [29 May 1905]
106. Moore, 618 [6 June 1905]

The Rectory, Morecambe
[n.d., c.24 May 1905]

My dear Sir Edward -

First business. I enclose cheque for 35 guineas for fee & travelling - and believe me we are only afraid we are taking advantage of your kindness in not sending it for a more satisfactory figure - I went for your hotel account this morning - & to my dismay found that you had paid it - I enclose a cheque for the amount -

It is not needful for me to add that we cannot thank you enough for all you have done for us - and you looked so splendidly well when I left you that I feel less scrupulous in making this inroad on your time.

I should like to get an opportunity before long of talking over the future with you of next year - For the Makers of Music, we would engage the London Symphony Orchestra[.] We might take the whole of the Bavarian Highlands - in 'the South'[sic], and have our own Elgar festival, or add some Palestrina -

I had a grand time with Coates[.] We only wished we could have had you on the climb also -

I trust that Lady Elgar is better -

Corder has written a notice for Musical Times, calculated to stir even the 'sleepy London Press'[.] I have had two applications from conductors for copies of my sketch [about King Olaf] - so that I hope Novellos will not prohibit the sale -

I trust the American tour will do much for you, and that your best will shoot at sight the intrusive American -

In all gratitude
Yours ever sincerely
C.V.Gorton

I am sorry to say that my dear friend Howson is very seriously ill alack! alack![107]

Elgar's continuing support of the Morecambe meeting justified Gorton's enterprise; for as the *Musical Times* commented: "The Morecambe Musical Festival has maintained its position as the leading event of its kind, not merely in the North of England but in the whole country".[108] In the same issue Frederick Corder wrote about his wholehearted approval of the competitive movement and its aims:

107.   EBML 2476
108.   vol xlvi, June 1905, 396

Let the blasé musician in want of a new sensation spend a couple of days at one of these wonderful gatherings and hear not only the best of good music, but music of a class to which he is probably an utter stranger. Beyond this he will have such a surprise as to the possibilities of choral performance as no words of mine can hope to describe. I have heard choirs of mill-girls that made me wonder what was left for the archangels; I have heard choirs of rough men brought to the fine edge of a solo quartet of trombones; but that crowning glory of the north, the well-selected mixed choir carefully trained by some local conductor, can touch the heart and compel the unwilling tear in a way that nothing else can. Here is England's strength and beauty: why is not the fact better recognised?[109]

Corder was equally enthusiastic in his covering letter to the editor, F G Edwards:

I am just back from Morecambe where I was with Elgar & McNaught. We were all perfectly intoxicated with the beauty of the things. I have had the same experience before but this time I can't help gushing a bit. It was too lovely.[110]

But any discussion of the 1906 Festival was not possible before the Elgars left for America (their first visit) on 9 June. There were going as the guests of Professor Sanford, who met them off the boat and made them most welcome: "our kindest of hosts made everything lovely",[111] Elgar wrote to Jaeger. But the weather was oppressively humid; and despite being made an honorary Doctor of Music by Yale University on 28 June, the Elgars did not really enjoy their stay.

While they were away, Robert Howson finally capitulated to the heart disease which had been plaguing him for years. He was fifty-two.

The Rectory, Morecambe
June 24 1905

My dear Sir Edward -

The blow which for 2 years I have dreaded has fallen and my dear friend Howson has been taken -When I was sitting by Lady Elgar at the Festival and saw him sitting below to hear his choir sing (for the last time) it came upon me that he was a dying man - He never left his bed since you and I were with him and after a discipline of pain which

109.   *op cit.*, 378
110.   BL Add MS 41574 fo. 245
111.   Moore, 619

made us welcome the end he passed away on Thursday morning - His body was taken to St. Laurence's church where we held the Eucharist this morning at 7. Oh how you helped us - He had arranged a Kyrie out of Gerontius (I must send it to you) and its wonderful unearthly beauty soothed many sad hearts - Then a few nearest to him laid his body to rest in his native village of Wray - where as a lad he 'dreamed dreams & saw visions' - He had that ground work which the mass of musicians think is not needful - so long as they can master counterpoint - viz the pure heart which answers and reflects beauty in nature, in art, and literature - He was essentially a reverent soul - and I lose in him a companion & friend hard to part with -

I am sure you will never regret holding out to him the hand of friendship like the gentleman you are - it was his crown in life, and he was proud of you for it -

I will not add more, a line from you to his wife wholly worthy of him would mean much -

I hope the change is not tiring you -

Much love from us all
Yours ever sincerely
C.V.Gorton[112]

Although Howson had never been what one could describe as a close friend, his death removed someone Elgar could trust and confide in. Like Rodewald, Howson was a gifted amateur musician, and his untimely death moved Elgar deeply. Writing to his friend Troyte Griffith some months later, Elgar said: "Howson, a good man, was Conductor at Morecambe (amateur - a fine fellow, he was really the Bank Manager in his meaner moments). H. was the *musical* soul of the Morecambe affair & chose the music".[113] And replying to a question about the choral singing at Morecambe, Elgar once told a journalist, "You should have heard Mr Howson's work; he alone knew completely the difference between sentiment and romance".

Undoubtedly Howson's death was a major blow to the continuing success of the Morecambe Festival. Within a week, across the Atlantic, there came another one: Elgar agreed to visit America again the following May to conduct at the Cincinnati Festival.

---

112.   EBML 2479
113.   Moore, *Letters of a Lifetime*, 172

CHAPTER 8
'EVENING SCENE' AND THE WORCESTER FESTIVAL

Gorton's obituary notice of Howson appeared in the press at the end of June. It began with the details of the funeral at Wray, and then continued:

> We came back, sad at heart, to Morecambe, when flags were flying and all the tokens of a busy day. The commonplace stood out by contrast. But was Morecambe unmindful? Not at all. It was the more wonderful to think of what he had been able to bring into a place apparently removed from all we had seen.

> His was an onerous part, and faithfully he filled it. He ever agreed with me that Morecambe ought to be made a place *not only to trip to but to live in*, and therefore he concerned himself keenly in the recreations and intellectual movements in the town...

> But in one region he was supreme, he was a master of music. Irritated by Sir Edward Elgar's famous words regarding 'the centre of music in England', critics who did not trouble to understand what he meant, or read what he said, have had their jibes about Morecambe music. But we would challenge any town to produce any organisation which surpassed the Morecambe Madrigal Society, or any event in music to equal our Open Night, taking into consideration the material with which its creator started, or the size of the place in which this annual event occurred. Mr Howson's business capacities had much to do with its organisation, it was sound throughout. He insisted on ideas never less than the highest, and all was concentrated on its achievement. Then he added to this, genius, that gift not to be bought with a price...

> Of the Morecambe Musical Festival I need write but little. Some of us have had the privilege of working with him - but the Festival is his Monument. It owes its success again to his double gift for business and music. He steadily opposed anything but the best attainable and our credit alone consists in the fact that we had sufficient loyalty and sense to aid him to work out his ideas. His was the gift of the inner ear - a glance at a musical score was sufficient, it needed no instrument to unravel the harmonies. No composer seemed fresh for him. He was supremely Catholic in his taste. The Old English Madrigalists were his first love, but Palestrina, Bach, Beethoven,

Wagner, Brahms, Schubert and Elgar would occupy their due place. He opened out each year fresh fields, and the lists of selections of music at other Festivals were 'the sincerest form of flattery'...

The Divine Presence is either realised or it is not. With him It was realised, and therefore the absence of individual intrusion, the perfect blend, the restrained feeling marked not only the anthems, but each response and prayer. May these traditions remain with us! May we make ours the two-fold principle of self-sacrifice and reverence! These memories of the past were faithfully reflected for us in the Memorial Service of the Holy Communion on Saturday last in S Laurence's Church. He spoke to us in the mystical strains of the Kyrie adapted from Sir Edward Elgar's *Dream of Gerontius*, linking as it did in memory the great English musician and him who first taught us to love him.

We can but thank God for the gift given, committing the spirit to Him who gave it, with the trust that there awaits him a fuller and unfettered service in that world veiled from our sight.

The following week saw the first annual general meeting of the Association of Musical Competition Festivals, which had been set up the previous year. The weekly journal *Truth* took the opportunity to poke playful fun at the new organisation:

The aim of the association is not in any way to interfere with the independence of the local festivals, but simply to further the movement generally and make converts. In fact, one of the announcements in connection with next week's meeting has quite a revivalist ring: 'Some member of the Executive will be willing to answer personal queries in an adjoining room throughout the day'. After which it would really not surprise one to read that the Rev Canon Gorton will take charge of the penitents.

Gorton had been due to attend the meeting, which was held on 27 June, and to speak on the Morecambe Festival and its finances. Out of respect for Howson he did not go but sent his paper which was then read out by the secretary. In it he laid down the principles on which the Festival was based. Morecambe had rejected the idea of financial guarantees, he said. "Guarantee involves representation. Mammon has been kept in the background. Patronage is not asked for on bended knee. No free tickets are issued: even the committee pays for tickets". And in an obvious tribute to Howson he concluded: "The chief cause of financial success is the excellent choice of music".

Mary Wakefield, no doubt thinking back to her disagreements with the Morecambe Festival, sought to qualify its achievements. If other districts had such fine halls as Morecambe, she remarked, half their difficulties would be dispersed.

> The Rectory, Morecambe
> July 6 [1905]
>
> My dear Sir Edward -
> I enclose you a memorial notice of Howson - We feel very helpless without him - his taste so unerring & his judgment so sufficient to work upon -
>
> I have written to Corder asking him to select the music for competition - and to keep us free from publishers - We certainly will include the part song you sent me from Hanley ['*Shall I compare thee to a Summers day*' by Havergal Brian] - It was the last music which Howson read, and he spoke very highly of it -
>
> We are of course most anxious to know what you can do for us - whether we can have Makers of Music - This with the whole of Bavarian Highlands, might form nucleus of our concert on Friday -the London Symphony Orchestra 70 strong would cost us £220. I do not know whether we dare risk this[.] We might have [a] fine programme -
>
> When you return I shall be glad to get opportunity of a talk with you -
>
> I do not feel desirous of putting my introduction to King Olaf in the paper basket - We paid Novellos £3 for use of libretto - and a bill of £107 for music - they gave kind permission to sell remainder of 300 copies if I paid them royalty of *One Penny* per copy -
>
> I am sending it to Scribner suggesting that they publish it with illustrations - It would help if you would send Scribner 5th Avenue New York, a line to say that you have read, and approve -
>
> I hope you are getting some quiet and that the change is doing you both good -
>
> With our united love
> Yours sincerely
> C.V.Gorton[114]

The Elgars returned from America to a backlog of letters and it was not till the end of July that Elgar informed Gorton, in a letter which is missing, that he would be unable to attend the next Morecambe Festival because of his American commitments.

114. EBML 2473

The Rectory, Morecambe
Aug 2 [1905]

My dear Lady Elgar -

It is too serious a loss for us to sustain without every effort that Sir Edward should not be with us - I propose to send out a circular to the conductors asking them whether June would be too late in the year to hold their choirs together - If we find this possible can Sir Edward promise us to come -We do not want to fall back into some well-worn ruts, and this we shall do without he stands by us -

Would it be convenient for me to see him about 14th of August[?] -

I have been spending the morning sailing with John Coates at Ambleside, but he spends most of his time wheeling his baby in a perambulator -

We are singing the Ave Verum on Sunday next at our Parish Church -

With our united love

Yours vy sincerely
C.V.Gorton[115]

But even the Canon's persuasive pleading was to no avail this time: Elgar had made us his mind. His popularity was leading to invitations from many places and, together with the Birmingham professorship, was making increasing demands on his time. Jaeger enquired about the second part of *The Apostles* and received the following depressed reply from the composer on 6 August:

> ...I know nothing about Apostles pt.2. or any analysis: if it is ever finished I imagined you might take on the analysis *if* properly recompensed: my life now is one incessant answering of letters & music is fading away.[116]

However, Elgar was keen to compensate for his absence from Morecambe. He invited the Canon to join the Elgars' houseparty for the Three Choirs Festival at Worcester, and two weeks later on 21 August Alice noted in her diary: "E. writing part Song with Coventry Patmore's words". Gorton had earlier given Elgar some copies of a small anthology of poetry entitled *Brotherhood with Nature*. It was compiled by Charles Rowley, a leading Manchester philanthropist,

115. EBML 2475
116. Moore, 619

Worcester Festival, September 1905, with (left to right) Canon C V
Gorton, Carice Elgar, Annie Gandy, Alice Elgar, Julia Worthington

and proceeds from the sale went towards the Ancoats Hospital. On page 20 were three stanzas headed *An Evening Scene*. They were an extract from a longer poem, *The River*, by Coventry Patmore. On 24 August Elgar, much brighter now, wrote to Jaeger:

> ...You will receive - the firm will - a new part-song - my best bit of landscape so far in that line[.] You won't make anything of it on the P[iano]F[orte]. - Morecambe is the place to hear it.[117]

Jaeger was delighted to know that Elgar was at last composing again, and replied: "Right you are, I'll *hear* it at Morecambe, if I'm alive".[118]

The same day Elgar wrote to 'the firm':

117. *op cit.*, 621
118. *op cit.*, 622

...With this I send a part-song. I have not yet heard as to permission to use the words but I do not think there will be any difficulty in that as they are by Coventry Patmore. If possible I should like it *printed quickly* so that it may be in time for *selection* for Morecambe & possibly other meetings which are now, or soon, making out their schemes.[119]

Naturally Gorton was also informed.

Plas Gwyn, Hereford
August 24: 05

My dear Canon Gorton:
I have written - or rather completed a partsong in memory of our friend Howson.

You will like it.

Now: the words are out of the Ancoats Book selected by Chas. Rowley. (You gave me some for distribution). "An evening scene" by C.Patmore p.20.

I must get permission to use the words & you can help me by finding out at once who publishes Coventry Pat's poems - (we have 'The Angel in the House' but no others) I thought you might get to know from C.Rowley who gave him permission to use the poem & I can go straight to headquarters

Be quick!

My love to you all:
Yrs ever
Edward Elgar

Looking forwd to seeing you at Worcester.
I *think* you sent me the words long ago in (*unreadable*) MS.

The Rectory, Morecambe
Aug 25 [1905]

My dear Sir Edward -
A thousand thanks. We are all greatly touched by your most kind thought - Nothing could be more acceptable & lasting as a memorial -

What a subject it is, and you will begin where we poor mortals leave off -

119. Novello archives.

["]The bees boom past, the white moths rise["] -

It is full of beautiful suggestions and quiet sounds -

I have written to Rowley - if he is away from home, I will find publisher in other ways -

Looking forward greatly to seeing you -
Yours gratefully
C.V.Gorton[120]

Elgar gave further details of the song in a letter to the chairman of Novello, Alfred Littleton, on 26 August:

> ...it is quite a short thing & will do for artistic singers but I fear it's not a gold mine & it certainly isn't a pot boiler - I think it's the best I've done & I put it to the memory of Mr Howson of Morecambe: one of the best men I ever met.[121]

Having discovered that permission to use Patmore's words was required from his widow Harriet, Gorton wrote to her telling of Elgar's plans, and she replied on 6 September: "It is with pleasure that I have written to Sir Edward Elgar to say that the verses you named might be published to his music". However, Elgar discovered that Patmore had later revised the poem, while Rowley had used the original words of 1844. Elgar preferred the original, and wrote himself to Harriet Patmore, who replied on 28 September:

> ...As you wish to retain the words 'The bees boom past, the White moths rise' and 'Bayeth the[sic] old guard hound', please do, especially as you think they are invaluable for the music. Thank you for writing to me about them.[122]

Meanwhile Jaeger had taken a proof of the song home to study, and found it "...altogether a perfect gem of a 'picture'. But it will require marvellous singing to bring out all the poetry that is in the piece. A rough performance will utterly ruin it & the average concert going ass 'wont see anything in it'. Anyhow, I congratulate you on the lovely

---

120. EBML 2472
121. Moore, 625
122. Patmore's revisions read: 'The chafers boom; the white moths rise'; and 'Bayeth a restless hound'.

creation & the Morecambe people on the chances they will have of hearing it properly performed".[123]

Elgar was represented at the Three Choirs that year by three major works - *The Dream of Gerontius* (conducted by Atkins), *The Apostles*, and the *Introduction & Allegro* for strings. In addition there was the first performance of Atkins' cantata *Hymn of Faith* to Elgar's libretto. And the new Mayor of Worcester, Hubert Leicester, one of Elgar's oldest friends, had arranged for the composer to be given the Freedom of the City at a special ceremony on the Tuesday.

The Elgars had taken Castle House in College Green for the duration of the Festival, as they had done three years earlier. The opening service was held in the Cathedral on Sunday afternoon, 10 September, but the musical part really began on Tuesday after the presentation at the Guildhall. Canon Gorton arrived in Worcester on the Monday, having travelled down from Morecambe with Mrs Gandy. Jaeger also arrived that day, although when originally invited he thought he would be too ill to attend. The other members of the Elgars' party were their daughter Carice, and niece May Grafton; Frank Schuster; Henry Embleton, a wealthy northern businessman and musical patron; Mrs Henry Wood, who arrived on the Wednesday; and three friends from America, Mrs Julia Worthington, Professor Sanford, and Frank van der Stücken from Cincinnati. Elgar also found accommodation for Havergal Brian, bought him tickets for all the concerts, and introduced him to all his friends.

On the Monday evening Elgar, Gorton and Jaeger went for a walk by the river Severn. Gorton wrote to his wife:

> ...Elgar was full of reminiscences of the place where he spent his boyhood[.] The house we are now in, he used to visit as a small boy and here improvise to two old ladies.

Everyone was up early on the Tuesday morning. Gorton put on his clerical robes and accompanied Elgar to the Guildhall, where the latter introduced him to all the officials. Elgar had decided to wear his new robes from Yale, and Gorton helped him with them: "a very splendid raiment of silk and velvet", he told his wife; "others all in war paint...It was a scene to remember". Hubert Leicester made a "most excellent" speech. In it he listed the previous eight Freemen, from the first one, Lord Nelson. "As the first freeman, Nelson,

123. EBML 9193 (29 August 1905).

relieved us of the reproach that England is not a fighting nation. Even so has Sir Edward relieved us of the reproach that Englishmen are not musicians", Leicester said.

"Elgar's reply was delightful with his lightness of touch & happy phrasing", Gorton wrote to his wife. In his speech, Elgar referred to his childhood and youth spent in the city, and how much he had learned from belonging to the Glee Club. "I regret that the day for that sort of thing has gone", he said. Using the opportunity to be slightly controversial, he urged the council to "build a large hall where performances might be given equal to those in other towns". Perhaps he was thinking of Morecambe's Winter Gardens.

> After the function we fell into procession, [*Gorton wrote*] the streets hung with flags, and lined with people - I think I was the only representative of any church present - and felt somewhat of a fraud, and much more of a friend to Elgar who as you know is always very sweet to me -
>
> Then to the Cathedral in state and to Gerontius - Coates was unrecognisable - and Muriel Foster angelical - the orchestra very excellent but we could give them points in brightness of tone, & attack etc,etc - Still it was most moving, and at times it breathes the Divine Presence & shakes one - there was a vast assembly, every corner. I had the millionaire's tickets[,] a prime seat -
>
> Afterwards I found May, she looks so splendid that she has quite won Carice, & the niece Miss Grafton -
>
> We went to lunch with the Mayor - Mrs.Gandy - Miss Burley - an American lady & Mr.Schuster & myself at a table - when we had great fun - Then back to [the] Cathedral[:] Ivor Atkins Hymn of Faith...- then a difficult Brahms[*Fourth Symphony*] - After I rowed Carice, M.Grafton & May up the river -
>
> Then dinner & great larks, Mrs.Gandy being in high form - Then back to [the] Cathedral: Cornelius [*eight-part motet 'The Surrender of the Soul to the Everlasting Love'*], Bach[*cantata no.61 'Come Redeemer of our Race'*] Beethoven[*Fourth Symphony*] - Mozart[*Requiem*] - but [the] singers were tired & so was I...It seems a shame for me to be revelling in these good things...

Annie Gandy was the ideal houseparty guest. Her quick wit and sense of fun were greatly appreciated, especially by Elgar. One particular incident of this Festival was recalled by Mrs Gandy's grandson, James Brandreth:

...Lady Elgar said to my grandmother that she found her husband was
in a bad mood as 'he had his trousers on'. My grandmother said she
would be surprised had he not, but it seems that, when happy, he
wore knee breeches.[124]

The following morning's concert saw performances of Strauss's *Tod
und Verklärung*; Parry's *De Profundis* (which left Gorton
"untouched"), conducted by the composer; and *The Beatitudes* by
César Franck, which "appealed most to me". Alice Elgar took Gorton
and Frank Schuster to lunch with the Bishop of Worcester, Charles
Gore, and Gorton sat next to him - "very kind, and courteous - but
no luminary", he commented.

In the afternoon came Mendelssohn's *Hymn of Praise*. John Coates
excelled as he had the day before in *Gerontius*: "Coates sang
'Sorrows of Death' and 'Watchman' very excellently". After the
concert Gorton spoke at length with Henry Walford Davies about the
possibility of his attending the next Morecambe Festival. With Elgar
absent, the presence of an up and coming young composer would be
a great asset: and Walford Davies's cantata *Everyman* had been well
received at its première at the Leeds Festival the previous autumn.

There were fourteen to dinner that evening with the arrival of Mrs
Henry Wood, "looking very splendid". Mrs Gandy was "in very great
form to the delight of Elgar". The evening concert was a mixture of
orchestral and vocal items. Harry Plunket Greene sang Parry's *The
Soldier's Tent*, conducted by the composer, and arrangements of
Irish and Welsh folk songs by Arthur Somervell. Frederick Austin
and Emma Albani also sang; and the orchestral items were
Schubert's *Rosamunde* overture: Strauss's *Don Juan*: and
Tchaikovsky's *Capriccio Italien*, all conducted by Atkins. However,
the highlight of the evening was Elgar conducting his own
Introduction & Allegro for strings. There was a "great crowd" at
Castle House afterwards, with much talking in the smoke room. The
ladies retired at 11.30, the men at midnight: Elgar and Gorton
continued talking in the Canon's room.

The following day, Thursday 14th, was the Gortons' nineteenth
wedding anniversary. Charles wrote to his wife:

I have just come back from the early service [at the Cathedral], when
I could but thank God for the gift, and pray that the bond might

124. Letter to the writer, 18.vii.1985.

strengthen continually - It is the loveliest September morning - 'On such a day did' - and as I am on the edge of going to Cornwall all seems more vivid - The love has grown much since then, though we did not know that it could.

The Gortons had spent their honeymoon at St Mawgan in 1886. Now he could have had no finer anniversary treat than the performance of *The Apostles* which took place that day, and which for him was obviously the high point of the week. It is best described in the Canon's own words to his wife:

What a day it was for me - After an ideal morning of sunshine with September in the air, the streets filled with expectant people - carrying Apostles in their hands - and (not a few the Interpretation). The Cathedral was packed - I sat in the millionaire's seat next to a delightful American lady, Mrs.Worthington, a great ally now of mine, Mrs.Gandy's, & May's - The service[sic] began at 11.30, the great want was Ffrangcon Davies[*Dalton Baker sang the part of Christ*] - the great gain was Plunket Greene[*as Judas*] Coates was admirable & M[uriel] Foster thrilled me - It was most moving - and the thousands crept out of [the] Cathedral, after 'Turn ye[sic] - to the stronghold' - I conveyed a party to lunch with the Mayor - where we had a high time[,] Mrs W[orthington] Mrs.Gandy & May being with me -Back to [the] Cathedral at 2.30 - I insisted on Mrs.Henry Wood taking my seat - and thus unconsciously won her most extreme thanks - I sat in a side chapel almost alone & out of view, near staging[:] and virtue had its reward[;] the isolation, and quiet were helpful - seeing no one, only floods of music pouring forth - The Ascension scene surpasses all - I was able to get out and recover myself before the huge gathering emerged - Then dozens to tea[.] I had a good talk with Sir Hubert Parry - and a dozen more people of interest - Then for a walk down river with May & Mrs.Worthington - Then to evensong. I saw dear May to the station - and then to Elijah - But alas! it sounded colourless - and I came out [at] half time despite Ag[nes] Nichols[sic] - [Andrew] Black etc - I spent the rest of the evening with Elgar - walking in the moonlight in the close - consuming endless pipes - and hearing much - Then in to Sinclair where a doctor who knew S.Hawker well gave us sloe-gin and so to bed.

One of the topics of conversation that week was the poet Browning. Gorton was something of an expert, and had already had articles published in the *Parents' Review*: on 'Browning and Italian Art' (1898), and 'Browning on the Incarnation' (1899). In the current issue (September 1905) was a seventeen-page article by Gorton entitled 'The Browning Letters', on the correspondence between Browning and his wife Elizabeth Barrett. In the Elgars' visitors' book Gorton wrote the following quotation from *Paracelsus*:

I go to prove my soul!
I see my way as birds their trackless way -
I shall arrive! what time, what circuit first,
I ask not: but unless God send his hail
Or blinding fire-balls, sleet, or stifling snow,
In some time - his good time - I shall arrive:
He guides me and the bird. In his good time!

                    Words dear to Gen. Gordon in Khartoum
                        C.V.Gorton   Worcester 1905

It seems likely that Julia Worthington was at this time given her nickname 'Pippa', after Browning's heroine: from now on this was how Elgar usually referred to her. "It exactly fitted Julia's charm, kindness and ability to bring out the best in all her friends, and her light-hearted and even mischievous influence upon them".[125]

Frank Schuster had passed on to Elgar an invitation from Lady Charles Beresford to join a cruise in the Mediterranean with the Royal Navy (her husband had recently been made Commander-in-Chief of the Mediterranean fleet). Elgar at first refused, but at the last minute changed his mind and then followed a rush to get him ready to leave. Gorton was travelling down to Cornwall on the Friday evening to see his cousin's wife who was seriously ill. He explained the day's events in a letter to his wife:

> Elgar started yesterday afternoon with Schuster to join the Fleet - he is going on flagship for Constantinople - & isles of Greece - Lady Elgar went with him to the station - I suggested that we should follow - Mrs.Worthington[,] Mrs.Gandy, Carice & Miss Grafton their niece - We just raced down the platform in time to see him & had great fun - I met coming back Muriel Foster, and had a long walk & talk with her - about Elgar & his future -I ended up by saying I had promised one of my daughters [to ask] whether she was as much an angel inside as she was outside? (not a bad speech for a married man) She smiled - and said 'I am trying'[.] I called to see Elgar's father at the music shop - He is 85 and told me many excellent things...
> We were quite a small party for dinner - Lady Elgar explained to me how much she owed me for coming! how kind it was, etc, etc, etc[.] I caught the 10 train, slept off and on[,] arrived at Columb Road at 7: left my things & walked the 6 miles, with memories crowding up from the lanes - the heather, ferns & gorse...

Now the fortuitous arrival of a cheque for £5 from Simrock for one of his translations prompted the Canon to invite his wife to join him

125. Atkins, 160

for a short holiday. She was reluctant to undertake the long journey without an overnight break, and wrote to Alice Elgar about the possibility of staying at Hereford.

S.Mawgan, S.Columb, Cornwall -
[n.d., c.17 September 1905]

My dear Lady Elgar -

Here am I on the side of one of the loveliest valleys in England[:] the Carnanton woods above clambering up the stream - the light and sound of the Atlantic, the convent and the church - side by side - and the church in this instance all it should be, beautifully kept, and a holy spot, and in the churchyard [an] Anglo Saxon Cross, the bodies of shipwrecked mariners & villagers -

The one shadow my dear friend Mrs.Gilbert lying in bed with angina pectoris, but it is hardly a shadow, for I sit and talk to this sweet soul, who bears her agony when it comes with a smile - Loving all beauty, with a sense of awe in the presence of all life - happy in any ten square yards of the earth so beautiful here, in the little room in the minute inn are the choicest of books - and holiest of pictures - yet music means most to her, and the name Beethoven quickens her face[.] Yet to her Elgar is only a name - and it is a delight for her to know of this new world - of which as an ignorant traveller I can tell her something -

Last week must ever be for me a joyous memory - You remember Fra Lippo Lippi's picture of himself in a high company - that expresses my sense that I received so much more than was my due - Your kindness & the friendship of Sir Edward is a mystery to me - it is the incident which makes other failures insignificant -

For the jests and larks we had were only a reaction after the exaltation of the music - It was wonderful to sit in the cathedral and think of that great minster of sound built by the magician - not (see Abt Vogler) as Solomon built aided by spirits summoned by his black art[126] - but aided by angels of sound - Surely he will be enheartened - to look up and give of what has been given to him so lavishly - The fact that it is wholly impossible for such an one as Mrs.Gilbert to know anything makes one bold to hope that he may in the next section [of *The Apostles*], be mindful not only of the great structure, but add some chapel of our Lady where humble sinners may worship - At present each is part of the whole - In the Messiah there is that which not only fills the temple, but which may rejoice the home - Surely this is not unworthy - I may be writing heresy and nonsense - but will he not sacrifice if only once the greater for the less[?] - He shall feed his flock

126. See the first stanza of Browning's poem *Abt Vogler*.

-and O rest in the Lord - are worth the sacrifice - though the other may be the greater art -

He too might suffer the little children - to enter - Of course it all lies in his power as we so well have seen in our Festival - in melodies which never fail to move the hearts of all -

Now shall I tear this up or send it? You will pardon me on score of my ignorance -

I sat down to thank you for all your kindness, but this sounds all too conventional - The word Worcester for me (despite the sauce) will have a glamour of its own - May I send you for criticism & suggestions my Pilgrimage - the music fetters one so much -

I hope you have good news of your husband - I was at first doubtful of the experiment, but I am now sure it will be all for good -

With most sincere thanks & love -
Ever yours most sincerely
C.V.Gorton[127]

Plas Gwyn
19 Sept. 1905

My dear Canon Gorton.
I have been wishing to write ere this & send you enclosed possession found in yr. room, but I have had so much to write entrusted to me by Edward, besides all the re-settling, I cd. not till now -

Now I have yr. letter full of beautiful thoughts & words wh. has given me great pleasure to have & wh. Edward will love to read on his return - I cannot tell you how much E. & I & all of us appreciated the pleasure of having you with us, how delightful it all was, & how touched E. & I were by the appreciation of his works, & the affection shown to him, I cannot tell you. He had just been expressing it when I left him in the Railway Carriage when the delightful troop of friends saved or rather cheered us a little of the pain in parting though I hope only for a happily short time & for his great good - I have just had a telegram I am thankful to say "all well" from Patras & it all sounds so delightful. I trust & pray he will return invigorated, he [has] not been really vigorous for some little time.

I am so delighted that Mrs.Gorton telegraphed about breaking her journey to you, we shall be so [pleased] to see her & will take every care of her & see [her] off on her way to you.

127. EBML 2474

I am so glad you are in such a lovely place & what you say of yr. friend is most touching. Edward can only write as it comes to him, at any rate he will like to hear what you say -

Now I *hardly* ever say anythg. about my literary endeavours, but somehow I feel a strong impulse to send you 3 sonnets, you have so much feeling & sound literary judgment that it wd. be a pleasure to know if anythg. in them appeals to you *at all*, severe criticism may of course be expected. They were written rather long ago, I have done so little lately, but any small things I can do to save E. worries are far more worth & important than the poetical attempts I cd. make, still I think of things sometimes - I will send them tomorrow when I can look them up & please do not let them bore you or trouble about them.

I trust you & Mrs.Gorton will have a lovely holiday & soon have your Alice Elgar with you again.

Yrs. very sincerely
C.A.Elgar
I shd. much like to see the Pilgrimage.

A postcard showing Constantinople from the Golden Horn, and dated 27 September, was sent to Morecambe Rectory:

Love to you all   Ed: Elgar

CHAPTER 9

THE 1906 FESTIVAL

Gorton's plans for the next Morecambe Festival were going well. He already had Elgar's new part-song, and Brian's: and as his letter to Alice mentioned, he was engaged in translating the libretto of a short choral work by Humperdinck, *Die Wallfahrt nach Kevlaar* (The Pilgrimage to Kevlaar), which he had heard at a Handel Society concert in London in May 1903, and which he hoped to include in the Friday evening concert.[128] Walford Davies was almost certain to attend. Yet Gorton was missing the unerring guidance of Johnstone and Howson, and was looking to involve gifted musicians in the planning. One obvious candidate was Ernest Newman, who had succeeded Johnstone as music critic of the *Manchester Guardian*. The Canon wrote to Elgar asking his opinion, and must have been staggered by the force of his reply, written on his way home from a rehearsal for the Norwich Festival.

> Langham Hotel, London.
> *Private*
> Just off home!
> [n.d.,13 October 1905]
>
> My dear Canon Gorton.
>
> I have just seen McNaught & asked him to say to you - if he sees you first - how *strongly* I feel the mistake you are making in taking any advice from Mr Newman. I do hope you will throw him over entirely: his influence is bad (& despicable) on all with whom he comes into contact.
>
> I do not interfere in things unless I am deeply interested. Morecambe, & anything of yours, interests me, but if you give a high artistic enterprise over to the evil one I leave you
>
> In great haste
> Yrs ever
> Ed: Elgar

128. Elgar's own Worcestershire Philharmonic Society had given the first English performance of the work on 7 May 1898.

Elgar had first met Newman in 1901 at Rodewald's house in Liverpool. He was impressed with the young man's musical perception and the strength and candour of his writing. Newman had called *The Dream of Gerontius* "the finest work ever produced at an English Festival", but recommended that Elgar give up writing oratorios for orchestral music. Newman was an atheist, and maybe Elgar suspected ulterior motives. In an interview with a young Manchester journalist on 23 December 1905 Elgar said: "[Newman] is an unbeliever, and therefore cannot understand religious music - music that is at once reverential, mystical and devout".[129]

The immediate reason for Elgar's antipathy was probably Newman's comments on the Birmingham lectures; and on Elgar's music in his new book on the composer, especially *The Apostles*, in which, he said "...the human element at times almost disappears and a frankly religious and didactic purpose flies out at us from the score..."[130]

The effect of such comments on the prickly Elgar can be well imagined: as he wrote to Professor Fiedler of Birmingham University on 14 July 1906:

> ...Newman appears to have deserted criticism to make personal attacks on such men as Richter...He seems to have quite lost his head out of pure (or impure!) conceit & seems to want to get cheap notoriety by abusing individuals. It is a pity.[131]

Yet Elgar's attitude towards Newman was ambivalent: in a letter to Walford Davies Elgar wrote: "Newman & myself are excellent friends".[132] The misunderstanding was eventually forgotten and Newman became once again one of Elgar's closest friends and advisers, receiving the dedication of the *Piano Quintet* in 1919.

However, Newman was not invited to join the Morecambe executive: and anyway early the next year he returned to Birmingham as critic on the *Daily Post*.

---

129. Gerald Cumberland, *Set Down in Malice* (Grant Richards, 1919), 83
130. Newman, *Elgar* (John Lane, 1905), 82
131. EBML 3270
132. EBML 2189 [19 November 1905]

At the beginning of November Gorton brought the Elgars up to date with his latest plans.

Morecambe
Nov 2 [1905]

My dear Lady Elgar,

The notice in M[anchester] Guardian of the lecture makes me want to read a fuller account - Can you kindly send me a paper[?] - I will return it - I am very anxious still further for news of all kinds -Was the voyage a success[?] - did Sir Edward translate the battleship into music[?] - What has he brought back with him, has he come back fit, did he have a good time, has he like a good man settled down to the Apostles[?] - this is the question of questions -

For a business question, what is to be the name of the part song? We are holding back our syllabus for it - I write to Jaeger[,] he tells me something else, to Dr.McNaught ard I get no answer - It is not 'Curfew Bell', but 'The *sheep* bell ringeth curfew time' - I think the whole line would do well, or the *River Brink* or a *river scene* - Will you kindly let me know what he has decided - ?

I have translated words of splendid part song for male voices - the Totenvolk - the Phantom host of Hegar's - only I am approached by Novellos - I wonder whether your husband knows it[?] -

I am very anxious to secure Frankoln [*sic*] Davies for our next Festival - I wish Sir Edward would send him a line - I am afraid we could not run to his usual fee - for last year we were £90 on the wrong side - Coates came for 20 guineas - I suppose Frankoln Davies could not accept this - perhaps he too is going to America

I fear I shall not be able to go to Gerontius at Manchester - as I have a big mission coming on here Nov 17-27 which consumes all time and energies -

What a delight it is to me to look back on our happy days at Worcester - but it must have taken you some time to recover from all it involved for you -

With much love to you all
Ever yours vy sincerely
C.V.Gorton

I am much concerned about the news about Jaeger - to whom I am greatly attracted[:] a man among a thousand - so different from the wooden people who run the concern & pocket the proceeds - He seems like a razor often used to cut cheese -

My writing is too vile, can you read any of it[?] - Sir Edward must get
me appointed to a canonry at Hereford, when I will buy a type-writer,
and bicycle with him along the Wye -[133]

On 3 November Elgar, back in Hereford after his second lecture at
Birmingham wrote to Jaeger:

Now Evening Scene seems best after all. I *did* like 'Curfew time' - but
the Curfew in the poem is ideal not real - & the title wd. be real & not
ideal. If you stick to the printed title 'Evening Scene' it will save
corresponding with Mrs. Coventry Patmore.

I think 'Evening Scene' a little prosaic, but there you are.

The first line is too long for a title & will be shortened ridiculously in
programmes.

I should like
Vesper   or better
Vesperal - a beautiful word which means everything & wd. make
people think.

I know I proposed it once before for some other thing but you thought
it churchy which of course it is *not* really[134]

So *Evening Scene* it was.

Elgar wanted to include a reference to Arthur Johnstone in his
lecture on critics at the beginning of December. He asked Gorton to
inform Lucy Johnstone of his proposed remarks.

The Rectory, Morecambe
Nov 11 [1905]

My dear Lady Elgar -

Many hearty thanks for your most welcome letter - I read the speech
with much interest, also an abbreviated report of the Brahms' lecture -

I obtained Mrs.A.Johnstone's address and wrote the message. It must
be obvious to her that Sir Edward could adopt no other course - While
I am writing I have no doubt that Olive is feasting herself at the

133. EBML 2483. An obituary of Jaeger in the *Manchester Guardian* [21
    May 1909] said: "Jaeger was keenly interested in the doings of the
    North-country competitive festivals, and assisted the Blackpool and
    Morecambe Executive in the Cornelius development, and was ever
    ready with helpful suggestions".

134. MS in possession of Felix Aprahamian.

Cheltenham concert [*the first in a tour by the London Symphony Orchestra conducted by Elgar*] - Would that I were with her -

Alas! how I miss Mr.Howson[!] it seems still impossible to believe I shall not find him in the town -and we feel the loss so greatly in music - he insisted on a high standard - and the absence of his personality tells at once on our Madrigal Society -

I had a most grateful letter from Mr.Brian for our selection of his song as recommended by Sir Edward - I will send on Monday a list of the music chosen -

I have translated 4[:] Hegar [*The Phantom Host*] Moellendorf [*Welcome to Spring*] -Brahms [*The Hump-Backed Fiddler*], and Humperdinck [*The Pilgrimage to Kevlaar*] - I will send copies as I get them from the publisher - Owing doubtless to the great man's introduction I find Schott willing to do anything I want -

You will be glad to hear that Ivor Atkins & Mr.[Walford] Davies are coming as judges in May next -

With kind love from all the family -
I remain yours very sincerely
C.V.Gorton[135]

Novello were now bringing out the new part-song, and on 30 November Gorton asked a favour in a letter to Alice:

...Would your husband kindly send Mrs.Howson 2 or 3 copies of The Evening Scene, she would greatly value the gift. Her sorrow is one which abides, for they were ever lovers and friends.[136]

Elgar gave a total of five lectures at Birmingham during the last two months of 1905. On 29 November his subject was 'English Executants', and in the course of this he spoke frankly on English choirs. His remarks were broadly complimentary, and his appeal for greater literary appreciation by singers was aimed as much at the education system as at the choirs themselves.

In England, in the north, choral singers are plentiful - it is possible to pick voices - to balance the numbers accurately and to turn out a machine as regular as a steam engine and perhaps as explosive. Every detail, every syllable is studied, but often there is something wanting - that something is an understanding of the subject sung about...I

135. EBML 2453
136. EBML 2430

want more intelligence from our Chorus singers - they should read up everything possible which bears upon the subject - the plot or story - of which they sing.[137]

Two weeks later, in the final lecture of the series, entitled 'Retrospect', Elgar affirmed his support for the competition movement, and spoke warmly of its aims and achievements:

> Larger audiences are being made and listeners educated by the Competition Festivals now, I am glad to say, being established throughout the Kingdom. When properly conducted, - and the English competitions are properly conducted on artistic lines, these gatherings are productive of good...
>
> It is a mistake to think that these competitors meet, in England at least (of the Principality I say nothing now), for the value of the prizes. They meet primarily - and this fact at least should ensure them a favourable eye from the critics - they meet primarily for criticism. The actual value of the prizes is so small that it need not be considered. And then the competition element - why should it be looked upon askance? On looking on Grecian land, two months since, and surveying the multitude of remains and ruins glorious in their surroundings, their nobility, their life history and their associations, the scenes of rivalry in athletics, poetry and song, were vividly brought to mind....
>
> I remembered also with joy that we have our own music - like this among the people. True, it cannot be picturesque in the way that ancient Greece was picturesque...but the feeling is the same - the rivalry - the chivalry and the song.
>
> Is the idea fanciful that from these gatherings much real good results? I think not.
>
> When the Salvation Army began in a small way, and even later, when its greater life astonished us, much was said against its methods and its aims. It has lived through this stage and it has reached the people in a way that religion - or it may be religionism has not done, and it is now looked upon by most serious churchmen as a valuable adjunct to their mission.
>
> The competition festival is in music doing similar work. Statistics are in some cases available as to the number of voices trained: we know in some places large choruses can now be got together where ten years ago no chorus was. It only needs to keep the standard of the music high, and the prize list low, to preserve the ennobling qualities of these institutions.[138]

137. Young (1968), 125-7, 143
138. ibid., 215-9

Early in the new year, Gorton wrote to inform Elgar that the Morecambe Madrigal Society had begun to rehearse *Evening Scene*. The annual Open Night on 20 February would be the first without Mr Howson. Ella Gorton wrote to her son Neville at Marlborough:

> I have just been making out a list of invitations to the Madrigal Open Night...I hope it will go well - though we miss 'our master' much...

Printed on the reverse of the evening's programme was a poem by Canon Gorton entitled *In Memoriam - R.G.W.H.* Two of the verses contained references to the part-songs by Elgar and Brahms which Howson had pioneered.

> Dear Friend, this hour recalls thy form,
> Thy well poised head, thy outstretched hand.
> Whilst thou didst hold all eyes intent,
> And music made with magic wand.
>
> What treasures didst thou draw for us
> From thy rich store, things new and old,
> Part song and glee and madrigal
> In mystic meaning manifold!
>
> The sounds came wandering like the wind
> Now fairy like with tiptoe tread
> Now bright with joy, now drear with gloom,
> And now with passion's hungry need.
>
> 'Those torrents' rose, from hidden source,
> Those deer stole out in moonlight wan.
> 'The Weary Wind' was lulled to rest,
> 'Those Happy Eyes' with love light shone.[139]
>
> Those Autumn leaves fell one by one,
> May dancéd in with glad surprise.
> 'In Dim-lit woods' we laid us down,
> 'The Night Watch' heard the lovers' sighs.[140]
>
> And didst thou lift our hearts with songs
> Which haunt our minds with mem'ries dear?
> And must thou not, dear friend, still make
> Sweet music - There as here.

139. Part-songs by Elgar: *As Torrents in Summer*; *My Love dwelt in a Northern Land*; *Weary Wind of the West*; *O Happy Eyes*.

140. Part-songs by Brahms: *Autumn*; *O Lovely May*; *Dim-lit Woods*; *Night Watch* (all in translations by Gorton).

It is easy, in an age more sophisticated and cynical, to smile at such an offering. Finer poetry has obviously been written: yet there is something touching in the genuine depth of feeling expressed.

After the outstanding success of the previous year it was inevitable that the 1906 Festival would be regarded as something of an anticlimax. The absence of Howson and Elgar was loss enough: but now the most successful choir of the last three meetings - Hanley Cauldon - had decided not to continue in competition. Its conductor, John James, had recently been appointed to lead the larger Hanley Glee & Madrigal Society (of which the Cauldon was part). He was quoted as saying:

> It is unwise to go further. If we win, and especially if we defeat a local choir, some indiscreet member of the choir may boast about it, even in the presence of the defeated singers, and that is not calculated to serve the best interests of music. The singers should ask whether the choir has beaten its own standard, and taken an interest in music for the cause of music, rather than in the defeat of an opponent. An ephemeral success in competition then becomes of more importance than steady progress.[141]

Gorton's preface to the programme book was largely devoted to a tribute to Howson.

> All who know the inner working of our Festival, and the cause of its phenomenal success, are well aware that it should rightly be called the 'Howson Festival'. It was Mr Howson who first gave it shape, his mind which guided its line of progress, his business capacity which dared fresh developments, his unerring sense of what was best in music, and his phenomenal knowledge which enabled us for fifteen years to supply test pieces which were often an education in themselves. He could tell at a glance what claimed attention; he could interpret the most subtle effects, and he therefore not only filled Morecambe with music, but he made it also overflow.

> There is not one of the Conductors who will not miss his presence, whilst as for Executive when we hold our meetings we do not miss him less, but more. Many of us seek to walk as well as we can in boots too big for us. Mr Howson never occupied a sphere in music, never had means at his disposal - either vocal or instrumental - which gave full play for his genius. I never look round on the thousands at our Festival without feeling that it is his work, and may the work now continue as his memorial; a memorial of a simple, honest and keenly artistic life - a life of service.

141. Quoted in Reginald Nettel, *North Staffordshire Music* (Triad, 1977), 32.

Henry Coward joined McNaught, Ivor Atkins and Walford Davies on the judges' panel. The Festival began on 9 May with the children's day. The *Musical Herald* praised the overall high standard:

> One fact stood out. Forcing of voices, which formerly spoilt the performance of most school choirs, was almost entirely absent. What one choir in a score could do twenty years ago all must do now. Our ears are educated, and voices must satisfy them.

One of the classes for choirs was won by the junior choir from Miss Ashworth's Ancoats Girls' Institute. The Girls' Friendly Society class was won by Ella Gorton's choir: the tests included Elgar's *The Snow*. At the evening concert, McNaught conducted the combined choirs in Roeckel's cantata *Merrie Old England*. The *Musical Herald* critic thought that "...the distribution of prizes was an anti-climax. Children are too tired at 10 pm to care about prizes".

The local competitions took place on the Thursday. Once again, the *Musical Herald* was very favourably impressed: "This was to me the most astonishing feature. Hour after hour, adult choirs passed in review. The proceedings on this day were not mere preliminaries to select choirs worthy of appearing at the concert. The contests took on their rightful importance as being the object of bringing the choirs to Morecambe. The whole of the choirs sang well. They were very small choirs, but the villages they came from are small. The standard, however, was high. Criticism is of little value when the performances are so much alike".

Walford Davies came in for criticism because of his churlish remarks. He said:

> Singers must realise their individual responsibility. An individual can bring down a whole choir, not so much by his stupidity as by his carelessness. Each singer should take a mental note of the pitch at the beginning of a piece, and compare it mentally at the end of each verse. I have said to a choir of boys, 'You are flat. You remember the pitch you started at. Get back to that'. They never failed to correct the fault. The flattening has spoiled this competition. If boys can set it right, surely an adult choir can do it.

The *Musical Herald* took the judge to task:

> I think it was too bad to accuse these choirs of carelessness in this way. They are models of earnestness. Flattening is a more serious matter than Dr Davies thinks, and he has not got the master patent for curing it.

The Festival concert on the Friday evening was conducted by Coward. There were three main works: Parry's *Pied Piper of Hamelin* (which had been premièred six months earlier at the Norwich Festival): Stanford's *Revenge*: and Humperdinck's *The Pilgrimage to Kevlaar*, in Canon Gorton's new translation. Preparation of both the Festival Chorus and the Lancaster Orchestra had been less thorough than for *King Olaf*, and it showed. "One expects so much from this splendid conductor", commented the *Musical Herald*, "but, given time and opportunity in the future, there can be no fear of the Morecambe chorus taking a high place". The *Yorkshire Daily Observer* discerned a relative indifference shown towards the concert: "One could not but remark that if half the finish shown in [the Challenge Shield] had been bestowed upon the three choral works sung at Friday's concert a much higher level of performance would then have been reached".

The rest of the programme was made up of prizewinners from the day's competitions, and song recitals from the three soloists - Mrs Henry Wood, Webster Millar, and Frederick Austin (who included Elgar's *Pipes of Pan* in his selection). The *Observer* noticed a worrying trend:

> One sadly fears that the festivals have not much educative value for the audiences which assemble in the Winter Gardens for the evening concerts. It was noticeable that the young lady winner in the obbligato class received more applause for her rendering of Braga's ineffably stupid Angel's Serenade than did Mrs Henry Wood for any of her songs by Brahms, Schumann, Grieg or Tchaikovsky.

Support for the final day's proceedings was as great and enthusiastic as ever, as the *Manchester Guardian* critic reported:

> To stand near the stage and look up at the vast audience of some five or six thousand people was to realise very pointedly the tremendous significance of these competitive festivals in the musical life of the North of England. The hall was filled too with a kind of electricity that one does not get at any mere concert, no matter how fine it may be.

The female voice class was won by Blackpool with 152 marks, two more than Barrow in second place. Ivor Atkins announced the result, and the *Musical Herald* critic disagreed with it:

> I preferred the Manx, Padiham, and Ancoats choirs to either of the winners, owing to their fine voices. Mr Atkins, however, is great at small details, and I hope he convinced the defeated competitors of

their faults. I should like to whisper to Mr Whittaker [of Blackpool] with the utmost deference to his fine choir, that tremolo ought to be suppressed.

In the smaller male voice competition (won by Lancaster) one of the tests was *Break, break, break* by Rogers, "the exquisite irrelevance and musical poverty of which suggested a sparrow calmly seating himself in the eagle's nest", wrote the *Manchester Guardian* critic. In the larger class Southport with 229 won by one mark from Habergham Glee Union, with Manchester Orpheus well beaten on 221. The three test pieces were *Counsel* by Spohr: *The Phantom Host* by Hegar (translated by Gorton); and Elgar's 'After many a dusty mile', from the *Greek Anthology* set. The *Musical Herald* criticised some of the pronunciation, but overall was very impressed:

> Mention of such points shows how hard it was to find fault. As Dr McNaught said, the three choirs were all splendid. A battle of giants. Each choir seemed to know that it was pitted against something worthy of its mettle.

The choice of the Lancaster orchestra to accompany the Festival Concert the previous evening allowed Colne and Nelson to renew their rivalry on equal terms, and this time Nelson won both classes. Runners-up in the full orchestra were the Potteries Orchestra, who "made a good impression", according to the *Musical Herald*.

In the Challenge Shield class the choirs began with Morley's madrigal *I follow, lo, the footing*, and Möllendorf's *Welcome to Spring*. Five of the choirs were selected to go on to the evening concert and to sing *Evening Scene* and Havergal Brian's *Shall I compare thee to a summer's day*. The *Musical Herald* critic raised an issue which was already contentious and becoming more so.

> Choirs in some classes have to be heard at two meetings, preliminary and final. Sometimes the judges add together the marks for the two performances, and sometimes it is announced that there will be no adding up of preliminary marks and final marks. Why add them up in any case? The preliminary is a contest for a place. The final is a competition for a prize. Each should be independent.

The final result was close, Barrow Madrigal Society with 309 defeating Blackpool by one mark. The Isle of Man Choir were eight marks behind in third place, Burnley were fourth and Nottingham fifth. The winners received full marks for *Evening Scene*, but the critic of the *Manchester Guardian* wrote:

Not one of [the choirs] gave even an approximately satisfactory rendering of Elgar's piece. This is a highly original bit of writing, a singularly faithful translation into tone of the drowsy, dreamy atmosphere of evening in the fields and its subdued sounds. Each choir took the music too fast, but apart from that, not one of them seemed to have really read and understood the poem or ever felt the magic and the mystery of such an evening in grey monotone as Elgar paints so wonderfully here.

The *Yorkshire Daily Observer* welcomed the song too:

At the first hearing it seemed scarcely distinguished, but it is eminently a thing which improves on acquaintance, and before the fifth repetition one recognised in it a gem of art, suggesting in a wonderful way the reposeful calm of evening, and investing the poet's words with fresh and subtle beauties. As a test piece in such a competition it was excellent, inasmuch as it provided an opportunity of judging of the ability of the several choirs to produce a good tone whilst singing in a sustained pianissimo, a most difficult thing to do.

The chief talking point of the Festival that year was the adjudication. The report in the *Lancaster Guardian* began by questioning the financial advisability of holding a Festival concert, and then continued:

There is another matter the Committee should consider and that is a more frequent change in the adjudicators. There are ominous signs which cannot be overlooked without injury. We do not say that there are any grounds for complaint, but unsuccessful competitors are often on the look out for some excuse.

Criticism there appears to be levelled at McNaught and Coward, as the other two judges were new to Morecambe: but generally it was Walford Davies's outspoken remarks which caused the greatest stir.[142] He was complimentary towards the meeting as a whole, calling it a "glorious festival of music". He continued, "It opens up vistas of glorious days to come when I hear four orchestras, mostly amateurs, playing the overture to Weber's *Euryanthe* so well as they did. Difficult modern works have a prospect of being done all over

---

142. It is instructive to keep in mind some later comments by Havergal Brian: "Walford Davies's pleasant manner at the microphone reminds me vividly of how he and McNaught alone among the adjudicators at Morecambe had the happy knack of getting on intimate terms with the audience" (*Musical Opinion*, May 1934, 603).

the country, even in villages". But he spoke critically as well. Southerners going there, he said, were inclined to be too enthusiastic at first. In the male voice class he said that too literal obedience was shown to the expression marks. In the Challenge Shield class he asked for a check to be put on over-emphasis, mechanically-made points in the music, renderings of the first magnitude spoilt by stupid carelessness in flattening. singers putting in *portamentos*, and making absurd *crescendos*, even those put in by the composer without reason. He said that even good music could be spoiled by the faults of performers, instancing a recent experience he had had in *The Dream of Gerontius* in which he heard the Angel's Song sung by a singer of the first rank "with a *portamento* from the top A down to the bottom A, which would have done very well for a demon in opera, but certainly did not do for an angel".[143] In conclusion, Walford Davies said that the South would pay the north the homage of flattery in its sincerest form - imitation.

The *Manchester Guardian* argued for a positive response to his speech.

> He used fairly strong language at times and hit the choirs very hard. but plain speaking of this kind will do them good. They will take the hard hitting with characteristic northern good sense and good feeling. because on reflection they will see that it is deserved, and they will appreciate the honest outspokenness of Dr Davies at its proper value and pay him the compliment of trying to get rid of the blemishes he has pointed out to them.

No doubt Walford Davies's remarks struck a sympathetic note in Gorton, always anxious to raise standards. Yet the Canon must have felt that the criticisms were a little harsh, particularly on the smaller choirs, in view of the problems they faced. The *Yorkshire Daily Observer* reported the thrust of his reply:

> The choral competitions are intended to foster the cultivation of choral music in the villages of the large agricultural and pastoral region which forms the Morecambe hinterland. Many of these places are so scantily inhabited that it is a matter of no small difficulty to get together a decent choir, and the difficulties do not always end with the collection of the material. This point was specially emphasised in a speech made by Canon Gorton...One instance related to a choir whose conductor has to walk fourteen miles for every rehearsal, and the rehearsals are held in a barn into which a piano has to be carried.

143. The passage referred to is on p 158 of the vocal score.

> There is something of a heroic cast about the pursuit of music in circumstances such as these.

Gorton also said he hoped that the philanthropic aims of competition festivals would stimulate charitable donations. "Ours is not a concert, but a school, with schoolmasters in the box. Such good work needs the aid of the wealthy. Some present libraries where people go to sleep or read novels. Others give thousands of pounds to clubs. Why not send some to our great club? A £5 note to a choir of working people that has heavy expenses would be a great help. Such things can only be done when the Festival has a balance". He finally paid tribute to Howson, whose monument, he said, "is in this hall".

Despite the slight decline from 1905 it was clear that the Morecambe Festival still led the way in the competitive movement. Writing in the *Musical Standard* W H Caunt said:

> The Morecambe gathering, although nine years[144] younger than that of Kendal, has a more far-reaching influence, covering the whole of the North of England, yet, be it remembered, its embrace is not limited. It may be truly called by this very comprehensiveness 'The English Eisteddfod'.

The *Yorkshire Daily Observer*'s congratulations were combined with a warning:

> The only doubt that can be cast upon the Morecambe competitions, as competitions, is that which is raised by the excellence of the results. When choirs arrive at such a supreme pitch of excellence one feels that their time should be employed on the greatest choral works rather than in polishing up pieces of smaller calibre...Unless these festivals make for an advance in musical taste and executive ability, their raison d'etre is gone, and when the technique is as advanced as it is in the case of many of these picked choirs the only thing that remains to be done is to look after development of taste. The lamentable exhibition afforded by the class of obbligato songs showed into what depths the amateur who is not protected against himself will plunge...

The *Musical Herald* also gave a warning:

> One danger of the festival is that Morecambe may become conceited. It would not be a matter of wonder if they did, considering the number of judges who have told them that there is nothing like their Festival to be heard elsewhere.

144. Actually six years.

But maintaining this pre-eminent position was bought at a price. Shortly after the Festival ended, Canon Gorton suffered a nervous breakdown and was forced to rest. It was the first serious attack of the chronic illness which eventually led to his death, but the more immediate cause was exhaustion from organising the 1906 Festival virtually single-handed. The future progress of the Morecambe meeting was now in serious jeopardy. In less than eighteen months it had lost not only its most perceptive and supportive critic, and its local musical genius: but now its founder and chief stimulus had been laid low.

CHAPTER 10

CAPRI

At the end of May 1906 the Gortons left for a period of convalescence in Norway. The report in the *Morecambe Visitor* mentioned local concern for the Canon's long-term health:

> General regret will be expressed in the town at the news that the Rev Canon Gorton is indisposed and has been ordered two months complete rest. The intimation came as a great surprise to almost everyone, for the happily phrased and witty speech which the Rector made upon the last night of the Musical Festival betrayed no sign of that nervous breakdown which it has since become known was then in progress. A man of lofty ideals, he has never tired in seeking to give practical expression to his sympathy with everything which he has thought was for the betterment of the people and the town. The worry and anxiety inseparable from so great an undertaking as the Musical festival will doubtless have contributed in no small degree to his present indisposition. We hope the somewhat alarmist rumours which have been current may prove to be unfounded, and that a period of quiet and freedom from anxiety will restore the rector to his wonted health.

The Norwegian holiday certainly appeared to bring about an improvement in the Canon's health. When the couple returned on 23 July the Canon threw himself into parish work with renewed vigour. There was a backlog of important matters to be sorted out, including the Festival accounts. These were published on 11 August, with the following explanation from Gorton:

> My long absence from home is the cause of the delay in issuing the balance sheet of our last festival...In spite of the increased magnitude of the work we only needed £5 to meet our expenditure. We have watched this expenditure with the utmost possible care - at the same time we believe that it would be but false economy to be content in any direction with less than the best obtainable.

The old fire was still there, and throughout the summer Gorton worked extremely hard. On 16 August General William Booth, founder of the Salvation Army, was in Morecambe to address a meeting supported by all the churches: Gorton led the prayers. At the beginning of September he wrote to the *Morecambe Visitor* suggesting a method to attract people to the town after the main holiday period had ended - a series of subscription concerts during the early autumn.

At this time Gorton was working on the Interpretation of *The Kingdom*, Elgar's new oratorio; and was also involved in producing a report by the Higher Education Committee on Art in Morecambe. Later that month he created a storm at a meeting of the Girls' Friendly Society when he spoke of the ugliness of the latest fashion in ladies' hats! He wrote to the *Manchester Guardian* on the question of buying Holman Hunt's painting *The Lady of Shalott* for the nation.

After attending the première of *The Kingdom* Canon Gorton went to London where on 10 October he officiated at the marriage of his younger brother. Much of his time now was spent in preparing for the next festival. It had been the original intention to give a performance of *The Dream of Gerontius* at the 1907 Festival concert, but it was now too late for this. The executive therefore decided to dispense with a large-scale choral concert altogether, and replace it on the Friday evening with a kind of recital involving professional as well as amateur performers. The Blackpool and Manchester Orpheus choirs were invited, and the Brodsky String Quartet and the tenor John Coates were engaged. Gorton was nevertheless determined not to abandon the *Gerontius* project, and in a letter to the *Visitor* on 12 November he was already looking eighteen months ahead.

> We are anxious to give in our Festival Sir Edward Elgar's Dream of Gerontius. But to give this work worthily we should need more time than it is possible to obtain before the next Festival. We propose therefore to give it in 1908...We are not without hope that choral singers will feel it a privilege to take part in this great work, but if it is to be given adequately it must involve regularity in attendance and most careful preparation. We trust that we may secure later combined practices under Dr Coward. The orchestral score is plainly beyond the scope of the best amateur orchestras. We should engage, therefore, the services of one of the best orchestras in England...

By the time this letter appeared in print, its author was on his way to Italy. His health had broken down again, and the Bishop of Manchester, on the advice of the doctors, ordered complete rest from the parish for six months. He arranged for Gorton to take on the Anglican chaplaincy in the island of Capri. The chaplain was sponsored by the Society for the Propagation of the Gospel, and came under the authority of the Bishop of Gibraltar. The island was immensely popular with wealthy foreign visitors, mainly Germans, and already had something of a disreputable name. "British society at Capri...was divided into those who were respectable but dull, and those who were entertaining but dissolute".[145] A building fund for an Anglican church had been set up in 1887, and the first recorded service was held in a room in the famous Hotel Quisisana in 1889. Chaplains came out every year from November to April, the main season for British visitors. In 1894 the church of All Saints was established in its own building in the Via Pastena.

In a letter to his congregation in the November parish magazine Gorton wrote:

> It is with a deep sense of regret and much against my will that I announce to my parishioners that I have to leave my parish again. There is very little matter with me but I am told that if I do not take in hand that little I shall be crippled in my work, and I have no fancy for being a half timer. I have put before the Bishop the many reasons why I do not want to leave the parish, to say nothing of my home, but in terms too kind for me to quote here, he has bid me go. It is a comfort to be a man under authority and as he has told me to go, I must. I am undertaking the chaplaincy at Capri. Capri I find is in the Bay of Naples, so that I am only exchanging the Naples of the North for the Naples of the South, and I have no doubt that I should be able to state on my return that it is not to be compared with Morecambe.

The *Morecambe Visitor* took the opportunity to pay the Rector a tribute.

> The departure of the Rector of Morecambe for a lengthy stay in Italy must be a source of sincere regret, not only to the members of his own church, but to the whole of the community. He will be greatly missed and his absence will leave a distinct void. A man of high intellectual attainments and clear views, his written commentaries on current events are acceptable in the highest places. His intellectual activities cover a wide field, but they always have for their aim the spiritual, moral, or mental culture of the people...Within the town the Rector has been a power for righteousness; not the mere exponent of a creed, but a practical minded man who realises that healthy morality is best attained by the provision of a good moral atmosphere in which a man ceases to do ill because he finds there is something better he can do...

145. Edwin Cerio, *The Mask of Capri* (Nelson, 1957), 77

Gorton left England on 12 November in order to take up his duties twelve days later. When he arrived in Capri he found the following letter waiting for him from the Rev E P Sketchley, assistant secretary of the SPG.

> I am not sure whether I mentioned it to you - but in any case you are likely to have heard that it has been for some time felt to be desirable that the Capri Church should be sold, and a new one built. Our solicitors tell me that the negotiations for the Sale are now complete. How soon we shall have to give up possession of it I do not know. But perhaps you will kindly be giving consideration to the question of a place where services can be held until the new Church is built. No doubt a room would be lent at the Quisisana Hotel. You might, perhaps, consult Mr.Seymour-Browne, whom you no doubt know by this time.[146]

The deterioration in the state of the building (no doubt caused by its half-yearly neglect) had persuaded the Society to take this action. Obviously the Capri chaplaincy was no sinecure: and all was not well among the congregation at the church. Sketchley wrote again on 3 December in a letter marked 'Private':

> I am sorry to hear of troubles at Capri - and think you are quite right not to be dragged into them. It is not for me to judge what would be the best action to be taken at Easter. My impression is that the appointment suggested would not make for unity.
>
> You ask for my definite opinion regarding the position of Mr.S.Browne - and I can only say that the sad intelligence in your letter is so entirely contrary to the opinion I had previously formed that I am almost compelled to think that you have been misinformed.[147]

Church politics and other troubles were unlikely to aid the Canon's recuperation.

But now Elgar was unwell. The writing of the second part of *The Apostles*, which became the oratorio *The Kingdom*, had occupied most of 1906 and had driven him to the verge of a breakdown. Once again only half of the proposed scheme was covered when he finished the work on 23 July. There was enough time to orchestrate *The*

---

146. United Society for the Propagation of the Gospel (USPG) X397 fo.229 [16 November 1906]

147. USPG X397 fo.277

Kingdom before its first performance at the Birmingham Festival on 3 October, and Canon Gorton was called upon to write an interpretation of the libretto, as he had for *The Apostles* three years earlier.

After the première of *The Kingdom* Elgar lapsed once more into depression and self-pity. Writing to Frank Schuster on 10 October he said: "I don't seem to realise that I have written anything & am trying to forget all about it & *myself*".[148] He was weighed down by thoughts of the next series of Birmingham lectures which was imminent. The first one, on 1 November, was on orchestration and was uncontentious enough. But the second, a week later, on the subject of Mozart's *G minor Symphony*, caused further controversy when Elgar seemed to suggest that Mozart would have scored the work differently were it not for the limitations of the instruments of the period; a reasonable sort of assumption, but one that was a gift for the critics. "Sir Edward Elgar expressed himself in favour of a revision of the works of the old masters", was one press reaction.

This was the last straw for Elgar. He offered to resign, and was relieved when the next lecture, scheduled for 22 November, was cancelled. His eyes had been troubling him, and when on 21 November a specialist insisted on "change and a warm climate", he and Alice decided to go to Italy. They booked a passage on a boat for Naples on 28 December. Elgar continued to be unwell right up to the time they left.

In Gorton's absence arrangements for the Morecambe Festival were left in the hands of John Hatch JP, the vice-president; and Mr Powell the secretary. Before the end of November they had good news to report to the Canon: Elgar had written to say that he would certainly be at the Festival if in England at the time.

Gorton's delight was increased when he heard that the Elgars were coming to Italy. His wife was due to join him later, and on 5 January he wrote to his daughter Helen:

> ...You must tell [your mother] that there is no need to bring a great supply of boots for the great luxury here is the Capri boot 3 francs
>
> I am not certain what the Elgars are going to do. I shall possibly go into Naples on Monday morning to meet them. They land tomorrow at 7 o'clock. I expect they have had a horrible voyage.
>
> You must correct this letter and see how many mistakes I have got through with. I can but make a poor show with my left hand.

148. Quoted in Young, *Elgar OM* (Collins, 1955), 135

The Canon did meet the Elgars, and he showed them round Naples and the surrounding area. They went to Pompeii on the 8th, but it was very cold and the rain turned to snow. Gorton and Elgar played billiards in the evening. On the 10th Gorton took the Elgars for a long walk which included seeing the octopus fed in the Aquarium. Alice found this "ghastly". In the afternoon Elgar rested while Alice and the Canon visited the museum.

The following Sunday, 13 January, the Elgars arrived at Capri. They landed at Marina Grande and made their way to the town of Capri, where they were staying at the Hotel Quisisana. (Typically the quick-witted Elgar transmuted this to 'Quasi-insana' on some of his letter headings). Later that day Elgar wrote to his daughter Carice:

> Canon Gorton came to see us and we had a short walk after lunch & it was lovely: warm at last & blue sky & *hot* sun. But we were tired & came in & slept...

Elgar had already discovered the 'Capri boot', for he continued:

> I cannot get much out of Canon Gorton who is not well & nervous about himself. I asked him how he could convert people with 'rope souls'... [149]

The next day Elgar and Gorton went for a short walk to the Certosa di San Giacomo, a partly-ruined Carthusian monastery. In the evening Elgar dined with the Canon at his lodging-house, the Pensione White in the Via Valentino. It was owned by an English artist, James Talmage White, whose son Alberto was the manager. After dinner White and the Canon accompanied Elgar back to his hotel, where Alice was "much amused" by White, who was something of a raconteur.

The two men continued their walks for the next two days, going as far as Anacapri on the 16th. On his return to the hotel Elgar wrote to Carice:

> I have been able to walk about with Canon Gorton & love it oh but now I have a throat! [150]

Alice had also taken a stroll with the Canon; but the hilly nature of the island was too much for her, as she told her daughter that same day:

149. EBML 103
150. EBML 101

> Canon Gorton took me a little turn but I fear walks will be rather impossible as it is so precipitous & my stupid head seems to go upside down...[151]

Like her husband, Alice was concerned about the Canon's poor health.

> I am afraid Canon Gorton is not better. Mrs.G. is to arrive next week which will be a great joy to him.[152]

Despite her reservations about walking, Alice went with the two men on the 18th when they undertook a long walk to the Villa Tiberio (also called the Villa Jovis), the site of the palace of the Roman Emperor of that name. From there was a fine view of the whole island and the adjacent mainland. After lunch Elgar and Gorton still felt fit enough to take a shorter walk to the ruins of a medieval castle, about a mile to the south-west. The next day, Saturday 19 January, was another time for walks, including one to Marina Piccola on the south coast by way of the Via Krupp. The narrow road, with many hairpin bends, had been built by the German arms manufacturer.

This spate of walks was to take advantage of the fine weather, as until then the winter on Capri had been appalling, so bad in fact that the wild flowers were blooming about a month later than usual. A report in the *Daily Telegraph* commented:

> Capri has lain a sad, drab-coloured heap of cloud-hung rocky heights and moist hollows, in which the gray olive trees shivered with the chill and dripped with continuous rain, and the stucco villas and contadino huts looked desolate and uncomfortable. Twice a day the quaking little boat from Naples breasted the rough water and disembarked a few forlorn passengers by means of small boats. The little carriages have gone up the winding road empty, and the hotel men have returned with sad faces.

The cold wet conditions had obviously not aided Gorton's hopes of recovery. After taking the Sunday service on 20 January he called in on the Elgars and looked so ill that they insisted on his staying for lunch. However, he was up early the next day to take the 6 am boat over to the mainland to meet his wife. She too was far from well, and that (coupled with the bad weather) limited them to just one walk during the next week. The following Sunday (27 January) Elgar wrote to Carice:

151. EBML 100
152. ibid.

...Mrs.Gorton has neuralgia & has only been out one day since her arrival a week ago: we are a set of cripples...

However he was still able to see the humorous side of life's problems:

Canon Gorton received a telegram today 'would he go over to Sorrento to bury an English gentleman who is dying'. Curious anticipatory idea. He went over by the afternoon boat & I hear he returned by the evening boat & I am anxious to know what happened.[153]

Elgar *was* feeling better: his eyes were improving, as a letter to him from the writer A C Benson shows:

I am delighted to hear that your eyes are rapidly convalescing. I wonder whether the necessity of resting them has been as profoundly boring as I can't help thinking it would be...

I have been at Capri, but twenty years ago: it seemed enchanting then, or seems so now in retrospect - I am sorry you have had bad weather; bad weather in Italy used to turn the landscape for me into a place like a theatre by daylight! [154]

On the last day of January Elgar and Gorton walked to Anacapri. Gorton was receiving treatment from Dr Vincenzo Cuomo, who lived there. The same man was attending to Elgar's eyes. The ladies drove there to join them after lunch. However the weather once more spoiled their day out: rain began, and the Canon lent Elgar his cape.

On 1 February Alice and Ella paid a call at the villa occupied by William Wordsworth (grandson of the poet), who was wintering there with his two sisters and a niece. He was a generous host and very popular with the English-speaking community. During the next week the weather brightened considerably, and the two couples were out every day, making the most of the improved conditions. Some of their excursions were quite adventurous, as Alice's diary for 7 February records:

After dinner, what to do? So E & A went to the Gortons groping in the dark. Canon G. lighted them into the road with a candle in a strong wind.

Gorton's chaplaincy continued to cause him problems. At the end of December the SPG had sent him the title deeds of the church so that

153. EBML 86
154. 29 January 1907

he could hand them over to the purchaser, one Joseph Bourdillon. Gorton's request to use the Lutheran church for Anglican services was refused by the Bishop of Gibraltar, and though the Canon tried hard to look for a new site he had no success. The SPG was anxious for the congregation to respond to the need, as Sketchley told Gorton on 23 January:

> We have the £200 - and although it is thought that a new site can be had for very little, any deduction from the £200 will be serious, as I suppose the Church can hardly be built for that money, and may cost a great deal more. The real question seems to be - is the little congregation at Capri prepared to go into this matter heartily & with spirit? We were advised & urged (after consulting the Bishop and others) that the sale of the old Church was most desirable - to say the least. Are the people now prepared to go forward?
>
> It is hardly necessary to emphasise the need for economy - both in regard to the land and the building. It will no doubt be felt by everyone that the Church should be a simple structure, and it might perhaps be well for its plan to be larger than the immediate needs so that only part might be erected now, and, if necessary, the rest later on..
>
> Is there any chance of erecting a church in time for the next winter season? If not, perhaps you will kindly make enquiries as to the best place to hire for the services, or to get free.[155]

By now the Elgars had less than a week of their holiday left. The morning of 8 February was wet but when it cleared up after lunch Elgar and the Canon walked to Anacapri. The ladies joined them later, and the four of them went on to the Piccola Marina. "Wonderful blue green waves & dashing spray", Alice noted.

On the Elgars' last day, 11 February, they all went once more to Anacapri, and this time on to Monte Solaro, the highest point on the island. When the Elgars left, Canon and Mrs Gorton accompanied them to the Marina Grande to catch the afternoon boat. Alice found it a moving occasion, as she told her daughter:

> We left yesterday at 3. Canon & Mrs.G. came to see us board the steamer & lingered & lingered on the quay till we started. It gave me a bad choke to part with them - & he will miss Faser[Father] so much.[156]

155. USPG X397 fo.448
156. EBML 88

On 1 March Elgar wrote to Walford Davies:

> I have been seeing that dear good man Canon Gorton & I fear he is ill:
> he is at Capri for a month or two longer, I hope & trust he will
> improve.[157]

But by then Gorton had written to SPG to inform them that he must
give up the chaplaincy. Dr Cuomo had diagnosed an abscess, and the
Canon underwent surgery at the International Hospital at Naples.
For Ella Gorton it was a very worrying time, and she shared her
feelings with her family. Her eldest son Neville wrote from school at
Marlborough:

> I got your postcard this morning & am thankful to hear the doctor is
> more hopeful - is he a good doctor? There must be English &
> American doctors staying at Capri whose advice you could get as well
> - do get the best.
>
> You must be having a terrible time of it dear all by yourself. I do hope
> your friends there are kind & help you. Poor mother - it isn't much of
> a holiday for you. But when Father gets better I am sure you will enjoy
> yourselves all the more & I hope for better news next post. I am glad
> you have written to the S.P.G. Sunday duty & preaching etc. must
> always be a strain, & the key fact that he has not got it must give
> Father a feeling of a more complete holiday & freedom from
> responsibility...

Fortunately the Gortons had made friends with some Americans,
and one in particular, Raphael Pompelly from North Carolina, was a
great help at this trying time. Canon Gorton also made the
acquaintance of the famous Swedish doctor and author, Axel
Munthe. He had two homes on the island - the Villa San Michele
above Anacapri; and Materita in the west of the island, from where
he wrote to Gorton in April:

> I think you are right in returning home to have your health attended
> to - Capri is a bad place for those who are not well. I hope you will
> return once more and in good health.

On 23 March Dr Cuomo wrote to Alice Elgar:

> Canon Gorton is recovered of what he suffered recently. He requires
> long bodily and mental rest.[158]

157. EBML 2193
158. EBML 6404

Canon Gorton had intended to be back at Morecambe in time for the Festival in May. But the poor weather, the difficult chaplaincy, and his unforeseen illness, virtually destroyed any benefit that his time in Capri might have brought. He realised that it would be morally indefensible and physically foolhardy to plunge straight back into the demanding task of running the Festival. This meant that for the first time he would not be present at the event he had brought into being. In the concluding paragraph of the preface to the programme book he wrote:

> I have been absent from my parish for six months trying to recover my fitness for work; I wish that I could feel that I had been successful. I have had a very trying illness in my absence, and I do not feel that I should be justified in re-commencing work with the strain of a Festival week - it would not be fair to my parishioners, who have borne so loyally with my absence. How much I shall miss, so much music which I want to hear, so many friends whom I want to meet, and who, I am sure, will reciprocate my regrets; but I leave the organisation in safe hands.

CHAPTER 11

THE 1907 FESTIVAL

Elgar had been very busy since leaving Capri on 12 February. He and Alice went on to Rome, which they both enjoyed immensely. When they arrived back in Hereford on 26 February, there were just four days before Elgar left for America, his third visit. This time he would be going alone; he insisted on Alice staying behind, as she had been away from home for so long. Artistically it was a successful trip: Elgar conducted *The Apostles* and *The Kingdom* in New York, and also gave concerts in Chicago and Pittsburgh. Yet America as a country gave him little pleasure, and he was grateful to be able to relax at Julia Worthington's New York home, from where he wrote to Ella Gorton on 14 April:

> My dear Mrs.Gorton:
>
> I have this moment returned from the West & find Alice's letter telling me, to my great grief, that dear Canon Gorton is not to be at the Morecambe Festival. I hasten to send a word by this mail to say how I will do anything I can at Morecambe to fill the void: of course the meeting will be nothing without the soul, bless him! I am asking Alice to send me full information to meet me at Queenstown: I sail on Ap.20 in the Campania.
>
> Well: I must not say, as post is going, to say all I would. After our sweet & delightful time in Capri it is a hideous change to be in Western America: here, in New York, I have that dear & wonderful woman, Mrs.Worthington, to speak to: she sends her love & is so sorry to hear of the illness & has great hopes to find Canon Gorton well in the summer when she comes to England.
>
> Now farewell [-] God bless you both!
> In frantic haste
> Yrs ever sincly
> Edward Elgar[159]

Elgar arrived back at Plas Gwyn on 27 April, and once again had only a few days at home before going to Morecambe. In one sense it was

159. Quoted in Young (1956), 171

good for him to be so occupied, as it helped him to forget that he had composed nothing of substance for almost a year: but even so it was with an air of drudgery that he and Alice started for Morecambe at 11.30 on Wednesday 1 May, the first day of the Festival. Alice wrote in her diary that he left "very reluctantly". Elgar used the train journey, as he so often did, to catch up on his correspondence. He wrote to his daughter:

> In train near Wigan
> My child,
> Why's Lancashire like a Judge?
> Because it has its Wigan
> (Joke)
> This is awful...[160]

They arrived about five o'clock and went straight to the Grand Hotel: Mrs Gandy was also staying there. But even her vivacious presence could not lift the gloom they felt at being in Morecambe without the Gortons: "dreary place", Alice noted.

The first day of the Festival was as usual devoted to the children's competitions, and there was an evening concert for the prize winners. Elgar did not go, but spent the evening with the other two main judges, McNaught and Walford Davies.

Thursday was given over to local competitions. The choirs performed in the main hall, and the instrumental ensembles in the ballroom next door. Elgar went first to the ballroom, where Carl Fuchs, cellist with the Brodsky Quartet, was adjudicating. "He...listened to the strings, and as an ordinary member of the audience warmly applauded some of the movements interpreted", said the *Lancashire Daily Post*.

The test for string quartets was Beethoven's *Quartet no 1 in F*, Op.18, and Fuchs regretted that there had not been more entries; the great masters had written their best work for string quartets, he said.

Shortly before noon, Elgar moved to the main hall. "The arrival of the distinguished composer and good friend of the Morecambe Festival...was marked by loud applause from the audience", the *Morecambe Times* noted. The competition in progress was for mixed voice quartets, who were singing Walford Davies's *A Song of Rest*.

160. EBML 92

The composer adjudicated, and complained that all the competitors had interpreted the *andantino* marking too slowly. Nevertheless, he said that the singing had reached a very high standard: in fact to an ordinary Londoner like himself it was amazing. He hoped that Elgar would supplement these remarks. The audience applauded vigorously, but Elgar merely smiled and would not be drawn to speak. "E. rather tired of it all", commented Alice, "but very dord [gorgeous] and busy".

The loss of Howson's critical judgment in the choice of the test pieces was being felt, and was noticed by the *Manchester Guardian*:

> The two pieces for female choirs were so poor that even the best of them shamed Dr McNaught into admitting that, although he had arranged the piece for ladies' voices himself, he had never intended it to occupy the time of such choirs as he had heard in it.

The writer went on to appeal for more intelligence in choral interpretation (much as Elgar had done in his Birmingham lecture):

> While it is certain that the singing at these Festivals has been to a great extent brought to its present high standard by a rigid adherence to marks of expression, metronome marks, and other indications of tempo...it is equally certain that the distance that still separates the singing from the ideal will never be covered until a much greater freedom is taken by the conductors who possess any genius.

The Church Choir Festival was held in the afternoon at St Laurence's Church. The Elgars dined at the Rectory where they were entertained by the Gorton children. The evening concert saw the finals of several of the local competitions, plus a recital by Plunket Greene. Elgar sat with the other judges: Alice found it a long concert. Her final diary comment for the Thursday summed up the Elgars' feelings: "Missed the dear Canon & Mrs G much".

There were no competitions on the Friday, and no combined rehearsals for the evening concert, so Elgar took the opportunity to visit Lancaster. He looked round the church and the castle, and had lunch there. The Festival concert that evening was well attended, but met with differing critical reactions. "The music lovers who assembled in such numbers...had a rich treat both vocal and instrumental", the *Visitor* said. However, Samuel Langford in the *Manchester Guardian* remarked: "Too much of the interest of the Festival was crowded into tonight's concert, which was too long and too incessant for enjoyment".

The concert began with the Blackpool Glee & Madrigal Society who sang ten songs, including *Weary Wind of the West* and three of Gorton's translations of Brahms. The *Morecambe Times* said that the choir sang "with charming delicacy", though the *Visitor* felt that the basses were too loud in the pianissimo passages. Langford was also critical:

> It being well understood how much we admire their singing, we may say that a little lighter treatment of unmelodic parts would make their work still better: and they do not always judge rightly the reason why the composer crosses his parts at times.

The Manchester Orpheus Male Voice Choir included songs by Hegar and Cornelius in their programme, and their basses came in for special mention in the *Visitor*: "They produce that deep diapason tone that is never heard anywhere but in the North of England and for which the great Leeds and Sheffield choruses are renowned". The audience particularly liked MacDowell's *Dance of the Gnomes.*

John Coates, who "sang splendidly", according to Alice, performed no less than sixteen songs, many of which he had translated himself. He included Elgar's *In the Dawn.* The Brodsky Quartet, playing Beethoven and Tchaikovsky, completed the programme.

Whatever the reservations concerning the first three days, the open competitions on the Saturday created the usual excited anticipation among the thousands of competitors and their supporters. Even Alice Elgar found it a "very exciting day". In the female voice class the winners were Barrow St James with 149 marks (the holders, Blackpool, were disqualified for being late for the 10.15 start). In the string orchestra class Colne with 70 marks beat Nelson by four, with Miss Cassidy's Orchestra third. Elgar announced the winners and "bestowed some very pretty compliments on Miss Cassidy's small band of players", according to the *Manchester Guardian*. The composer also presided over the class for smaller mixed voice choirs (not exceeding thirty-five voices). Here the tests were *The Clouds* by Rheinberger, and Parker's madrigal *Come Away*. In announcing the winners (Mr Poulter's choir from Douglas) Elgar took the opportunity to make a plea, albeit in light-hearted vein, for a continuing high standard in the selection of test pieces. "When I first came to Morecambe", he said, "the greatest interest centred on the Challenge Shield class, and although it must still take first place in the public mind, to a man like myself the smaller classes have a greater interest. The test pieces today were a great advance upon the part-songs which years ago always related to Phyllis, Phoebe, and Corinna, and all the other ladies with their 'tra-la-las' which choirs were expected to sing. I am very pleased to find in the part-songs we have just heard that those ladies are alluded to only very slightly: the words largely refer to the beauties of nature and contemplation. Singers nowadays are expected to use their brains, and to give expression to a much higher class of words. The execution generally showed a vast improvement as compared to a few years ago, and in this way these festivals are justified by bringing out the smaller choirs to sing in such a splendid way. I hope Corinna and Phyllis and all the rest of those respectable ladies will be allowed to rest for the next century. Corinna may very well sing herself to sleep, and if Phyllis in this lovely May weather can find enough flowers to dress herself in, she ought to do her dressing by herself, and not worry us about it".

Elgar was in his element, and thrived on the adulation he received. It was all so different from the nervous, unsure Elgar which characterised some of his other public appearances. Here in Morecambe he reigned - and it showed. "E. so dord in red box", wrote Alice.

The Elgars took lunch at the Midland Hotel with Walford Davies. In the afternoon came the chief male voice class, where the tests were MacDowell's *From the Sea* and Elgar's 'Yea, cast me from heights of the mountain' from his *Greek Anthology* set. The Habergham Glee Union were awarded full marks for the Elgar, but in fact all the choirs sang it so well that few marks were lost. In the Challenge Shield class the seven choirs sang Morley's madrigal *Arise, awake* and Elgar's *Evening Scene*. The latter had been a test piece the previous year, and now became the first music ever to be used for a second time at Morecambe. It was altogether much better this time, as Samuel Langford noted: "Sir Edward Elgar must have been a happy man to hear one choir after another sing his *Evening Scene* in the way they did...The piece seemed as fresh and beautiful after the seventh performance as at the beginning. Elgar's music enfolds the clear details of Coventry Patmore's words just as the shadows and mists of evening soften objects to our vision. In the words there is no single syllable wasted on vague sentiment; it is a great feat, to have found musical expression in them; to have done it without vulgarising them in any way and at the same time without exposing the inability of music to express details, to have kept the reticence and quiet of words and to add the softness that only music can give, is what only the finest and most gifted nature could accomplish. Far off, in the Isle of Man, along the coast of Lancashire from Blackpool, along by Lancaster, Morecambe, and Barrow; at Burnley, where the men look of hard mould; in the heart of England at Nottingham, this delicate music, wed to the sanest and purest poetry of our day, has been sung and sung over and over, until it has become more perfect than they who have not heard it could believe. It is only by looking at the matter from this point of view that we can get any idea of the far-reaching good of these festivals".

Five choirs went on to the final in the evening, Nottingham and Lancaster being eliminated. The *Musical Herald* writer resumed his criticism of this procedure:

> ...I think the time has arrived when the system of examination should be revised. The afternoon contest only resulted in scratching two choirs. It was a great expenditure of effort for so small a result. It would have been better to excuse all the choirs the attendance in the afternoon, especially if the choirs have such ups and downs that the fourth choir in the final becomes the first in the award.[161] Another more excellent way is to have 'heats', half the choirs to be heard in the afternoon and half in the evening, and the best one in each section to sing for the shield. I would let the choirs choose one piece both in the preliminary and the final. Is taste so well defined a thing that the committee have a monopoly of it, and can insist on all the tests being to their liking? For years I have pleaded for liberty in this direction. It is the old-fashioned plan, and the new one has not proved to be better.

The Morecambe Madrigal Society under their new conductor only just qualified for the final, but their singing had caught the attention of Samuel Langford, who wrote:

> In Morley's madrigal Mr Smale's Morecambe choir made the construction of the piece clearer than the other choirs - it was a feature that showed the thorough musician.

As usual, the afternoon schedule overran. "E. not back till just in time to dress", wrote Alice. McNaught and Walford Davies thought so highly of the singing of the Elgar piece by the male voice choirs that they arranged for the combined choirs to sing it again in the evening, with the composer conducting. It was well received by the audience, including Langford:

161. The overall winners of the Shield were only fourth on the evening's marks alone.

The singing had the same unity as the separate choirs. As the piece is very short and the expression ranges from the most profound piano effects to the most abrupt fortissimo, the unity was wonderful.

However the *Musical Herald* thought otherwise:

It was a scratch performance, and, as [Elgar] called it, 'an experiment'. Its only justification, to my mind, was that it gave the evening audience the chance of hearing one of the finest pieces of music performed during the day. The words lent themselves to the contrasty, descriptive power he so well possesses, and the tone of the choirs was big and grand, but the second tenors spoilt the blend, and the 'experiment' further proved that composite pictures are blurred compared with the finished word-painting obtained by a single conductor-artist.

The final test piece for male voices was *The Desert March* by Hegar. Walford Davies called attention to the grisly subject the song portrayed. "Why picture these ghastly things?" he asked. *Musical Herald* (published by Curwen) smugly endorsed his views:

It may be mentioned that a few years ago the British rights in Hegar's men's choruses were offered to Messrs Curwen, who are the leading publishers of this class of music. They declined them, feeling that the style was laboured and ungrateful and that the subjects were unpleasant. However, the pieces have taken the fancy of someone at the Morecambe Festival, Messrs Novello have brought them out, and the unfortunate choirs have been compelled to get them up.

"I fancied that the Manchester Orpheus Glee Society had given the most correct interpretation", wrote the *Visitor* critic, "the other competitors taking the 'tramp, tramp' sound at the commencement a great deal faster than it would be possible to imagine any army in a burning desert go, considering all the attendant horrors which are so realistically depicted in the song".

The winners in this class, with 234 marks, were the Habergham Glee Union. Elgar said he felt overwhelmed by the magnificence and beauty of the tone generally of their rendering of the test pieces. Manchester Orpheus and Southport tied for second place on 231. Langford criticised the music (except the Elgar) in this class:

As for the other two pieces sung by these choirs we can only express our sorrow that such good singers had to spend their time on them.

He was equally outspoken about the choice of music generally:

> Excepting the two pieces of [Elgar], one by Cornelius, and an old madrigal by Morley, the music sung during the day had been either crude and false or negligible.

The full orchestra class was won by Nelson with 73 marks, two more than Colne, so that the two orchestras shared the spoils.

The five choirs left in the Challenge Shield class now had to sing J B McEwen's *Let me the canakin clink*, and Cornelius's *Stormwind*. Dr McNaught told the choirs that in the McEwen piece they were out of tune at times. "Quarter-tones which were not designed by the composer were heard", he said. "It is, in fact, an extremely difficult piece to sing in tune". Samuel Langford was in no doubt as to where the blame for that lay: "The faults of intonation made by all the choirs in this piece ought with justice to be laid at the door of the composer, as they were only caused by bad modulations...The Isle of Man Choir...imparted some little meaning into a few passages that to the other choirs meant nothing. We say 'imparted' because we do not think the composer himself put any meaning into them".

Habergham Glee Union.
Ernest Hitchon is in the fifth deck chair from the left.

It was hard to choose between the leading choirs. "Difficult for judges", noted Alice. In the end they opted for the Isle of Man choir with 301 marks, with Barrow second on 300, and Blackpool and Burnley third equal on 299. The result was seized upon by Langford:

> By an award of 301 marks to one choir, 300 to another, and 299 to the next two choirs in the Challenge Shield class, and an equally uncertain verdict in the Male Voice Choir Competition Sir Edward Elgar and his colleagues had stated their inability to come to any real decision as to which of the choirs they had been hearing was the best, and so the competition as such had developed into a farce, and the music chosen was open to criticism.

In the absence of Canon Gorton, the President, the prize giving was chaired by Mr Helme, the local Member of Parliament. He invited Elgar to speak.

> Since I came to the Festival four years ago, I have seen it grow in the best possible way. I have taken an interest in it I have not been able to take in other things of its kind. I think it is owing, in a great measure, to the care of my friend, Canon Gorton, that he has presented you with this great institution. I know there are other officers, and nothing could be better managed and run more machine like than it does. But having advanced so far, I would like to ask, 'What are you going to do next?' You must think of the future. You have led the way at Morecambe. You have had the opportunity with so fine a building. You have now set a standard here which has been emulated in other districts. That, of course, is all for good, but you must keep that standard up. You must keep your pre-eminence. (Applause). I read in the preface to the Festival book that Canon Gorton says that he has been unable hitherto to secure the presence of the London critics. Believe me, you want London reports, but you don't want London criticism. You must set a standard for yourselves. The chorus singing we have here is of a kind which you do not find in any measure farther south. The social conditions are different. In London I know that they have large choral societies, but this sort of thing they have not. In some ways, the Londoner, superior as he is, is about 150 years behind the age in the matter of music. (Hear, hear). Lord Chesterfield, in his advice to his son, tells him not to fiddle himself, but to acquire fiddlers to amuse him. Well, most of the Londoners do that. They hire people to amuse them, and they like music most when it is expensive. (Laughter). When I said three or four years ago that the living centre of music was not in London but somewhere further north, I meant it, and it is so still. (Applause). My critics who grumbled at that expression did not notice until about four years afterwards that we were talking of two different things. They were talking about the music they paid for; I was talking about

the amount of music you made in your hearts and in your own homes. Occasionally you come for criticism - only for criticism - to a gathering like this. There is a difference: you have music and you make it. That difference remains still, and possibly will remain. (Applause).

I am pleased to hear that notice has been taken of your doings, because you have set a standard which is worthy of being followed all over England. You are being closely followed in many parts and you must keep it going. I said last time - my remarks were infamously reported - that here the commercial element in the matter of prizes had never come in. I was reported to say that I advised you to keep the commercial element out, which is quite another matter. I made a calculation last Festival, and it seemed to me that the most anybody could win was 7s 6d. (Laughter). Well, you know that if a critic is terrified that a man may become commercial in music for the sake of 7s 6d, I pity that critic, and I pity the man who reads his criticism, because if you would sing music for 7s 6d, what would you criticise for 7s 6d? (Laughter). That phase has gone. This Festival now is being treated with that importance which is its due. People are beginning to understand that these are not mere musical performances done for money, but for the improvement of taste and the elevation of the people generally. Sorry as I am that my dear friend Canon Gorton is away ill, still in one sense I am glad he is away from this gathering, for now you see what you can do without one of the main springs - if there can be two main springs. I have not been here since the death of Mr Howson. I had the honour to write a small part-song to his memory. To him you owe the great artistic feeling that comes down to you now. I have warned you now that the Morecambe Festival occupies great eminence; you must keep it up. Some of the pieces chosen this year are open to criticism as compositions, but that point is not for me to deal with. I would ask you in all sincerity to keep up your enthusiasm, and keep up your high standard. Let nothing fall, and be, as you have been, a pattern and guide for other festivals of this kind.

Once again, Elgar had provocatively stirred up the London v North controversy. Perhaps he would have been wiser to refrain, but in fact his original assertion as to the musical state of the capital was still being confirmed by other observers. The previous February, for instance, Arthur Fagge analysed the membership of his London Choral Society and discovered that less than ten percent were London-born. Most of the choir came from Yorkshire and the Midlands, he said, and had settled in London. That same month, in an article entitled 'Are we growing more musical?' the composer and conductor Frederic Cowen wrote:

One thing we must learn to do...is to form a more free and independent judgment of the merits or demerits of musicians: in the provinces people do this more readily than they do in London. It is, to be sure, only human nature for people to give a more favourable hearing to a musical artiste who comes among them with a great reputation than to an unknown and untried individual. If, however, we are ever to lay claim to being a musical nation we must be ready and willing to judge for ourselves as to the merits of a musician's claims to our attention, irrespective of the fact that he (or she) may have either won a big reputation elsewhere or whose advent among us has been skilfully and widely advertised. Our progress in this way has been very little, in London especially. An unknown artiste will get a far more favourable hearing and a much-boomed one an infinitely more unprejudiced judgment passed on his merits in the provinces than in the capital. I do not say that provincial people are always right in their judgment, but they are less prejudiced than Londoners.[162]

After Elgar's speech, Dr McNaught got up to announce the winners. Before giving the judges' verdict, he delighted the large audience by describing himself as a "meek, moody, modest, miserable metropolitan".

The next morning Alice went to Mass on her own: Elgar was tired after his exertions of the previous day. In the afternoon they had a "restful" drive to Hornby Castle. In the evening Deaconess May Gorton and the Canon's daughter Helen called in to see them. The Elgars returned to Hereford on Monday 6 May.

Press reaction to the Festival was varied. Some of Langford's criticisms have already been mentioned, but he was also constructive:

> Sir Edward Elgar manifested a certain amount of anxiety about…the future of the competition movement. We do not wonder at his anxiety…'What are you going to do next?' he asked. It was a pertinent question, for it is certain that the limits of development on present lines have been reached, and unless some new field of work is opened out the enthusiasm that is connected with the movement will begin to abate.

Langford then suggested the performance of large choral works, and also the possibility of setting up a new class for unaccompanied Bach singing. He continued:

> Another direction of development is perhaps indicated by the statement made in the preface to this year's Festival book, that no less

162. *The Tatler*, 20 February 1907, musical section, 4

than nineteen new names are added this year to the list of composers whose works have been heard at the Morecambe Festivals. So far as this means that our English composers are being stimulated by the prospect of a perfect performance to write good choral music in order to get it sung at these festivals it is a very good sign; and to some extent this is the case. But the present Festival book also shows signs of a laxity of taste in the choice of foreign music, and a restless desire for what is sensational; this feature is wholly bad. A weakness of the competitive movement at present is that it causes one choir merely to duplicate the work of others. To some extent this result might be avoided by encouraging choirs to search out good pieces for themselves, and giving part of the marks for the freshness and beauty of the piece, part for the merit of the performance. Freedom and originality of performance might also be encouraged if Sir Edward Elgar or some other composer of richly expressive music would compose a piece for the Festival and give it into the hands of the conductors without indications of pace or expression of any kind.

The 'special representative' of the *Musical Herald* discerned a loss of interest:

The Morecambe Festival did not present so much attraction as usual to an outsider - not sufficient attraction to lead me to sit it out for four days as I did last year. The number of choirs were fewer, there were scarcely any new-comers, Canon Gorton's genial presence was missing, and there was a gap of a day and a half in the middle of the Festival during which concerts and promenades took the place of competitions. The audiences also were slacker both in size and enthusiasm, and bad weather did not account for this entirely.

The *Daily Telegraph* writer called for greater expression:

Beyond a doubt the most vivid [impression of the Festival] is that of the wonderful pitch of perfection to which choral singing has been brought. On its technical side, certainly in this part of the country, so finished was the ensemble of the vast majority of choirs that the tone produced had all the roundness and balance of a chord struck on a sweetly-tuned organ...Now that these choirs in the North-West have perfected their technique so remarkably their next advance must be in the domain of expression. It was, indeed, surprising to notice how frequently many of them failed to realise the possibilities of the verbal text. That is one reason why one has the less hesitation in reminding certain of the competing choirs that, after all, they may not be the salt of the earth in choral singing. Sir Edward Elgar is fond of taking his musical bearings from a point well to the north of London, but there be choirs even further north than Lancashire which, with little to learn from Morecambe in technique could perhaps teach it something in emotional and dramatic expression. Nevertheless, to listen to the magnificent tone of these festival choirs is a great treat which one does not easily forget...

Musical Standard picked up Elgar's reference to the commercial aspect and gave it an emphasis of its own, possibly as a side-swipe at the composer:

> It is difficult to see how the commercial element can be eliminated entirely from either competition or ordinary Musical Festivals unless composers are really to subsist on air. The music performed naturally becomes more widely known and with obvious benefit to the composer...

Most daily newspapers and musical journals cast a veil of silence over the details of Elgar's speech, feeling perhaps that enough had already been spoken and written on the subject, and that little would be gained by re-opening old wounds. However, *Musical News* once more took up cudgels on behalf of London, as it had done so forcibly three years before. On 11 May a correspondent spoke of Elgar "putting forth a new edition of his annual diatribe against the unfortunate metropolis. Amidst much that should be the subject of critical examination his amazing statement that London was one hundred and fifty years behind the age in the matter of music is indeed a ludicrous as well as an ignorant assertion...Sir F Bridge, Dr Cowen, Dr Borland, Mr Betjeman, Mr Gill, Mr Fagge, Dr W Davies and Mr Venables...are conductors of many more highly-trained choralists than the much-flattered Morecambe can boast of inhabitants..."

Official reaction followed in the next issue on 18 May: first, from the journal's leading feature writer, W H Caunt:

> Sir Edward Elgar seems to be a man full of words, and to say many things in haste which he would find difficult to justify in his contemplative leisure. That he spoke without due consideration is the most charitable view we can take of his latest outpouring at Morecambe...With six million or more of inhabitants, it is small wonder that a considerable proportion hire people to amuse them, and like music mostly when it is expensive. We may be very thankful that this is the case; if it were not for the moneyed folk who pay others to amuse them, it would fare badly with musical bread-winners, including Sir Edward himself...We would remind [Sir Edward] of the legion of professional musicians in London who earn their living by the exposition of their talents and gifts. True, music is to them a

trade, but they could not, and would not, have adopted music as their life work if they had not been possessed with the spirit of music, and the temperament which is indispensable for all who call themselves musicians. This then is the condition of London; is it 150 years behind the age? Perhaps Sir Edward will name the place which can be compared with it.

The journal also referred to the matter in an editorial in the same issue, entitled 'The Appreciation of Music':

> It would be easy to say a great deal about the eminent composer's unfortunate speech, but we have no desire to emulate his example by indulging in comparisons. It is quite possible to defend London from the aspersions cast upon it without depreciating Morecambe...Against the hypocrisy of supporting music simply because it is fashionable or for the sake of ostentation, no words can be too strong, but Sir Edward Elgar does not and cannot prove that this is applicable to London as a whole, or even in any great measure. If he would only get rid of that unreasoning prejudice against the Metropolis, and would only cultivate the open mind, he might in time arrive at a just and dispassionate judgment.

The same issue contained several letters on the subject, some of them vehement in their condemnation:

> Does it very much matter what the Birmingham University Professor of Music says about art, its composers, conductors, and teachers? Those who know can afford to be more amused than angry. In 1905 your columns chronicled the highly complimentary opinion he expressed that 'English composers after fifty years of age had dwindled into nonentities'. Shortly afterwards...when on a visit to America he is reported to have said:- 'The English National Anthem is the silliest thing imaginable; the words are stupid, and some of the lines won't rhyme, and altogether the man who sings it and thinks of what he is saying can't respect himself. The music is good enough, because it was stolen from the Germans'. There's patriotism - and ignorance!

> At the Birmingham University lectures in the autumn of 1905 Professor Elgar sneered at English conductors...At the same series of lectures [he] went for performers and actors...Now we are told that London is still in the Handel period of 150 years ago. Pleasant reading for men like Parry, Stanford, Mackenzie, Bridge, Cowen, and others who have had much important vocal music performed in the metropolis during the past decade!

> But, after all, Sir Edward Elgar has been so often rebuked by responsible men speaking for our profession that does it much matter what he says?

Another letter was more reasonable and placatory in tone:

> I was present at the Morecambe Festival on the 4th inst, and took
> special notice of Sir Edward Elgar's remarks. To me, Sir Edward
> made his meaning very clear, and I am astonished at the wilful
> manner in which these remarks have been misunderstood and
> twisted...I am not connected in any way with the Morecambe Festival,
> and though I may see where a little improvement might be made...I
> believe that Canon Gorton and his excellent committee have the cause
> of music at heart as one of the best means of elevating the people.

Also on 18 May the 75-year-old Joseph Bennett wrote an article in
The Daily Telegraph entitled 'Of Elgar and the North'. Bennett's
beautiful style, lightness of tone, and gentle irony cannot disguise the
depth of his feeling on this issue.

> ...By 'Elgar' I, of course, mean the famous and fortunate composer
> who, at the present moment, occupies a position both social and
> artistic never before attained by an English musician - the composer
> upon whom Fortune showers favours unweariedly; all well deserved,
> no doubt, and to be worn with pride and honour. But what of the
> North in this connection? Is not Sir Edward Elgar the pride of the
> pastoral Midlands, where he was born, and is he not the boast of
> embowered Hereford, where he resides? If this be so, how link him
> with the bleak and stormy North, whence come the freezing winds of
> our English spring, and with strenuous stentors whose speech, unlike
> his own, conveys no music to the ear? The reason is that the North
> has taken very kindly to 'competition festivals', as borrowed from the
> Welsh Eisteddfod, and that one of its most important gatherings is
> held, from time to time, at Morecambe, on the sandy shore of the Irish
> Sea. Sir Edward has friends at Morecambe, as in most other places,
> and these, we may well believe, have found little difficulty in
> persuading him to go down occasionally and act as adjudicator.
> Depend upon it, the Morecambe public did not examine him for his
> fitness. They took the southern knight upon the strength of his
> renown, and great distinction came to them, and to their competitions
> because of it.

Bennett proceeded, in a lofty and disdainful way, to refute Elgar's
remarks about London and the North. "I...do not pretend to teach Sir
Edward Elgar. He is wiser than is his tongue in the speech-
stimulating air of Morecambe".

The following week, *Musical News* was still publishing
correspondence on the issue. One writer went so far as to say:

> ...Sir Edward is not an adept in expressing himself very plainly in words, and unkind people have said that he does not always do it in his music.

Yet once again Elgar was not without his supporters:

> Some of us are deeply pained at the recent outbreak against our great leader. There appears to be much wrath because in a public speech he has ventured to allude to London without at the same time falling down to worship in uncontrolled ecstasy...If there be falsehood in Sir Edward's words it will very surely fall to foolishness without need of mud thrown to help it do so; and if there be truth in them, it remains but for us to seek it, test it, and take it to heart.

The most sensible press reaction came from *The Reader*, which sought the views of Elgar's fellow-judges, McNaught and Walford Davies, both based in London. Their remarks appeared on 25 May in an article entitled 'Is London Unmusical?'. McNaught wrote:

> My loyalty to London induces me to say that I think Sir Edward compares things which are quite unlike. When, for example, he remarked that Londoners mostly like music when it is expensive, and that they do not make their own music, but have it made for them, he had in his mind, I imagine, a musical public recruited from the wealthy West End patrons of opera. But 'Society' is a small and not very representative body of the music-loving public of the metropolis...To give point to his remark, Sir Edward ought first to show us what the 'comfortable' classes of Manchester or Liverpool do to demonstrate their taste in musical matters. Judged from this standpoint, I should say that Liverpool and other northern towns are not in advance of London.
>
> The fact is that little attempt has yet been made to organise and concentrate the popular musical activities of London. The spread of the musical competition movement in the north of England has, I think, done more than anything else to foster the belief that the north is the real living centre of music in this country.

McNaught then gave the history and aims of the movement, before continuing:

> On the whole, then, I am of the opinion that the high reputation of the north for excellence in musical matters is largely the result of careful organisation and the focusing of district talent, and I am convinced that if similar organisation were brought to bear upon the musical activities of London, it would not be long before at least comparable results would ensue. People in the North do not realise the immensity

of London, and the difficulties of unifying its musical efforts. Talent and activity there are in plenty, but they flourish often in gloomy isolation...

Walford Davies was also full of praise for what the movement had achieved in the north, but added:

> ...my present experience goes to show that however much the north is ahead in actual choral technique, it is not so in the power of intelligent interpretation. Surely, also, the question as to whether a district is really 'musical' or not is largely to be decided from the character of the audiences to be met there; and in this respect London is certainly not unmusical...
>
> In two senses I agree with Sir Edward Elgar's criticisms:
> (1) We want competitive festivals among the people; London itself ought to have a magnificent musical 'tournament' each year; and (2) it is to our detriment that all famous players and singers are 'on show' in London. This, of course, brings all the follies and drawbacks of 'lion-hunting' and of showy and expensive performances...

And there the matter rested, some four years after it had begun. Elgar gave no more Birmingham lectures (he resigned the professorship about a year later), and within two years his success as a symphonic composer began to draw him inexorably towards the very place he had so often denigrated.

CHAPTER 12

'THE CAPTAIN LEAVES HIS SHIP'

The Gortons left Capri on 27 April 1907, accompanied by Pompelly, and arrived back in England the following weekend. They stayed in London so that the Canon could see a specialist, and he had the opportunity to catch up with news of the Morecambe Festival.

148 Manchester Street, London -
[n.d., 6 May 1907]

My dear Sir Edward -

How often I have thought of you with gratitude for all you have done at our Festival - All our letters have been full of glowing accounts of your speech - and of the help your presence has been - The papers give mangled reports - but I could recognise the cut and thrust of your sword - Clearly the two events were the 'Evening Scene' and the Greek anthology - It must do you good to hear your work stand out pre eminent, and makes us cry out in reason for more -

My voyage home did me more good than anything - I was quite free from pulsations while on board - and am better now - I see Sir William Gowers, with Dr Oldham tomorrow - I truly never feel my old self - in unconscious health - but have a pressure at the back of my heart: but as I was so well at sea, it gives me hope that I may yet be fit once more -

It is a delight to get back to England - I could have cried at sight of the king-cups, the lank woods, and the meadows - and a well set up clean Englishman is so good a sight after the fat Germans -

I can't write with any comfort and if I could I could not tell you how grateful I am to you both - We hope to return home Saturday or Monday - I am glad you think [well] of Smale - who is a gentleman in ways & thoughts -

There is so much I would write about but I hope we may meet before long - that I may be regaled with your American experience -

We have met some of the most delightful Americans - and have with us now a young fellow who has the frame of an Apollo - and the soul of a Galahad - I hope to carry him with us to Morecambe -The children were full of pride & pleasure at entertaining you both.

With united love -
Yours most affectionately
C.V.Gorton[163]

Plas Gwyn, Hereford
May 7: 1907

My dear Canon Gorton
Welcome to England!

We missed you dreadfully at Morecambe but all worked with a will &
the whole thing was splendid. I *wish* you could have heard the
combined men's choruses sing Cast me on Saturday evening: not
because it was the best thing to hear but because it was a new idea,
unpremeditated & effec*tual*.

We do hope you are feeling better & have fewer worries: it is too much
to expect that you are entirely free from all your anxieties but we hope
& trust things are smoother now you are safe in this blessed land.

I will not refer to my American experiences now: let us have a hearty
laugh over them together.

All the 'staff' at Morecambe were splendid again I thought. Hatch &
Powell giants!

My remarks are not accurately reported but they will serve: I cannot
take the trouble to amend them.

I am glad the Shield has gone to the Isle of Man: the victory seemed
popular but I hear Blackpool is darker in spirit than even its name
would warrant.

Our love to Mrs. Gorton & to you
Always sincerely yrs
Edward Elgar

The Arch-chanter John [Coates] was the greatest success & a joy to
see.

Canon Gorton's visit to Sir William Gowers, the most eminent
neurologist of his day, was not encouraging. His condition had
deteriorated, and Gowers held out little hope for a complete
recovery. However, in view of the improvement Gorton felt during the
journey home, Sir William suggested a long sea voyage to somewhere
like South Africa (Gowers himself had been there in 1894 to recover

163. EBML 2486

from a bout of sciatica). Ella Gorton broke the news to Neville at Marlborough, who replied:

> I got your letter this morning, the bravest letter I have ever read. I know how much it means to you, to Father & to us all. It seems terribly hard that he should have to give up his work just at the time when he might have been most successful. But after all he has done a great work already - I never realised how much until I saw this year's festival & saw the choirs coming up from all around & heard the kind things everyone said about him...

The following Monday, 13 May, the Canon wrote to Neville, seeking to moderate his wife's reaction to the doctor's verdict:

> I think your mother must have given you somewhat of a wrong impression...The great consolation for me was to know that it was not mischief in the brain - but muscular. Of course when I told him that I had been free from palpitations at sea, it was natural for him to say "Go back to the sea"...I am going to try first a very quiet time at Morecambe and if that does not bring relief I will take a voyage. I am so glad you took to Dr [Walford] Davies.[164] I was with him at the Temple [*Church, where Davies was organist*] service yesterday. We must go together there some day. It is an ideal act of worship: the music occupies its rightful place, and Davies fills it with [a] spirit of reverence...
>
> How much your loving thoughts for us both have been to me I cannot try to tell you. God will bless you for it and make your life a blessing.

The Gortons arrived in Morecambe later that day, and a large crowd gave the couple a warm reception. The Canon gave a short speech, in the course of which he said: "I had bad weather and a serious illness: from the latter...I have not recovered, and Sir William Gowers after a careful examination, ordered me to take a voyage to the Cape". The *Lancaster Guardian* reported: "Although much improved in health the reverend gentleman is not yet strong enough to get into the full stride of his work..."

So Gorton had decided not to wait, but to proceed with the voyage. They arranged to sail on 31 May, less than a month after their return from Italy. For the Gorton family it was a worrying time. On 28 May Neville wrote in his diary: "Expected to hear from Father - but was disappointed. Feel anxious about them & not keen on their going

---

164. Sir William Gowers was a close personal friend of Walford Davies, who presumably recommended him to Gorton.

away again but hope S.Africa & the voyage will do him good." Two days later he wrote: "I am afraid they will feel leaving home very much so soon - mother most of all. But I pray it will do Father real good...He loves the sea & it must be great fun [-] a voyage on a big liner..." The following day Elgar wrote to his friend:

Plas Gwyn, Hereford
May 31: 1907

My dear Canon Gorton:

This brings you & Mrs.Gorton every good wish: all our thoughts & prayers are with you: I know how trying this enforced rest is to you & how hopeless it is to try to say anything to an active man which will be un-irritating.

I had hoped I might have seen you before you sailed but it has not been possible:

Let us hear of your travels as often as you can. I will not enter into Festival matters now.

We are well here & have slowly subsided, through various stages of disgust & despair, to resentment at this truly awful weather. I have ridden very little but have been over some of the spots consecrated by your company[.] I thought of you

God bless you!
Yrs ever sincly
Edward Elgar

I shall write to the Committee later.

The Gortons arrived in Capetown on 24 June, and reported progress to May, who passed on the news to the rest of the family. Neville wrote in his diary: "Heard from S.Africa...at least a card from Aunt May to say Father only 'fairly well' - not very encouraging". They left for home on 1 July. The Canon certainly enjoyed the voyage, even if it did not bring about the improvement in health for which he had hoped.

One preoccupation the Canon undoubtedly had on his mind during his enforced rest was the problem of restoring the 'pre-eminence' of the Morecambe Festival. The postponement of *The Dream of Gerontius* in 1907 had been a bitter disappointment, and Gorton was determined to proceed with it the following year. Shortly after his return to England at the end of July he prevailed upon Elgar to approach Hans Richter with a proposal, and on 31 July Elgar wrote to the famous conductor:

The Morecambe Festival authorities are anxious to know if you would consider a proposition to conduct Gerontius there next May: they propose your own orchestra & the best soloists: they ask me to speak to you of the chorus, which will be well trained & will be a most admirable body of voices which you would delight to lead.

I fear the date, which would be probably in the early part of May, wd be a difficulty as the Opera season will be on then. They ask me to tell you that the Chorus will be worthy of you if other things can be arranged - this I testify with the greatest pleasure.

Elgar's fears about the clash of dates proved to be justified, as Gorton discovered when he wrote to Richter himself, formally asking him to conduct. Richter replied:

Excuse kindly the delay of my reply, but I could not give you a decisive answer before I have seen what I have to do at the Opera. Unfortunately I cannot accept your offer to conduct in May the Dream of Gerontius, as I shall be fully occupied at the Covent Garden Opera from 15th of April until 12th of June.

Canon Gorton was still far from well as he returned to parish work at the beginning of August. He was forced to cut down on his work, in particular his membership of various committees. Another enforced rest in September took him for treatment to Bournemouth and the Isle of Wight, accompanied by Neville. He was thus forced to miss the Three Choirs Festival, where Elgar conducted *The Apostles* on the evening of 10 September, followed by *The Kingdom* the next morning. After the Festival Elgar wrote to Gorton:

[Plas Gwyn, Hereford]
[16 September 1907]

My dear Canon Gorton,

We thought & spoke much of you at Gloucester & longed for your company. We are glad to hear that you have received some benefit from your Ryde treatment.

Things went well at Gloucester, helped much by the glorious building.

I am not supposed to read or write much & have during the summer not been quite idle: several small mostly old things will reach you in a post or two: one new part song, too small for any purpose of yours, also was written & a new march which is gaudily gay & brilliant.

The serious work waits for Rome. I am not sure as to our movements which are not conclusively arranged: you shall hear what we do if not all we plan to do. In the meantime all good wishes & love from us all.

Yours ever
Edward Elgar.[165]

The "small mostly old things" included two church anthems from the
St George's days: and the music to a children's play *The Wand of Youth*
dating from the 1860s, which Elgar was now arranging as an orchestral
suite. The part-song was entitled *Love*, and dedicated to Alice on the
composer's fiftieth birthday on 2 June: and the new march was
number four in the *Pomp & Circumstance* set, and destined to become
almost as popular as the first march. The "serious work" probably
suggested to Gorton the third oratorio: but Elgar had by now given up
the idea of completing his trilogy, and was working on a symphony.

Despite his illness, Canon Gorton's mind and interests were still as
active as ever. On 17 September a long letter from him defending the
Three Choirs Festival from criticism appeared in *The Daily
Telegraph.* Objections had been voiced for some time by those who
resented the transformation of a "sacred" building into a concert
hall, where the audience paid for seats. After dismissing such
protests, Gorton continued:

> To shake oneself free from irritating quibbles and to come to the root
> of the matter, music in its highest form has its claim on the cathedral,
> has its part to play in the work of adoration. Into the Temple 'the
> kings of the earth bring their treasure', and first among these kings
> are heaven-given artists...Our greatest interpreters of music have a
> ministry in the Kingdom of Heaven as real as our bishops; they do not
> cease to fulfil this ministry because they are paid. Truer still is this
> for the composer. With him religion is no excuse for music, but music
> is the expression in natural form of the faith. Who that has heard *The
> Apostles* and *The Kingdom* has not felt that he has heard a more
> potent argument for the faith than in any sermon? Here the
> Incarnation is set forth as a living power; here are arguments which
> reach men where words fail. They are listened to by thousands with
> bowed head, and not seldom with tears in their eyes. And yet we are
> to be told that these and such works are to be given under the
> conditions of a magnified evensong, or are to be banished to the
> concert-halls, where applause and not the bowed head is to follow
> those movements which open for us the gates of heaven.

As indicated in his letter of 16 September, Elgar was planning to
spend another winter in Italy and so was unable to commit himself

165. Quoted in Young (1956), 190

definitely to attend the next festival, but in spite of this uncertainty Gorton decided to proceed with the recruitment and training of the festival chorus. On 25 September he made another appeal to the public via the pages of the *Morecambe Visitor:*

> ...I remember Canon Allen telling me with natural pride 'that he had once spoken to Mendelssohn'. I believe that he even sat on the same organ stool with him...The days will come that we may boast to our grandchildren, if we live to have any, 'that we once saw Elgar', or that we even sang under his baton.
>
> Those who have not heard Elgar's oratorios may be slow to realise what I have insisted from the first in our festival book, that he is the greatest of our living Englishmen, and I can imagine no greater delight than being the humblest instrument in assisting to produce that stupendous masterpiece, *Gerontius.* I know how the real author of our Festival, Mr Howson, looked forward to the day when we should produce this work in Morecambe. Now the time is come. Either we must produce a worthy rendering of this work, or the structure which we have raised with so much effort will begin to totter. But to produce this work means much. I know that the demand which music makes on the time of many is very exhaustive....
>
> I must appeal to all these music makers in Morecambe to join in the coming season, to put 'first things first', and to devote themselves heart and soul to the strenuous practising of the *Dream of Gerontius...*

During the first week of October Elgar was in London for rehearsals of the orchestra for the Leeds Festival. He met up with Walford Davies, who shared his feelings about the need to encourage choral conductors to develop the interpretative aspect of test pieces, rather than to concentrate solely on technical excellence. To do this, Davies recommended Langford's suggestion of using compositions with few, if any, expression marks. Elgar wrote to Gorton:

> The Athenæum, Pall Mall S.W.
> Oct 4 1907
>
> My dear Canon Gorton:
>
> There's no real reason for this letter, only to ask how you are finding things at Morecambe: I trust well.
>
> I have been going through the Kingdom with the orchestra for Leeds & thought of you & I saw that dear good fellow, Walford Davies: we talked of Morecambe matters & I fully approve of his idea: the ptsng without expression marks: the 'class' wd. throw a lot of responsibility on conductors but it is quite time they shd. have it.

I go home today

We sail for Naples in the first week in November: then Rome till May
I hope.

Ever yours, and with much love to you all,
Edward Elgar

Elgar was evidently concerned about the Canon's health. A few days
later he wrote to Walford Davies:

> I wrote to Gorton at Morecambe a few days ago but have heard nothing
> in return: there is no reason why he shd. have written quickly but he
> usually does and has not - so I don't know where or how he is.[166]

The great impression which Rome had made on the Elgars earlier in
the year encouraged them to go there for the winter. They left
England on 5 November, taking their daughter and niece with them.
A postcard showing the statue of Marcus Aurelius was sent to
Morecambe Rectory with the following inscription:

> 38 Via Gregoriana
> Rome III
> 9 Nov.

> A line to tell you we are safely here & feel so settled. We arrived on
> Thursday. Edward loves Rome so much. Carice & May are delighted.
> This is a splendid situation [:] we see all over Rome. & have taken the
> flat for the winter. We do trust you are keeping better

> Our love to you all: E. hopes to write soon.
> Yrs.
> C.A.Elgar

Soon after arriving, Elgar wrote to Frank Schuster: "Here is my
Mecca & I love it *all* - Note the fact that I am pagan not Xtian at
present...We are very comfortable here & see over the tops of the
houses across to S.Pietro with fine sunsets thrown in. Yes: I am
trying to write music - but the bitterness is that it pays not at all & I
must write & arrange what my soul loathes to permit me to write
what *you* like & I like. So I curse the power that gave me gifts &
loathe them now & ever. I told you a year ago I could see no future:
now I see it & am a changed man & a dour creature".[167]

166. EBML 2192
167. Moore, *Letters of a Lifetime*, 191

Novello had asked Elgar to write "a marching song for soldiers"; McNaught wanted a male voice song for the next Blackpool Festival: Sinclair had asked for a carol for his Christmas concert at Hereford Cathedral[168]: and F G Edwards requested a small part-song for the *Musical Times*. Elgar was aware of the financial benefits which might accrue from writing such music, yet his creative instincts were looking towards large-scale orchestral expression (the "serious work" he had mentioned to Gorton): hence his frustration, and his remarks to Schuster.

He got down to his task. A simple hymn-like part-song *How Calmly the Evening* was sent to Edwards on 2 December. Three days later Alice wrote some words for a carol entitled *A Christmas Greeting*, and in another three days Elgar had set it to music and sent it off to Sinclair. The *Marching Song* was already begun, and on 16 December McNaught sent Elgar some words by the American writer, Francis Bret Harte, a poem entitled *The Reveille*. McNaught wrote:

> You will remember that I pressed you to compose a biggish male voice chorus (unacc) and you said find me the words. I have sought in many places in vain and at last came on to the enclosed. I do hope you will like the poem for the purpose. Mr.Littleton agrees with me as to its suitability.
>
> We have had an enquiry from Morecambe as to your coming 'Marching Song'. If it could be in the Morecambe programme it would be a capital start...[169]

Ten days later Elgar completed his setting and posted it to McNaught, who acknowledged it with delight on 1 January 1908:

> I am so glad you have taken to the 'Reveille' so kindly.
>
> The setting is splendid - the high B at the end will be a roof raiser up in the North and I hope in Wales.
>
> Mr Clayton is seeing to the words - as to permission - and when that is settled the world will soon come into its inheritance.[170]

---

168. Elgar's sketches and letters to Sinclair can be found in BL Add MS 49973B.
169. Moore, 686.
170. *op cit.*, 687

Elgar had been impressed with the way that the best choirs at Morecambe could interpret part-songs of an extended nature, and in response he had now written one of his own. *The Reveille* was a dramatic and musically complex song of one hundred and thirteen bars - almost the length of the five *Greek Anthology* songs put together.

Yet as well as these commissions, Elgar was in the process of writing four part-songs for mixed voices. They are all dated 'Rome, Dec.1907' and were given the opus number 53. (The last one, *Owls*, is dated 31 December). It is curious to reflect on the fact of their composition at this time, when Elgar was keen to proceed with his symphony. Are they to be seen as compensation to Gorton for Elgar's absence from the 1908 Festival? They were certainly written with Morecambe in mind, and represented an enormous technical advance on Elgar's last mixed voice part-song, *Evening Scene*, written two and a half years before.

The first song, *There is Sweet Music*, used the opening lines of Tennyson's poem *The Lotos Eaters*. Elgar wrote at the head of the score "To my friend Canon Gorton". The tonality of the song was very unusual, as Elgar described in a letter of 17 January to Ivor Atkins:

> I write a little & have furnished (good word) four part-songs, one whereof is in two keys at once! that is to say, the S[oprano]. A[lto]. & right hand PF bear the signature of $\flat^{\flat}_{\flat}$ while simultaneously the T[enor].B[ass]. & left hand PF are in $\sharp$. It will sound very remote & will please village choirs.[171]

That last remark must have been Elgar's little joke, for none but the best choirs could hope to do justice to such a demanding song. Difficulties in maintaining pitch arising from the antiphonal writing were aggravated by the subdued dynamics - a maximum marking of *mf*, and most of the song sung *pp*. And Elgar, taking up Walford Davies's idea, was more sparing than usual with his expression marks. The opening is marked *legato ed espressivo*, and the only other marking is *cantabile* for the men's voices at the words "that brings sweet sleep" in bar twenty. There is almost no sense of pulse, as within the basic 4/4 metre are inserted bars of 2/4, 5/4 and even 10/4 to accommodate the words.

Elgar was immensely pleased with what he had written, as he told Alfred Littleton on 12 January:

171. Atkins, 169

> I am dispatching 3 partsongs somewhat *advanced*...There should be four in the Op[us]. but I send *now* only Nos. 2, 3 & 4. The last is a 'clinker' & the best I have done.[172]

The second song, a setting of Byron's *Deep in my Soul* was dedicated to Julia Worthington; and the link between these songs and Morecambe was further underlined by the dedication of the third song, Shelley's *O Wild West Wind* to "my friend W G McNaught, Mus Doc". Elgar had also set the "west wind" to music in 1903 when he had first shared the judges' box at Morecambe with McNaught, and now once again in the same key, E flat. But unlike *There is Sweet Music*, this third song is littered with expression marks,[173] and Elgar asked McNaught to check them for him. Replying on 8 January, the doctor confirmed that he would, and thanked Elgar profusely for the dedication. "It is a great honour", he wrote.[174]

The final song was entitled *Owls*. Elgar himself wrote the words, and the dedication is to "my friend, Pietro d'Alba" (his daughter's white rabbit, Peter). Basil Maine describes the song as "an essay in queerness", and Percy Young says "in this Elgar's imaginative dread of darkness and obscurity, pain and death is set out in broken fragments of melody".[175]

McNaught wrote again on 9 March:

> I have been gazing at 'There is sweet music' and am longing to hear it done by a real live choir. It will give some conductors a bad quarter of an hour
>
> I have decided not to use it on a sight test at Morecambe...
>
> ♩ = M.44 for Sweet music seems slow for some parts.
>
> But I can see that anything like a jaunty rhythm will upset the idea.[176]

---

172. Moore, 689. There is a certain ambiguity as to which song Elgar is referring. The "last" could be *Owls*, as the final one in the set (no 4); or it could be *There is sweet music*, as the last to be sent. Either would justify the description "clinker".

173. Young, in a memorable phrase, describes the song as being "notable for its general congestion" (*Elgar OM*, 296).

174. Moore, 688

175. Young, ibid.

176. Moore, 693,

The following month Elgar shared his views on the new songs with Jaeger, who was writing an article about them for the *Musical Times*:

> ...I do not think I have overdone the marks [of expression:] you see nothing emotional is ever performed in strict time & it takes conductors *years* (literally) to find out a reading...I have only put sort of *emotional* marks for the conductor to do the best he can with. I wish you could have heard the *Morecambe choir under Howson* sing four or five years ago: you wd then fully appreciate what I have tried to do...[177]

Arrangements for the next festival at Morecambe were well in hand, although Gorton was unable to give it the same personal attention as before (in November 1907 an additional priest was appointed to Holy Trinity to share the burden of parish work). Walford Davies had been commissioned to write a short cycle of unaccompanied part-songs for the Challenge Shield entitled *England's Pleasant Land*. The first song, 'The Green Fields of England', to words by Arthur Hugh Clough, was written without expression marks, and the conductors were invited to interpret the piece in their own way. The other two songs were 'England' and 'And did those feet'. The fourth song in the Challenge Shield class was also specially commissioned - *Justice* by Joseph Hathaway.

The chorus had started work on *The Dream of Gerontius* in the autumn, and at the beginning of November 1907 the secretary of the Festival Chorus appealed in the press for singers, as Gorton's earlier plea had not produced sufficient numbers. The danger signals were clear to see. Then, towards the end of January 1908, it was announced that *Gerontius* would not now be performed at the forthcoming festival. A disappointed Gorton wrote in the preface to the programme book:

> I had hoped that this Festival might have been marked as the 'Gerontius Festival' but we have been compelled to postpone giving this work owing to the difficulty in securing an adequate chorus. This difficulty has arisen, paradoxical as it may seem, from the plethora of choral singing in the district; but it will be readily understood that when in any town or village practices are being held of mixed voice choirs, male, and female voice choirs, Girls' Friendly Society choirs, and Church and Chapel choirs, not many days remain in the week for any added effort. The difficulty is even greater in securing practices in towns than in villages: because in the former people naturally plead that they must occasionally see after their business...

177. Moore, 694

The *Morecambe Visitor* was not slow to criticise:

> It is discreditable to local musicians that they have failed to support
> the Festival Executive in this venture. It must be noted that it is the
> male voices who have thus failed, for quite a strong choir of ladies has
> been available. It is not from any dearth of good male voices that this
> unfortunate result has come to pass, but it is rather the outcome of
> the demands which a considerable number of small choirs make
> upon the time of their members. Apparently the patriotic spirit has
> not been strong enough to lead these many capable singers to make
> the small extra sacrifice which the Festival Chorus rehearsals
> demanded. It is much to be regretted that this is so...We shall surely
> be asked "Where is our vaunted musical superiority now?" The fault
> lies at our own door. Verily, what a pity.

Apparently there were often twenty to thirty ladies at the Morecambe
rehearsals, but sometimes only two or three men, and the same
indifference had been shown in Lancaster. In his book *Musical
England*, written the following year, W J Galloway commented on the
decision:

> So much was being done that it was impossible to do more; and as
> long as the present standard of excellence in part-songs and
> madrigals is maintained, there is really no need to press forward with
> undue haste to the introduction of more extensive works.[178]

Certainly there was no obvious reduction in public enthusiasm when
the festival began on 13 May. Almost 5000 competitors entered the
thirty-nine classes, and the audiences were as large as ever. Elgar
had kept his options open on attending the festival, and as late as 22
April the *Morecambe Times* reported: "Sir Edward Elgar is out of
England, but should he return before the Festival is concluded he
will certainly visit Morecambe". Possibly a performance of *Gerontius*
might have brought him back sooner: as it was, Canon Gorton read
out a letter sent from Rome in which Elgar conveyed his greetings to
the Festival.

On the first day the combined children's choirs gave the first public
performance of Walford Davies's cantata *Humpty Dumpty*, with the
composer conducting. On the second day the local competitions took
place and in the mixed voice class (open to Lancaster, Morecambe,
and all villages and towns of under 800 inhabitants within a 35-mile
radius) one of the test pieces was Elgar's new part-song *Love*. The

---

178.　W J Galloway, *Musical England* (Christophers, 1910), 174

Musical Times wrote of the local choirs: "It speaks volumes for the educative effects of the festival that the standard in these classes has now reached that of the open classes of a few years back".[179]

Langford in the *Manchester Guardian* agreed:

> [The Festival] has altogether banished harsh singing from choirs of quite country places. The delicate mystery of Elgar's music has done more than anything towards this result, and his new part-song *Love* was given by nine choirs this morning, in each case with an insight which was most creditable considering the districts from which the singers came. The words of the piece are among the weaker things Elgar has set, and lack clearness and hardness. It is a natural fault in Elgar that he sometimes falls a victim to such things, when he himself needs a little stiffening, and is at his best with words clear and hard like those of Patmore and Newman.

Langford praised the singing of the G F S choirs in a motet by Mendelssohn, but went on: "The other pieces chosen for these singers were not worthy of them, like a fair number of pieces sung during the day".

The Festival concert on the Friday evening included a recital of twenty songs given by Agnes Nicholls, accompanied by Hamilton Harty. Herbert Brown sang six of Parry's *English Lyrics*, and a performance of Mendelssohn's *Piano Trio in D minor* was given by a group led by a twenty-five-year-old violinist from Preston named Arthur Catterall, who later found fame as leader of the Hallé and BBC orchestras. The current holders of the Challenge Shield, the Isle of Man Choir, sang a group of six songs. Once again Langford felt led to disapprove of the repertoire:

> Their choice of music was most disappointing. Only two of the pieces they sang had any real worth, and these were pieces of small scope - the carol from *The Childhood of Christ* and Elgar's *O Happy Eyes*. The other pieces were unworthy of the singers and of the occasion. Things like Leslie's *Lullaby of Life* are of the type which it is the special glory of Morecambe to discourage.

"Despite the increase in the number of festivals the choirs entered are even greater in number than ever", Gorton wrote in the preface. As well as those from Belfast and the Isle of Man, competitors on the final "open" day came from as far north as Newcastle and as far south as Melton Mowbray, totalling forty choirs and five orchestras.

179. vol xlix June 1908, 399

The men from Newcastle won the male voice section, in which the three test pieces were all in English translations by Canon Gorton: *Happy Light, Happy Day* by Scharwenka; *Media Vita* by Bruch; and *Sturmlied* by Fauth. However, Langford was not slow to speak his mind:

> Canon Gorton had written very singable translations, but the music of Fauth's piece was unvocal...Scharwenka's piece was a weak thing in a style that is dead long since. Max Bruch's work was the best of the three...Altogether it was a case of importing music that was hardly worth the trouble.

The victory of the Newcastle choir was largely due to their fine performance of the Fauth. They scored 283 marks altogether,[180] three more than the Manchester Orpheus, and five more than Habergham. Nelson won the two orchestral classes, scoring 86 marks in each. Both the female voice class and the Challenge Shield were won by Mr Aldous's Lancaster Choir. In the former, with 187 marks, they were no less than twenty-two marks ahead of Barrow in second place. There was a sensation in the first round of the Challenge Shield, when three of the favourites - the Isle of Man Choir, Blackpool, and Morecambe - failed to qualify for the final in the evening. Lancaster, with 368, won by five marks from Southport, with Barrow third and Nottingham fourth. The winners also received a special prize of five guineas for the best interpretation of the song without expression marks, *The Green Fields of England*. "Mr Aldous' choir gave the only thoroughly good reading of the piece", Langford wrote.

It was a notable triumph for Aldous, who seventeen years earlier had been the festival's first secretary. Neville Gorton, now in his first year at Balliol, wrote to his father:

> I was very surprised to see Lancaster did so well in the Festival. Mr.Aldous ought to be quite unbearable. I am very sorry Morecambe did not do well: Smale must be disappointed. I think the Manchester Guardian's criticism of the music - from what I heard of it - was rather justified...
>
> I hope you have not been knocked up. It must have been a very tiring week but I hope you enjoyed it.

180. Marks for each test piece were now out of 100, ie. 20 marks for each of the five sections.

The *Musical Herald* renewed its attack on the Morecambe system of adjudication:

> When the turn comes for sympathy with the defeated, it is easy to suggest changes of plans which would have been fairer to Barrow and Southport choirs, which gained the same number of marks in the final as the winners. People who came fresh to the evening audience could not agree with the verdict because they were unable to add marks gained in the afternoon. Morecambe has borne with this plan for many years in spite of the vexations it causes. There should be a clean slate for the final, or the preliminary should be in 'heats', as in races.

However, the Morecambe executive could afford to ignore such criticism as its policy was clearly vindicated by the number of choirs wishing to compete. Yet Langford had noticed a distinct decline, saying that the festival would have been "poor indeed" without the presence of Walford Davies.

It was now becoming clear to those close to him that the Canon's health was deteriorating to the point when he could no longer continue to work. On 15 July Elgar wrote to Walford Davies: "I...heard of your being at Morecambe from Canon Gorton: I am so very glad you were there, I fear our friend is in a bad way - I wrote some time ago & have no reply. It is sad".[181] Davies replied on 21 July: "Poor Gorton seems ill & fighting the natural depression which nervous illness must bring".[182]

At this distance, and working with incomplete evidence, it is not possible to give an accurate diagnosis on what exactly Canon Gorton was suffering from. The commonest cause of progressive paralysis in this age group is motor neurone disease, which is a wasting and weakening of the muscles: however, it is not primarily a painful condition, and there is evidence that the Canon was in severe pain at times during the last few years of his life. (Having said this, patients with motor neurone disease often suffer pain or discomfort because of bad posture etc, consequent on the weakness[183]).

181. EBML 2198

182. EBML 2199

183. I am indebted to Professor John Marshall of the Institute of Neurology at the National Hospital, Queens Square, London, for suggestions on this topic.

Although becoming increasingly incapacitated, Canon Gorton pressed on with his work as best he could. He obtained another of Hegar's male voice songs, *Walpurga*. Ella translated it as usual, and the Canon sent music and translation to the Elgars for their comments. The letter contained the news that *There is Sweet Music* and *Deep in my Soul* were to be test pieces at Morecambe in 1909. Alice replied:

Plas Gwyn, Hereford
2 Augt. 1908

My dear Canon Gorton

I waited to answer your letter until Edward could play through the Hegar pt.Song. That he has just done & tells me to say he does not care for it & does not think it so good as the others -

I can find no direct *Walpurga* legend, Grimm in his "German Mythology", says that amongst the North German people, these "wilden Weiber" play an important part during the 12 nights from Christmas to the Holy Kings,&c-&c- they belong to the heathen ghoulish goblin domain. Even amongst the Germans in Vicenza & Verona, (see Boccaccio & Grönfelte,) at that special time, the boldest hunter dare not visit the woods, for terror of the "Wilder Mann" & the "Waldfrau"......The people were terrified at any sign of communication with the powerful spirits & he who braved the terror has to pay a heavy penalty....

Of course you are familiar with all this but I thought it sheds light on the subject.

What a brutal sort of poem it is. Do you think "witch" quite represents "*Elf*"[?]. It feels to me as if "witch" belonged to a later period - but that is only an idea of my own -

I think Mrs.Gorton's translation gives a faithful rendering of the 3rd verse, I think one can give any interpretation one fancies symbolically, but as you wish, I write out a literal (almost) version of 3rd verse.

It grieves us deeply to know you are suffering, I so wish you could be in the country as you wish. Edward sends much love, he is rapt in his Symphony & can hardly bear to leave it. I trust you & Mrs.Gorton will hear it some day, it seems to me *wonderful*, so noble & beautiful.

Best greetings
C.A.E.

How lovely to have the pt.Songs, E's at yr Festival.
I do not think you *could* have a better rendering of 3rd verse so do not send my attempt.

Two weeks later, on 19 August, the *Morecambe Visitor* carried the news that Canon Gorton was to resign. Tributes came from many quarters, and the following week's issue contained many of them. Above them all was a drawing of the Canon in the dress of a naval captain leaving the bridge of a ship whose lifebelt carries the word 'Morecambe'. The caption read: "The Captain leaves the ship". All writers acknowledged the Canon's kindness, wide interests, and zealous efforts on behalf of the town. A letter spoke of his concern for the welfare of the fishermen.

There were other generous tributes in the press. The *Morecambe Times* commented: "The resignation will be received with a general feeling of regret, more especially as the cause of which leads to it has meant the imposition of bodily suffering upon one who was the embodiment of kindness and sympathy towards others". The *Lancashire Daily Post* was similarly eulogistic:

> A man of expansive ideals, and broad and generous sympathies, his work and usefulness were not confined to any narrow groove or limited mould, but he found touch with the whole life of the people amongst whom his labours were cast...His activities outran his physical fitness, and it is sad to reflect that one who upheld the honour of his university in the domain of athletics should in the prime of life be compelled to relinquish all.

> He stood for everything that was robust, whether in Churchmanship or civic life...In the pulpit and the Press he spoke and wrote with power and conviction. He expressed himself with no uncertain voice on the social questions of the day. He proclaimed a high ideal of civic life and responsibility, and no man was more sensitive of the honour of the town in which his life's great work lay...

> He had calls to many, and even more lucrative livings, but his affections were with the people and town of Morecambe. Had he been blessed in health there can be little doubt if higher honours in the Church than the well-deserved hon. canonry conferred upon him in 1902 had not fallen to his lot, and the Church and its institutions would have been enriched by his sagacity and zeal.

The musical press also contained tributes, like this in the *Musical Herald*:

> Morecambe suffers a great loss by the retirement of the Rev.Canon Gorton from the Rectory...Ever happy and genial, always frank and free, his voice was good to hear. Without being a practical musician, he did a great work for music. No labour was too great if he could help the art or the town. Pessimists capitulated before his high-souled optimism. Obstacles disappeared. Whether as chairman of the

musical festival, translator of German choruses, speaker or writer, he has been a model to admire. His recent illness was deplored by everybody, and now his removal from Morecambe is irreparable.

Canon Gorton wrote the following letter to the people of Morecambe.

For nineteen years now I have worked here and during this time the population has more than doubled, the town was spread out in all directions, responsibilities and anxieties have increased. I sought, as best I could, to meet these increasing needs, and to identify myself not only with the church, but with the town as a whole. Much work has come to me from which I have tried not to run away. Perhaps I have tried to do too much for the work's sake. One thing is clear: that, now, I can do too little and I have no wish to stay on and leave as my memorial a ruin. I desire now to go as quietly as possible. I think I address a larger audience than my own people. Among my fellow townsmen, from my many fellow workers in all classes and creeds, I count up numberless acts of kindness and words of sympathy. One and all will know what it means to break up a home, to part from friends, to let go hold of work at a time in my life when I might have hoped to gather the fruit of experience. It is to pull up the plant by the roots. I shall preach no farewell sermon, or hold farewell services.. Speech is more than I can at present endure, and I trust that I shall not be misunderstood when I say that the greatest kindness to me will be to accept this my act in silence. I shall not fail to watch over you in prayer and, in turn, I believe that many will not fail to ask for me strength to endure.

In acknowledging Gorton's letter of resignation, the Bishop of Manchester, Edward A Knox, wrote:

...I know what you have been to Morecambe, and to the Diocese, and to myself personally.

To Morecambe a very true Shepherd of your people spiritually, bringing to your work intellectual vigour & that rare freshness of enterprise which counts for so much in a parish like Morecambe.

To the Diocese a wise counsellor and a most welcome example of a faithful parish priest, who can yet understand that his parish is not the whole world, but part of a Diocese and a Church.

To myself from the first day that I knew you a genuine, and most delightful friend, refreshing me spiritually and mentally whenever I met you and helping me with loyal and unstinted service. Such friends lighten the burden of Diocesan anxiety, but they are very rare and very precious...

God bless you, my dear brother, and help you to bear what He has laid on you.

CHAPTER 13

'THERE IS SWEET MUSIC'

In June 1907 Mary Wakefield wrote once again to Elgar. The annual meeting of the Association of Musical Competition Festivals was approaching, and she invited him to attend. He replied on 25 June:

> Dear Miss Wakefield,
>
> I am sorry I cannot be at the meeting. I should not have had so much to say, but amongst other things, I feel that at every competition a prize should be offered for the "most artistic" effort. I say "effort" because the best work during a whole festival might be done with a conductor with an inadequate choir: that is to say, the judges should bestow the award on that person, or on that choir, which they think has shewn the greatest artistic perception, - possibly apart from actual execution.
>
> Providence, it was irreverently said, is on the side of the big battalions and, judged from the standpoint of tone, choirs large in numbers, or drawn from large districts, must necessarily have an advantage.
>
> The award should be an important one in every festival: ie, of considerable value in relation to the other prizes offered.
>
> Believe me,
> Yours very sincerely,
> Edward Elgar[184]

The following month, William McNaught gave a progress report on the movement in *The Musical Times*: "The spread and progress of the competition movement shows no sign of abatement", he wrote. McNaught estimated that 50,000 were involved in festivals that year, and went on to list some seventy centres, of which thirty-two were in the North of England. He defended the competitive principle although he referred to the dangers:

> The aims must be high and always educational. If the movement drifts into providing arenas merely for a sordid struggle for a cash-down

184. Elgar's suggestion was taken up at the Kendal Festival in 1908 (letter from Mary Wakefield, EBML 3048).

prize, it will sound its own knell and there will be no mourners. This view is consistent with the belief that money prizes of a reasonable amount are not open to objection, when it is clear that the prize, if won, merely contributes to the unavoidable expenses of competitors. It is absurd to suppose, for instance, that the working men who mainly compose the Habergham Choir (Mr E Hitchon) - one of the best-equipped choirs it has ever been my good fortune to hear - gain pecuniarily as individuals by their achievements in the North. To those, who, like myself, mix freely with the enthusiastic and obviously altruistic promoters,....there would seem to be no danger of the festivals under their benign sway degenerating.

As the number of meetings grew, a problem arose in the *Musical Times* because the reports were taking up so much space. From August 1908 therefore, Novello published the *Competition Festival Record* as a supplement to the *School Music Review*.[185]

The Blackpool Festival of 1908 was an enormous triumph, and one of the highlights of the final "open" day on 17 October was the first public performance of Elgar's *The Reveille*. McNaught referred to this the following month when he contributed an article entitled 'The Great Choral Revival' in the *Daily Mail* on 5 November:

> In some countryside districts the results achieved do not as yet reach a high standard. The movement being one not to award prizes to the efficient, but to educate the inefficient, much has to be suffered in the early stages. At a village competition you may hear an ill-balanced choir, composed of children, women and rough men, who sing clumsily, and yet with a simplicity and earnestness that invite sympathy rather than criticism.

> It is a great day for these folk. They have practised zealously, albeit not scientifically; they have given up a day's occupation to attend the festival. Arrived at the hall they are cordially received by the social powers that be, they hear other choirs perform, and when their turn comes they find themselves before a generous audience, a kind they have never sung to before. They may not win a prize, but instead they get sound advice, unexpected encouragement, and a new outlook.

> In a large town or at a popular seaside resort the scheme works out differently. A day or two of the festival are reserved for local competitors, who often display great merit, but the chief musical glory is the open day. Choirs and other musical organisations led by conductors of great ability come in gorgeous succession. Their singing inflames you and paralyses criticism.

185. It appeared in the *School Music Review* until December 1922, and then in *The Musical Times* from June 1923 to December 1931.

We are in one of Blackpool's sumptuous halls. The choir of working men comes from Habergham, a pit district not discoverable on the map or in the "Post Office Guide". With resonant rich voices they sing appallingly difficult music and make an audience of five thousand eager listeners hold their breath with excitement and emotion.

The piece is Elgar's recent setting of Bret Harte's *Reveille*, a wonderful composition born of the composer's experience of northern choir singing. How did this choir - as fit to sing before King and Queen as any choir in the land - gain this splendid technique, this power to interpret the moods of the modern composer?

In the first place, by virtue of their natural capacity and the genius of Mr Hitchon, their conductor, and for the rest by lessons in the severe school of criticism...

About 50 pieces are scheduled every year at Blackpool, and it is the boast of the management that no pieces are repeated. A pamphlet recently issued gives the titles of 356 compositions by 150 composers selected as tests from 1901 to 1908. It is a remarkable list, and a striking testimony to the high aims of the promoters of the Blackpool scheme, which, it is only fair to add, is modelled upon that of Morecambe.

There was more than a hint of the past tense in that reference to Morecambe. McNaught clearly believed that it was Blackpool's star that was now in the ascendancy, and he was in the best position to judge. The future did not seem too promising for the older festival. The Gortons were preparing to move from Morecambe. They had chosen Hereford: the climate was warmer, and they would be near the Elgars. Ella Gorton paid some preliminary visits to the city in the early autumn, and on 15 October Elgar, who was in London to hear his new orchestral work, the second *Wand of Youth* Suite, wrote to her from his club:

Oct 15 1908

Dear Mrs.Gorton:

I hear from home that you have been with them & looking at a house in Hereford. I am so sorry that for a second time I should have been prevented from welcoming you in person. Nothing wd. give me greater pleasure than to have Canon Gorton & you near us, but I am not sure if your invalid does not require a somewhat bracing climate.

Hereford is very relaxing & enervating: on our hill it is not so bad but in the valleys it is well-known that the air is - somewhat.

Forgive me presuming to interfere & I hope my description of the climate may lead you to come - that it may be what is best for our dear invalid.

Give him my love & with all good wishes
Believe me
Yrs v sincerely
Edward Elgar

Mrs Gorton's visit on 16 November was to confirm the purchase of a large house in Castle Hill, close to the Cathedral and with a garden leading down to the river Wye. It was called Vaga House, after the old Roman name for the river. The Canon was not able to resign his living until early in the new year, and he stayed on in Morecambe for several weeks on his own after his wife and family moved to Hereford on 12 December. On 3 December Gorton had attended his fourth major Elgar première at the Free Trade Hall in Manchester when Elgar's Symphony in A flat was given by the Hallé Orchestra conducted by Hans Richter, the work's dedicatee.

Alice Elgar was kindness itself to the Gorton family during this settling-in period. They went to tea at Plas Gwyn the day after the move, and the following day Alice called in on them with some flowers. The family often went to tea with the Elgars in the week before the Canon finally arrived. As he had requested, there was no formal farewell: he said his in a letter in the December parish magazine:

> ...I have ever in my mind's eye, my old home, the streets of Morecambe, the sea front and the good fishermen, and then the familiar forms and faces, the Churches in the parish, and my many fellow workers. I have not been, and cannot be unmindful. I have you in my prayers. It is not the parting I had looked for, but life is full of surprises, and I must believe that God knows best. May He give me grace to submit...

The momentous arrival of Elgar's symphony marked the start of a new phase in the composer's career. He had had successes before: but with the first symphony he had really arrived. As Neville Cardus wrote some forty years later:

> Elgar put English music on the map of Europe: we could play a work by him in any programme of symphonic dimensions and pretensions. I cannot hope, at this time of day, to describe the pride taken in Elgar by young English students of that far-away epoch.[186]

186. *Ten Composers*, (Cape, 1945), 126

The symphony was played eighty-two times in its first year. Many of these performances were conducted by Elgar himself, and of course this increasingly kept him away from Hereford.

The Gortons quickly settled into their new home. Carice Elgar became a great friend of the two oldest Gorton girls, Olive and Helen. The Canon was now quite severely crippled and could not walk any distance. Eventually a donkey named Sebastian (after Bach) was bought in order to carry the Canon around Hereford in a chaise, and he became a well-known sight in the city. The money for Sebastian came from the royalties on Gorton's translations of German part-songs.[187]

Elgar suffered from his usual melancholy following the première of a new work, and a bad cold only deepened the gloom. Then Julia Worthington, who had taken a villa near Florence, invited the Elgars to stay with her there. Edward left at the beginning of April to spend some time in London and Paris, while Alice stayed behind to make arrangements to let Plas Gwyn in their absence. Elgar wrote to Gorton from Paris:

> Hotel des Deux Mondes, Paris
> Sunday [18 April]
>
> My dear Canon Gorton
> I hope you are enjoying such weather as we have been blessed with here: Paris is alive &, in a curious way, inspiring: all cities are built on seven somethings. Rome on seven hills[,] Hereford(!) on the cardinal virtues I suppose very much buried & Paris certainly on the seven deadly sins - which make life worth *looking at* if not worth living: this is nonsense & wd. 'go' better in French than in English - or in Ovid's Latin.
>
> I send a rough proof of your chants.[188]
>
> Alice & Carice have arrived & send all messages
>
> We travel to Florence on Tuesday. Send me a reprimand or anything else you think I deserve to
> > c/o
> > Thos.Cook & Sons
> > Florence

187. Information from Priscilla Thouless, in conversation with the writer, 1983.

188. These were the four Anglican chants which Elgar composed for the *New Cathedral Psalter*, published in September 1909.

which is a certain address in much travail & travel

Love to you all
Yrs ever
Edward

The move to Hereford had made no appreciable improvement in the Canon's health. On 10 March Ella Gorton wrote to Neville at Oxford on the occasion of his twenty-first birthday:

...I am afraid that Father will have written sadly about himself. He is very stiff & has many aches I fear & just lately he has been more depressed which is bad of him. I mean he ought to make the effort. The weather has been very much against him & affects him very much though he will not own to it.

The following month Gorton went for further treatment to a nursing home in Bath. In the period following Easter he read from St John's gospel chapter 21 the account of Jesus' post-resurrection appearance to the disciples in Galilee, and was inspired to write a poem which expressed some of his own innermost thoughts.

By the Sea of Tiberius

Through the chill hours of the long night
The fishers toiled, yet toiled in vain;
But with the dawning of the light
A voice said, "Children, cast again".

They cast and gained their faith's reward,
Their doubts like morning shadows flee,
And one cried joyous, "'Tis the Lord!"
And one plunged headlong in the sea.

Weary with toil, drenched with the spray,
They drag their nets towards the shore,
The mists dispelled by dawn of day,
Their Lord is in their midst once more.

And on the solid shore they tread,
And after toil find grateful rest;
They look, and lo! a table spread,
And Christ once more their Host and Guest.

How oft in loneliness we ask
"Where is Thy promised presence, Lord?"
How weary grows the daily task,
How long Thy time, how dark Thy word.

Is there no Form upon the shore?
Is there no royal Voice which saith
"I am alive for evermore,
I hold the keys of hell and death"?

Is there no Watcher of the night?
Are there no gleams of coming day?
When in the dawn of Easter light
The shadows dark shall flee away?

Then may we stand with Thee at last,
Thy voice to hear, Thy face to greet,
To feast with Thee, from labours past,
To cast some treasure at Thy feet.

C.V.Gorton
April 1909

The Canon hardly felt up to attending the Morecambe Festival, but he decided to pay a visit to his old parish: the prospect of the first performance of the part-song dedicated to him must have been the deciding factor. The 1909 Festival was the biggest yet. There were forty-three classes, and the ones for children and local competitors were as popular as ever. Elgar's small part-song *How calmly the evening* was a test in the local mixed voice class on the Thursday.

A more ambitious Festival Concert than usual on the Friday evening included a performance of Mendelssohn's *Scottish Symphony*, given by the Hallé Orchestra under Richter. A Festival Chorus of more than 300 voices was formed from eleven local choirs, and they sang Bach's cantata no 106 *God's own time*; and *Hero and Leander* by C H Lloyd. The choral items were conducted by Henry Coward, but most of the preparation had been done by Smale, the Morecambe chorus-master, and as the *Morecambe Visitor* noted, "Dr Coward found it an easy matter to put on the finishing touches necessary to a smooth and meritorious performance". The report continued:

> The Festival Executive have added another to the admirable educative purposes of the Festival, by their training of village choirs to sing choral works which a small choir on its own would not dream of attempting. The individual members of the choir too are to be commended on their musical enthusiasm, which led them to attend many a rehearsal, for the works sung last Friday meant almost incessant practice; but they have had their reward in the gratifying success which attended their labour of love.

The main interest on the final day obviously centred on the two new Elgar part-songs. "The promenades and streets were thronged with visitors", reported *The Yorkshire Post*; "the performances in the principal competitions, which were of a very high order of merit, aroused keen interest and excited customary enthusiasm". But not among some of the choirs, it seemed. Only five had entered for the Challenge Shield class, and notable absentees were the choirs from Blackpool, Nottingham, and the Isle of Man. Rumours spoke of the insurmountable difficulties presented by *There is sweet music*. Yet even in the male voice class there were only three entries, with Newcastle and the Manchester Orpheus amongst those missing. Also missing, for the first time since 1898, was William McNaught. It was at his own request, as he felt that it was time for new blood in the judges' box. In the preface to the programme book, Gorton had written:

> One leading feature of this year's Festival is the absence from among the judges of Dr McNaught. In the last eighteen Festivals he has acted as judge on no less than twelve occasions. We have not asked him this year to occupy his usual seat in the red baize box, perhaps for the sake of variety, and certainly not because our faith in him as a Judge, "and a good Judge too" is anything but strengthened as the years pass on...

The full orchestra class had only one entry - Nelson, who played the *Karelia* Suite by Sibelius. They won the string class, too, by twenty-one marks from the Cumberland String Orchestra, whose "increased numbers and efficiency" was "a most hopeful feature of the Festival", according to Langford.

The judges for the final sessions were Walford Davies, Coward and Sinclair; and they were joined by Sydney Nicholson, the new organist at Manchester Cathedral. The smaller mixed-voice class was won by the Sheffield Tabernacle Congregational Choir, much to the delight of Henry Coward, who having taken a Sheffield choir to Canada the previous autumn was now contemplating a round the world trip. He invited members of the winning choir to volunteer for an audition.

Barrow Ladies won the female voice class from Lancaster and Morecambe, and here again the number of entries was down, to just four choirs. The men from Habergham were clear winners in the larger male voice class. The *Lancashire Daily Post* confirmed that their victory was "thoroughly deserved...In all respects they were the superior choir". Southport were nine marks behind in second place, on 383, with Lancaster third on 372. Canon Gorton had translated three of the test pieces: Hegar's *Walpurga*; Feodor Berger's *The Hunter, the Rabbit, and the Moon*; and Scharwenka's *When shadows flee away*. (The fourth piece was Coerne's *Sadly the moon*). Gorton had also translated Max Schilling's *New Year Greeting* for the smaller mixed voice class. Langford was once again highly critical of most of these pieces, his chief complaint being the "unvocal style" of the compositions.

With only five choirs contesting the Challenge Shield this year, the vexed question of "singing off" was not relevant. There was time for each choir to sing all four test pieces. The two chosen for the afternoon session were Bach's 'Death, I do not fear thee' from the motet *Jesu, priceless treasure*; and Elgar's *Deep in my soul*. The Lancaster choir under Aldous sang superbly, scoring ninety-seven out of 100 for the Bach, and ninety-nine for the Elgar. They built up a lead of three points over Smale's Morecambe choir in second place. Barrow slipped badly in their performance of the Bach piece, and were a poor fourth at the end of the afternoon.

The evening concert was preceded as usual by impromptu singing from the vast audience. Just before the start, when the Nelson Orchestra was tuning up, someone struck up *Lead, kindly Light*. A solo violin took it up, then another, until finally the whole band was playing. "The effect was electrical", wrote the *Daily Post* reporter, "for immediately the whole gallery joined in the hymn, making a mighty chorus whose voices filled the hall. At that moment the judges entered their box, and the opening verse would have ended the unrehearsed excerpt, but Dr Walford Davies would not have it so. A motion of his hand, and the whole orchestra was at work again. Dr Davies looked up expectantly to the gallery, and as if divining his purpose they gave forth of their best in superb volume. Thunderous applause from the other parts of the hall crowned the effect, and Dr Davies clapped his hands in unaffected delight".

The two tests in the evening were John Munday's five-part madrigal *Lightly she tripped* from 'The Triumphs of Gloriana'; and *There is sweet music*. The critics were quite fascinated by Elgar's new song. "Its production had been eagerly anticipated", wrote the *Post*, "and as it was performed by five successive choirs, the public were given ample opportunity of appreciating its uncommon beauty and delicate structure". Langford was similarly captivated. Describing it as "what may possibly come to be considered the most beautiful of all English part-songs", he continued:

The subtle compliment paid to our Northern singers by the choice of the text was almost surpassed by that implied in the extreme difficulty of the music, which contains the most daring experiments in tonality ever made in an unaccompanied choral work...Unaccompanied voices always test the naturalness of musical progressions and combinations, for voices cannot be made into machines. The poetical object of using the vacillating tonality is in this case easy to see. It is only the most extraordinary of the many means adopted by the composer to express the languorous mood, the 'wavering lights and shadows', and the uncertainty of voices 'thin as voices from the grave', of which the poem speaks. What is new in Elgar's piece is not the connection of keys, but the antiphonal overlapping of them. For this he has found the excuse in the ninths, elevenths, and thirteenths of modern harmony. In practice the ladies' choir managed to begin their A flat chord over the sustained G with ease, but in no choir did the men quite convince the judges that they had introduced their key of G well under a sustained A flat, as must be done in one place. After a few chords the fine blending of the voices put all right, and except for this little flaw each time the piece proved entirely practicable and beautiful. The many alternating chords of A flat and G to the words 'sleep' were done perfectly by all the choirs, and had an exquisite effect. Our own feeling was that in this particular piece the Barrow choir did the best, singing most perfectly in tune and binding and shading the phrases best. The one defect of the music to the words seems the false scansion introduced in the line 'Like tir'd eyelids upon tir'd eyes', especially when it is broken up.

All agreed that Barrow had given the outstanding rendering: Walford Davies said later that he could not recall a finer one at Morecambe. They had sung it, he said, "with surprising excellence and beauty". Lancaster were let down by their men, who occasionally became ragged, and were uncertain in the rhythm. They scored only ninety-one marks, but had done enough in the other three pieces, and with 382 marks they retained the shield by one mark from Morecambe. Thus for the fourth time since the Festival was extended to four days in 1899, Morecambe finished in second place. The *Post* recorded:

That Morecambe, who did so well in the Bach piece, and scored higher marks in the evening than the winners, should still lose the coveted award was thoroughly provoking to the local patriots, but the disappointment was borne with becoming fortitude.

Langford was once again impressed with Smale:

They probably owed their position to the musicianship of the conductor, shown on the spot by his capable management of the tempi, indication of the form, and convincing style in the contrapuntal music...None of the other conductors show the same confidence in dealing with Bach's music.

When the judges appeared on the platform to announce the results, they were accompanied by Canon Gorton, who was "warmly greeted" by the audience. The occasion of the first performance of Elgar's part-song, dedicated to him, was also to be his last appearance at the Festival he had brought into being.

Walford Davies said that he was full of praise for the work done during the week, and said that the Festival had been a greater one than was generally imagined. He had in mind, he said, the production of the Elgar part-song, which carried his mind back to the time when the chord of the dominant seventh was discovered 300 years ago. The influence of this upon harmony was revolutionary, and something of the same kind was happening now in relation to choral music. Things usually associated with the orchestra, and thought impossible vocally, were shown by our inspired men both here and in France to be by no means impossible for the voice, and would, perhaps, carry its influence forward for the next 300 years.

Walford Davies then read out, to great acclaim, a telegram from Florence: "My love to you, and best wishes to all at the Morecambe Festival. Edward Elgar". On 20 May Walford Davies wrote to Elgar:

> ...Gorton has sent me your address. I never thanked you for the welcome friendly telegram. I read it, and they cheered you. Lancaster kept the Shield, but Barrow sang your 'sweet music' gloriously. The double-stopping part in the alto was wonderfully done. But unfortunately they utterly failed to do the splendid Bach bit...and could not have the shield. There was some rebellion, I understand, as to the difficulty & complexity of the Test pieces. I tried to suggest to them that it was a greater Festival than they knew. I hope they may become reconciled to their sweet yoke, and that you will write a great many such works which shall be heard at Morecambe and elsewhere, and together make a chapter in choral history.[189]

On their return to Hereford, the Gortons wrote separately to the Elgars.

189. EBML 7932

[Vaga House, Hereford]
May 12th 1909

Dear Lady Elgar

I am sorry to have been so long in writing but I waited until my husband returned from Bath: for I knew you would want news of him. & then we went off to Morecambe. I am glad & thankful that we managed to get to the Festival for in spite of pain & weakness I know the joy it was to my husband to hear 'his partsong'. How keenly he would have felt afterwards if he had missed it. I cannot speak of the wonder & joy of There is Sweet Music but it is in our hearts & the great audience on Saturday night felt this I am sure. The telegram was received with warmest applause & pride, that Morecambe Festival should be remembered on the very day. I wish you could both have been there. My husband is tired after the journey & excitement & I fear may have written rather sadly about himself. He felt the contrast of other years of course but I thought that he managed wonderfully. I hope tomorrow he will feel more rested. I enclose some lines my husband wrote & sent to me a fortnight ago. We are so glad to hear of your happy time. Olive & Helen send their love to Carice & all of ours to you.

ever, dear Lady Elgar,
Yours affectionately
Ella Gorton

Please remember us both to Mrs. Worthington.[190]

The Canon's letter to Elgar had been started before the Gortons went to Morecambe.

[Vaga House, Hereford]
[n.d., c.12 May 1909]

My dear Sir Edward,

It was good of you to write and to send the chants. I hope we may get them in the cathedral here. I have been at nursing home in Bath where I spent three weeks. I got rid of some acid [-] mental, moral, and physical [-] and can use my right arm better, but oh, the woeful thing it is to feel to be lacking in backbone and to move the least with discomfort, however I saw many patients there worse than myself who continued to smile, so I must try to cultivate one. I find it more cheerful to live among cripples! It is very trying to hear some breezy normal mortal say he has just come in from a 20 mile walk, whereas if they boast that they have crossed the room without crutches, I feel quite bright at being able to struggle for a half a mile.

190. EBML 2494

I send you the Festival book. Olive, Helen and John will be there and if my back will mend a little, I may go for two days. McNaught suggested that I should tone down the preface it might give offence, so like the Firm to want as M[usical] Times to tone down black that it might be mistaken for white.

It is all very well for you to luxuriate in Florence, but the beauties of this Hereford spring and the tender dainties of the trees leave it all far behind!

I stopped here to go to Morecambe, it was a great effort[.] I found the journey very trying, and the revisiting in my altered state my old parish, and the welcome of friends, but I was very anxious to hear the part song. And oh my friend, what a wonderful man you are and with what a stupendous gift; as one of the papers said, it is no light thing for me to see my name on the finest part song ever written. I found several of the conductors in fear about the result, but when Barrow began under Mrs Bourne, the thing unfolded itself in its consummate beauty and the audience were entranced. Nothing else was talked of. Walford Davies said it opened out new possibilities in music and in my happier moments wafts of the sweet sounds come to me as refreshment. The singing was wonderful, not one of the choirs failing to keep perfectly in tune to the last note; at the same time the great difficulty had caused half the choirs to give up before entering and yet when mastered it seems so natural. It would require me to get back my sense and a sheet of paper to tell you half of what I think of your wonderful creation. But dear man with all this do go on and give out while you can.

We had a splendid day's music on Saturday. I managed to crawl on to the platform on Saturday and people were very kind. The bay was very beautiful, I went out sailing every day, but now I have got back again I can but feel I am losing strength, when there is much which makes life precious, walking through weakness becomes so painful & difficult. I know how much you both will feel for me, we have sent you a book & some papers[.] I can write no more

God keep and bless you all
Much love from yours affectionately
C V Gorton[191]

The letter was type-written: the Canon's "wretched fist" had become even more illegible with his developing illness. The papers Gorton sent included Langford's criticism of the scansion in *There is Sweet Music*. Elgar's reply took up this point, and also contained details of his latest composition - another large scale part-song:

191. EBML 9141

Villa Silli, Careggi
May 18 1909

My dear Canon Gorton:

I was so happy at receiving your letter & to know that you had been
to Morecambe: also, in a less way, happy that you liked my partsong
- I wish I could have been present: we must talk over this & other
things when I return, but it is good to know you were able to be
amongst the music & see the good you have done. I am glad the
papers give Morecambe its due credit as pioneer.

We are having glorious weather & feel too lazy to do much sightseeing
- I have been writing some things [-] a big part song to *fine* words by
Cavalcanti - translated by Rossetti - very well done & only one word
which betrays a translation. I give you them on the other side

> "Dishevell'd, and in tears, go, song of mine,
> To break the hardness of the heart of man:
> Say how his life began
> From dust, and in that dust doth sink supine:
> Yet, say, the unerring spirit of grief shall guide
> His soul, being purified,
> To seek its Maker at the heavenly shrine.["]

I think that is fine & have given it a big setting

By the way as to that verse of Tennyson '*Like tir'd eyelids* &c' the
elision is T's own & there is a special note in the son's edition (which
you shd. see if you haven't got it) quoting T. who emphasises the fact
that he so desired the printing and the pronunciation.

Love to you all
Yours ever
Edward Elgar

The musical critics, while recognising that all was not well at
Morecambe, were generally very positive about the 1909 Festival.
Samuel Langford, acknowledging that "the standard of the best
singing was more than kept", commented:

> The saying that nothing succeeds like success is only one side of the
> truth, for success too brings its difficulties, and to every successful
> institution there comes a time when it must suffer for its own good
> influence - when its imitators or its own offshoots begin to act
> powerfully against it. Morecambe Festival is in every practical sense
> the mother of the Northern festivals. Its influence for good has gone
> far and wide, past all reckoning. Its work, so far as it affects the outer
> world, is in a sense complete, for there are now other festivals,

managed with no less energy and zeal by men who have caught the same ideals, in centres where for purposes of further development there may be a more open way. But whether the next move forward comes from Morecambe itself or from one of these places matters little if only the Morecambe ideals inspire it.

The *Competition Festival Record* urged the festival not to allow its standards to slip:

> This premier event did not reach its best record in the matter of entries or audiences. There are special circumstances to account for this. Trade languishes, and this depression rapidly tells upon a place like Morecambe. Then, the institution of so many similar competitive festivals in the district is apparently offering a supply greater than there is demand. But notwithstanding these setbacks, which all who value the need of the festival must hope are but temporary, the executive musical standard of the performances in the chief classes were still of the highest. It is rumoured that some choirs kept back because of the difficulty of the pieces set as tests. This may very well be true: but are Morecambe standards to be whittled down to the capacity of second-rate choirs? It must never be forgotten in this discussion that during the last ten years or so Morecambe tests have not merely revolutionised the choral technique of many of the best equipped choirs in the country, but in turn have reacted upon the ideas of composers. If Mr Aldous's Lancaster choir could gain nearly full marks by a marvellous performance of Elgar's epoch-making part-songs, it is shown that such compositions are possible to good choirs when led by a man of insight and skill... Broadly, in this particular at least, the festival maintained its lead. Much of the musical success of the event was due to the long-sustained and untiring efforts of the music librarian and conductor of the Morecambe Madrigal Society.[192]

The town of Morecambe itself was not unaware of an impending crisis in the affairs of the Festival, and the *Visitor* brought the matter into the open on 12 May in a leading article entitled 'Is the Morecambe Festival declining?':

> There was noticeable in this year's Festival an apparent lack of that local enthusiasm and interest which has characterised the movement in previous years...Is the immense influence that it has wielded among the music lovers of the country waning, or has it achieved its mission

---

192. *Competition Festival Record* June 1909, 10. In the absence of McNaught, the report was almost certainly written by Walford Davies.

as an educational factor, so far as competitive music is concerned? Admitting then, at the outset, that some retrogression has set in, the other questions which arise are 'who is to blame?' and 'where is the remedy?'

The writer went on to berate the town for failing to be enthusiastic about this great event. Other causes for the decline, he said, were the number of festivals, the absence of Elgar, and the difficulty of the test pieces. The paper enlarged upon this last point in its comment column:

> The nineteenth annual Festival which has just concluded will probably not outwardly rank as one of the greatest successes since the inauguration of these big musical competitions which have made Morecambe famous throughout the Kingdom, but although the entries were fewer in the chief competitions, the musical standard was higher than ever, and therefore what was lacking in quantity was made up in quality. There are divided opinions, however, as to whether the character of the music selected for the Festival is likely to make for its continued popularity...

> The crux of the matter appears to lie in the answer to the question: Are those responsible for the selection of the Festival tests, choosing works that are not only difficult for competitors, but above the heads of the masses? Are they, in fact, overdoing the educative side and losing their hold upon the populace of the North who flocked in their thousands to the Festival in the past? The 'man in the street' is not disposed to sit and listen to a piece highly technical in character, and from his point of view possessing very little music...We agree that the primary purpose of the Festival is educational in character, and that it is the desire of the promoters to keep on raising the musical standard, but is there not a danger of raising it to such a height that it ceases to appeal to any but the 'faithful few'? When music gets up 'into the clouds', so to speak, the democracy will turn their attention to something else that is within their ken.

The 1909 Three Choirs Festival was to be held at Hereford, and the Gortons were looking forward to it immensely. On 27 July Elgar called in on the Canon to talk about the Festival. There was to be a good deal of Elgar, most notably the symphony, and *The Apostles*, and the first performance of *Go, Song of Mine*, the part-song he had written in Italy earlier that year.

Carice Elgar was nineteen on 14 August, and on her birthday she went for supper at Vaga House. The Elgars went to Mass at nearby Belmont Abbey on 22 August, and they took the Canon with them. It was now two weeks before the Festival, and Carice was not feeling well. She contracted scarlet fever, and had to be quarantined at Plas Gwyn along with Alice. Elgar took Harley House for his guests, who included Frank Schuster and Julia Worthington. Elgar's setting of the *Te Deum* (written for the 1897 Hereford Festival) was performed at the opening service on Sunday 5 September.

[Vaga House, Hereford]
[n.d., 6 September 1909: typewritten]

My dear Lady Elgar

You may be sure that you are constantly in our thoughts[.] My associations of the festival are so interwoven with your many acts of kindness that I perhaps especially regret the disaster which keeps you a prisoner. Your husband seems in excellent spirits and it seems to do him good. In his great kindness to me he came down to ask whether 'Go song of mine' appealed to me, as if my opinion were worth having, such acts make me feel less the burden that is placed upon me. I heard for the first time the Te Deum and it came with a definite message and was an act of worship. The Ter Sanctus[,] the et Incarnatus, When thou tookest upon Thee to deliver man, the Future judgment, we believe that Thou shalt come again[sic] to be our Judge, and the last phrase of trust were to me especially moving.

We had a memorable afternoon in the garden with a stream of friends till I became quite exhausted. John Coates made me laugh so much that I forgot some of my woes, among other things acting with the help of the baby's barrow an overworked & idle gardener. We had among others the charming Miss Phyllis Lett for supper, I hope she may rise to her great occasion tomorrow [*The Apostles*].

You will do us the great kindness of letting us know if there is anything we can do. Please give my love to the interesting "convalescent" and with sincerest sympathy

I remain yours
C V Gorton[193]

The Gortons saw hardly anything of Elgar that autumn. He was busy conducting in the north for most of October, and was also in London a good deal. He had begun to compose some important new works - a violin concerto, and a second symphony. There were also some solo songs with orchestral accompaniment. Three of them were first given at the Jaeger Memorial Concert at the Queen's Hall on 24

193. EBML 2484

January 1910, sung by Muriel Foster. Elgar was now living in a flat in Queen Anne's Mansions, and in March he and Alice let Plas Gwyn again and took a flat at 58 New Cavendish Street, where the composition continued amidst a whirl of social activity. Elgar was really enjoying his fame and success, so much so that he was even able to write music in town. Only six years before he had told a foreign journalist:

> This London is too noisy for me: one cannot formulate any peaceful thoughts and can work even less.[194]

At the end of March Frank Schuster suggested to Elgar a motor tour of Devon and Cornwall. Elgar immediately accepted. Their itinerary included a visit to Charles and Alice Stuart Wortley, friends of the Elgars, who had a holiday home at Tintagel on the north Cornish coast. Elgar's visit there was inspirational, and 'Tintagel' is one of the places he wrote at the end of the score of the *Second Symphony.*

Arriving back in London on 11 April, he found a letter from Gorton enclosing the programme book for the Morecambe Festival.

> 58 New Cavendish Street, W.
> April 12 1910
>
> My dear Canon Gorton
>
> I am just home from a long & wonderful tour in Cornwall & Devon & found the Scheme of the Morecambe festival with your kind introductory words. I wish I could promise myself the pleasure of being present but I fear I shall be otherwhere.
>
> I hope you have been having *passable* weather: we had east winds most-ly but glorious sun & it seemed difficult to believe we were in England when walking amongst the gorgeous rhododendrons & camellias in full bloom in the open air, to say nothing of the groves of palms
>
> I am sure you know St Cross at Winchester - too lovely for words & Romsey Abbey also.
>
> I have *much* to do here & cannot see myself back in Hereford for a long time
>
> My love to you & all of the family
> Ever yours
> Edward Elgar

194. H Conrat, 'Edward Elgar' in *Neuen Muzik-Zeitung* 24 December 1903 (translated in *Elgar Society Newsletter* May 1976, 21-26)

58 N[ew] C[avendish] St W
May 5 1910

Dear Miss Helen Gorton

Please give my love to your father & thank him for the programme of the Morecambe festival. I wish I could hear some of the singing. I regret very much we are not all there together as in days gone by.

I hope you are having better weather & are able to be out

With kindest regards
Believe me
Yrs v.sincly
Edward Elgar

The 1910 Morecambe Festival broke no new ground, and it was clear from the preface he wrote that Charles Gorton was already looking forward to the following year:

This is our twentieth Festival. Next year we come of age. The steady growth of the movement permits, I hope, some flourish of trumpets. I have before me the syllabus of what we boldly called the 'Second Annual Music Competition'. It included classes for Solo (what we suffered!), for Male Quartette, for Local choir, for Open choir, for Sight reading: these five classes have now extended to 40, and a single fly leaf has grown into a book of 46 pages. Nor do I think that we shall be accused of bombast, when we suggest that the influence of our Festival has been widely felt.

We propose then to celebrate this our coming of age by inviting those interested in the Festival to assist us in choosing the music from the programmes of past years. For this purpose we are issuing a list of music rendered in the competition...

We have Sir Edward Elgar's permission to say that if he is in England next year at the time of the Festival he hopes to be present at our meeting...

In his preface Gorton also referred to the address given by Ivor Atkins at the AMCF annual conference in June 1909. Atkins' talk was entitled 'Combined Music', and in it he was highly critical of certain aspects of competitions. "The plan of making up a whole concert of items given by winners of first prizes is one which cannot be justified on any grounds so far as I can see", he said. Rather, "each singer...should be made to feel that the final rehearsal and combined performance of the work are *the* things to live for..." [195]

195. Association of Musical Competition Festivals, Annual Report (1909), 19-20

Gorton strongly opposed this in the preface.

> I entirely dissent from this statement. It is the natural opinion of one
> accustomed to associate the word Festival with the big chorus, backed
> by an imported orchestra, with certain soloists to brighten the
> firmament. I have yet to learn that the value of any art work depends
> on its size. We do not most of us buy our pictures by the square yard;
> personally I should prefer to be asked to hang in my house one of
> Raphael's silver-point drawings to one of his cartoons. But our critic
> adds: 'That it is not enough to teach people in our country districts
> part-songs and glees, you must bring them into touch with the great
> music of the earth'. Here again size is taken as the test of merit. I
> would on the contrary suggest that when a choir is striving week after
> week to get at the heart of a part-song by Brahms, or Cornelius, or
> Elgar, it is as near the great music of the earth as when digesting
> *disjecta membra* of some well-known oratorio. At least I would say
> that the climax of our Festival must not be sought in the rendering of
> music by combined open choirs, highly as we value such work, for
> this music can obviously be better rendered in large centres of
> population by more thoroughly trained choruses; but the climax must
> be sought in the perfection of rendering some part-song or madrigal
> which is worthy to have its place 'with the great music of the earth'.

This led to some spirited exchanges in the pages of the *Competition
Festival Record*, including a reply from Atkins and a letter from
Herbert Thompson. Langford joined the argument in a leading article
in the *Manchester Guardian* headed 'Musical Festival Policy', in
which he made a telling point:

> Canon Gorton, it is well to remember, has been found in some very
> enthusiastic moments to be at heart on the side of his critics. It is not
> many years since he rejoiced at the prospect of having "The Dream of
> Gerontius" at the Morecambe Festival. And we may venture to think
> that if it had been possible for Canon Gorton to have continued
> unabated his own active support of the festival, that prospect would
> by now have been fulfilled, and neither would Mr Atkins's criticism
> have been offered nor Canon Gorton's defence been ever thought of.[196]

The 1910 Morecambe Festival began on Wednesday 4 May, with the
church choir festival conducted by Sydney Nicholson. This included
the first performance of a Creed Processional for choir and
congregation, *God enthroned in awful night* by Walford Davies, to
words by Gorton. The local competitions took place on the
Thursday, and the male voice class sang Feodor Berger's *Song of the*

---

196. Quoted in *Competition Festival Record* July 1910, 1

Pied Piper and Kaun's *Praise God* in translations by Gorton. At the evening concert the highlight was a performance of Mendelssohn's setting of *Psalm 95* by thirteen local choirs, comprising over 400 singers, conducted by Percy Smale. The accompaniment was provided by the Lancaster Orchestra, who also played Weber's *Oberon* overture. Webster Millar sang lieder, the Morecambe Madrigal Society sang two songs by Hathaway; and Elgar's "marching song" *Follow the Colours* was performed by the 5th King's Own Territorials.

Friday was the children's day, and there was a full attendance for the first time. At the evening concert a new junior cantata, *Jack Horner's Ride* was performed by the combined children's choir conducted by the composer, Joseph Hathaway. He had dedicated the work to Canon Gorton, but the festival's president was too ill to be present. The *Times'* correspondent was favourably impressed by the work, calling it "tuneful and rhythmical and at the same time full of touches of refined musicianship". The review went on:

> The combined choirs formed a huge chorus, which sang from memory and with unfailing spirit, while the children who assumed the principal characters enacted their parts with an intelligence that made one feel what wonderful possibilities a sympathetic and inspiring teacher may discover in a child of fair average intelligence.

The 1910 Festival played its part in creating a little piece of English musical history. One of the judges in the children's section Rev H Dams, asked Sydney Nicholson to listen to a twelve-year-old boy whose musical ability had "completely stumped him". The boy was from Wyke, near Bradford, and was very gifted: two years earlier he had won the ear test with full marks. Nicholson was duly impressed by a great natural talent, and on the strength of this meeting the boy became a chorister at Manchester Cathedral. Twenty years later he succeeded Adrian Boult as conductor of the City of Birmingham Orchestra, becoming one of the great interpreters of Elgar's *Falstaff*. His name was Leslie Heward.

Early on Saturday morning, just after midnight, news reached Morecambe of the death of King Edward VII. The executive met hurriedly to discuss the situation, and worked hard throughout the night to inform all the choirs and orchestras that as the Winter Gardens were licensed premises, there was no option but to close them, and to postpone the final day's proceedings until 18 June. The special train from Cockermouth and Workington was turned back at

Penrith; that from Newcastle at Barnard Castle. But having got so far, the choirs decided to continue and spend the day by the sea. Most of the Yorkshire choirs decided to do the same.

The postponement was a tragic blow. Under normal circumstances the 'open' day was the culmination of the four-day festival and eagerly awaited. Now there was a distinct sense of anticlimax. The new arrangements did not suit all competitors, some of whom were already booked elsewhere on that date. Nicholson was the only judge who was unable to return, so Granville Bantock, Corder and Tertius Noble shared the adjudication between them. Despite all this, the most serious problem was the loss of revenue. "At no time did the audiences approach what we have been accustomed to see on the closing day of this great meeting", noted the *Competition Festival Record*. The *Morecambe Visitor* spoke of "hundreds of empty seats", and the *Lancaster Guardian* commented: "The gathering lacked to some extent the enthusiasm and virility which has marked the open day of previous festivals".

Yet again reports criticised the choice of test pieces:

> The selections in the female voice, the 'alto-lead' male voice, and one piece in the 'tenor-lead' male voice classes left much to be desired; such aimless selections in the past would never have raised this festival to its commanding eminence, and nowadays both choirs and audiences know 'what's what' in the quality of works chosen for performance, and those in authority should find no room for fifth-rate compositions when first and second-rate are not exhausted.[197]

In the absence of Habergham, the main male voice class was dominated by Manchester Orpheus, who with 286 were seven marks ahead of Colne in second place. Lancaster won the female voice class from Penrith; and once again Nelson were clear winners in both orchestral classes. Bantock was evidently impressed with them, and said that many bands of professional musicians played with less certainty and precision. England was much behind other nations in the matter of orchestral music, he said. Every encouragement should be given to the formation of orchestras, but the only way to arouse interest in orchestral playing was to prescribe modern works and not such old-fashioned things as Gade's *Novelletten* and the familiar *Prometheus* overture of Beethoven.

---

197. *Competition Festival Record*, July 1910, 8.

The nine choirs in the Challenge Shield class sang Marson's madrigal *The nymphs and shepherds danced*, and Brahms' *Abendständchen*. From this preliminary round Barrow, Blackpool, Lancaster and Southport went on to the evening's concert, where they were called upon to sing *Love and Youth* by Cornelius, and Elgar's *Go, song of mine*. The *Morecambe Visitor* reported that the audience "were fairly carried beyond themselves" during the singing of the latter. Lancaster had built up a considerable lead of eleven marks in the afternoon, and though they slipped back in the Cornelius they recovered well in the Elgar, scoring ninety-eight marks. They thus won the Shield for the third year running, emulating Blackpool's feat in 1900, 1901 and 1902. Their total of 378 was seven more than Barrow, and seventeen more than Blackpool.

A telegram from Canon Gorton was read out at the evening concert: "May the meeting prove happy and harmonious...and may the judges discover the best". But McNaught and Walford Davies were badly missed, as the *Visitor* remarked:

> The proceedings throughout lacked the general sparkle associated with these Festivals...Neither Professor Bantock or Professor Corder seemed to rivet the attention of the audience in the remarks they made, and only Mr Noble seemed to get on terms with both competitors and listeners.

The critic Gerald Cumberland found an enormous change at Morecambe since his last visit four years earlier.

> There was an electric feeling in the air [in 1906] - a manifestation of the true festival spirit -and I left Morecambe the following morning with the conviction that here music was understood and loved for its own sake; and that, come what might, nothing could destroy the hold that it had upon the imaginations and the emotions of the people. Well, I was mistaken. I returned to Morecambe this year and found everything changed. The orchestral concerts had been abandoned, they did not pay; Sir Edward Elgar had not been to the town for several years; Canon Gorton...had left to live in Hereford; and the attendance had decreased considerably, it being but the ghost of what it had been only four years previously...Morecambe - full of enthusiasm in 1906 - was dull and enervated in 1910. Why?[198]

Meanwhile Elgar had been busy writing his violin concerto. Most of the early part of June he spent at The Hut, Frank Schuster's house

198. *Musical Opinion*, November 1910, 90

by the Thames at Bray. By the end of the month the work was approaching completion. Billy Reed, the leader of the London Symphony Orchestra, had become a close friend of Elgar, and the composer had invited him to Plas Gwyn to try through parts of the work. Gorton was also invited.

> Plas Gwyn, Hereford
> June 30 [1910]
>
> My dear Canon Gorton
>
> Mr.Reed will be here today to play through some of the Violin Concerto: if you would come up to tea - say about 3.0 I would ask him to play the Andante to you. It would give us the greatest pleasure to see you - I shd. like you to hear some of the new music.
>
> Yrs vy sincerely
> Edward Elgar
>
> 3.0 is too early for tea I know but Mr Reed goes to London tomorrow evening & he may have to catch the 4.20

Reed was not the only one "going to London". On 14 July Elgar told his visitors, Sinclair and Percy Hull, that he and Alice intended to give up Plas Gwyn and to leave Hereford to live in the capital.

CHAPTER 14

VAGA HOUSE

On Tuesday 26 July Billy Reed was once again at Plas Gwyn, this time to play through the whole of the *Violin Concerto*. Alice Stuart-Wortley was staying there at the time, and the Gortons also came to hear the work. It was a thrilling occasion, and everyone was full of anticipation of the magnificent première at a Philharmonic Society concert in November. The work was dedicated to the world-famous virtuoso, Fritz Kreisler, who was to give the first performance. He was reported as being delighted with the concerto.

Canon Gorton was by now badly paralysed, and life for the whole household was not easy. Neville Gorton recorded in his journal some of his father's expressions from about this time: "I have singularly little brain power and suffer from acute mental depression...Every day at noon till six a depression settles down on me that is hard to shake off".

Alice Elgar continued to be a close friend, inviting the Gortons to tea, and taking them flowers and other gifts. Miss Alice Underwood, known as 'The Duchess', and her friend Miss Lily Thomas were also great friends of the family, often accompanying them to tea at Plas Gwyn. The Elgar family referred to these ladies as 'the 44s', after the number of their house in Bridge Street. During the period of the Gloucester Three Choirs Festival in September 1910 Mrs Gandy and Julia Worthington called at Vaga House to see the Canon.

The successful première of Elgar's *Violin Concerto* took place on 10 November in the Queen's Hall. Canon Gorton wrote to his friend:

[Vaga House, Hereford]
[n.d., 9 November 1910]

My dear Sir Edward -

My thoughts are full of you and the concerto, and I know that amid all the plaudits which will greet you tomorrow - you will not be wholly unmindful of one whose small bucket you have so often filled - 'It is not so much what men suffer as what they miss' said Ruskin - of this

I know alas more day by day. Still I need to be thankful that it was given to me to hear among the first - The Apostles - the Kingdom [-] in the South, and the Symphony.

I fear that you will find these days very exhausting, but then no man can give of *himself* without some sacrifice

I am trying to relearn how to write: it is a slow & humiliating process -

May all blessing be yours tomorrow and may others give out your message to men. You will not have forgotten the word [:"]And the Lord took me as I followed the flock and said unto me 'go prophesy unto my people'[*Amos* 7:15"]

Much love to you all
Ever yours sincerely
C.V.Gorton

Many thanks for the splendid picture[199]

Two days later he sent a telegram: "Heartiest congratulations on great triumph. Canon Gorton"[200].

If the concerto confirmed Elgar as the indisputable head of musical art in England, the Morecambe Festival by contrast was conscious that its pre-eminence was a thing of the past. Those entrusted with the organisation of the 'Coming-of-age' festival hoped that such a celebration would re-kindle enthusiasm. Percy Smale, the conductor of the Morecambe Madrigal Society and now secretary of the festival, called a meeting of conductors for 1 October 1910 to discuss the arrangements. There was a large attendance of nearly seventy (including McNaught), and the Mayor of Morecambe presided. In his opening remarks, Smale said that the history of the festival could be summed up in the words "Success makes success". Yet they had had several drawbacks, chiefly the death of Howson, and Gorton's early retirement. He also mentioned the two-year absence of McNaught, which the doctor himself had initiated, saying that it might be in the festival's interest if they gave him a rest. Smale then came to the subject of the last festival, which he described as "a calamity". They had sustained a serious financial loss of £325, and they did not know how it could be met, but felt that the executive in going ahead with the next festival "should be credited with great pluck". There was to be no real change in the way the event was run, except for the inclusion of a second major concert on the Thursday evening.

199. EBML 3590
200. EBML 3588

McNaught, in his speech, paid eloquent tribute to Mary Wakefield, who had died a fortnight earlier. He too gave credit to Howson, whose "fine taste was only equalled by his modesty". To him they owed the high standard of the test pieces adopted at the festival, McNaught said. He went on to discuss the main problems - 'singing off', and the choice of music for tests. They must have fine music, splendid music, and of the highest order. "We must not choose music because it is difficult", said McNaught. "We have to take care whether we shall govern the movement, or whether it shall govern us. We have ideals of the movement, and it is for us to see to it that we keep it pure".

The meeting was felt to have been very worthwhile. "There was an atmosphere of expectancy that could not be overlooked, and the perfectly harmonious spirit that prevailed was significant", commented the *Visitor*. As a step towards paying off the deficit and raising funds for the 1911 Festival, a Grand Concert was held in the Winter Gardens on 2 November. Webster Millar sang lieder, and the Morecambe and Lancaster choirs took part.

Elgar visited Canon Gorton at Vaga House on 23 December and told him of the success of the concerto, and of how the new symphony was taking shape. The composer promised to do his best to attend the next festival if at all possible, but he had undertaken to conduct several concerts in North America during the spring with the Sheffield Choir, which Henry Coward was taking on a six-month world tour. Then there was the work which had to be done on the second symphony. Elgar left the Canon optimistic, but unsure.

Gorton realised that his connection with the Morecambe Festival must now come to an end. It was an agonising decision, but he was no longer in any condition to play an active part in the running of the festival, and being merely a figurehead meant nothing to him. He therefore took the opportunity of the 'Coming-of-age' festival to resign and to hand over to the vice-president, John Hatch, who in the preface wrote the following tribute to his predecessor:

> Of all the features of this year's gathering, at once the most outstanding and the saddest, is the resignation of the Rev C V Gorton. He, since the inception of the Festival, has stood at the prow and guided us through many anxious moments to safe waters, and only consideration for his health could deter us from seeking to dissuade him from his purpose. His devotion to the work and living interest in all affecting it are shewn in the characteristically graceful retrospect to be found on another page. None, we are assured, will spare effort to safeguard and maintain that fruitful heritage to which he has led us.

Canon Gorton's 'retrospect' traced the history of the festival, and concluded:

> We stand now on Pisgah heights[201], some of us looking backward, some looking forward. As we look back on the past and trace the path we remember chiefly the difficulties we have overcome, the friendships made in pleasant places. It is now for others to go forward seeking 'fresh woods and pastures new'.

Sadly he was unable to attend the festival, and during the latter half of May 1911 stayed with the Walker family, some friends from Ben Rhydding in Yorkshire. In their visitors' book he wrote: "Then said he to the host: take care of him and when I come again I will repay thee. S Luke X. C V Gorton. hors de combat"

Elgar arrived back from North America on 9 May, a week before the Morecambe Festival. The first performance of the new symphony was fixed for 24 May. However, several rehearsals had been arranged to take place during the week of the festival. Morecambe was extremely disappointed that Elgar could not attend, especially as Walford Davies would be absent too. The latter's health had not been good, and he was heavily involved in the preparations for the Coronation of George V at the end of June.

Over 5000 competitors took part in the 'Coming-of-age' Festival, which began on 16 May. The judges were McNaught, Nicholson, Noble, Hathaway, Fogg; and Harry Evans, conductor of the Liverpool Welsh Choral Union. The test pieces had been selected by the participating choirs and orchestras, who were able to choose from what had been given at the festival in previous years. There was a good deal of Elgar. On the Thursday the G F S choirs sang *Fly, Singing Bird*; and *As torrents in summer* was given in the smaller of the local mixed-voice class. On the Friday, the local female voice choirs sang *The Snow*.

The first of the Festival concerts on Thursday evening saw a performance of Haydn's *The Creation* given by eight local choirs and the Lancaster Orchestra under J W Aldous. The second concert was conducted by Harry Evans, and was a mixture of solo recitals and choral works. Twelve local choirs, accompanied by the Nelson Orchestra gave Walford Davies's cantata *Hervé Riel*, and Elgar's choral suite *From the Bavarian Highlands*.

201. See Deuteronomy 34: 1-4

The final Saturday was more like old times at Morecambe. Forty-nine choirs and four orchestras were contesting the seven major open classes. Barrow Ladies with 378 marks were clear winners over choirs from Carlisle and Penrith in the female voice class. Elgar's *Serenade* (Op.20) was the test for string orchestra (at it had been ten years before), and for the fifth time in six years Nelson were the winners. They also won the full orchestra class for the sixth year running. Some indication of the progress made in choral singing was shown in the choice of Elgar's *O happy eyes* and Brahms's *The Maiden* for the smaller mixed voice choirs (maximum thirty-six voices): in 1902 they had been used in the Challenge Shield class.

There were five test pieces in the larger male voice choir class: *Feasting I watch* and *It's oh to be a wild wind* by Elgar; Hegar's *The Phantom Host*; MacDowell's *From the sea*; and Scharwenka's *Happy light*. Manchester and Southport being absent, the outcome was predictable, as *The Times* reported:

> In the male-voiced class...one choir coming from Habergham, conducted by Mr E Hitchon, went far beyond the others in perception of the meaning of the music and their power of drawing out that meaning and impressing it upon their hearers. Mr Evans was justified in speaking of them as great artists - a phrase too often grievously abused - because they had the artist's method...The men of Habergham were content with what they could draw out of [the music]. Consequently they were nowhere more wholly satisfying than in Elgar's tiny part-song, *It's oh to be a wild wind*, for it will not bear the addition of a thought which the composer has not put there. There is nothing to be made of it; it must make the performance.

> The inclusion of this exquisite miniature in the programme of one of the biggest classes of competition seemed to point out what is the future hope for festivals such as these...The time for sensations of astonishment seems to be past. Pieces of mere vivid picture-making, such as Hegar's *Phantom Host*, already begin to sound stale. Choirs cannot go on curdling their blood and that of their audience to stone, as Canon Gorton's translation puts it; the attractions of the process begin to pall...Now is the time, when the possibilities of brilliant choral technique have been probed to the uttermost, to go forward with the real business of artistic interpretation. It will soon become quite impossible for any choir to make an impression by means of mere technical equipment; it is almost so now. But the possibilities of artistic interpretation are boundless, and the genuineness of the movement will be tested by the desire of the choirs to devote themselves more and more to it. Both the mixed and the male-voiced choirs who won on Saturday did so because they entered into the

music in the spirit of artists. Some of the others did so too, but less fully. As this becomes recognised as the only possible means of distinction, the wretched 'pot-hunting' spirit of which we sometimes hear must be killed.

Habergham won with 478 marks, twenty-four more than Todmorden in second place.

And so to the Challenge Shield. Nine choirs began in the afternoon by singing *O lovely May* (Brahms) and *O death, thou art the tranquil night* (Cornelius) from 1902 and 1905 respectively. To everyone's great surprise the winners for the previous three years, Lancaster, were eliminated, as were the 1904 winners, Nottingham. In the evening the four finalists sang Elgar's *Evening Scene* and Morley's *Fire, fire, my heart*. In a close contest Barrow with 356 won by two marks from a revitalised Blackpool. Sale were third on 348 and Morecambe fourth.

The *Times'* critic did not altogether approve of using test pieces again:

> ...Since all the music had been done before, and done by certain choirs almost perfectly, it followed that one did not come to this meeting with the expectation of being thrilled with new sensations of wonder at hearing choirs from unknown places, conducted by men of no great musical reputation, achieve feats of consummate virtuosity. Every one knew that the music had been sung in the past by such choirs under such conductors, and that men who have spent their lives in music have been astonished into silent admiration by the result, so that the question was rather whether the level would be maintained.

Many commentators were now becoming aware of the true significance of the contribution made by the competition movement to the musical development of the country. In the *Contemporary Review* for March 1911, in an article entitled 'The Prospects of Choral Music', Gerald Cumberland wrote:

> Now that the orchestra has already reached the climax of its power and has become practically a social and economic impossibility, the creative energy of many European composers is being directed into channels where it may most quickly reach large masses of the people - that is to say, it is exploring the possibilities of the human voice and creating music which, intended as it is for mixed voice choirs, is largely experimental in its attempt to arrive at hitherto undreamt-of effects in tone colour, dramatic description and lyrical expressiveness. This sudden growth of interest in choral music on the

part of composers of genius is due in a large measure to the inception of the competitive festival movement, instituted as a result of the enthusiasm of Mary Wakefield in 1885...

The test pieces chosen...were at the outset taken from those already available in print...But the difficulties presented by the music of the past were so readily overcome...that search was made for more exacting material, and here and there it was found. Cornelius, for example, was discovered to have written no small amount of choral composition that had never been published, and on examination it was discovered that some of his work was so modern in spirit...and presented both technical and æsthetic difficulties not contained in other available music, that steps were taken by the Morecambe Festival Committee to have various part-songs by Cornelius published in England and Germany. In the meantime a few composers of distinction had acted as adjudicators at some of the festivals, and had been brought into the closest possible touch with the festival movement. The immediate result of this contact of the creative and interpretative elements in modern music was a crop of fresh choral work, both original in idiom and new in its whole method of expression. For the first time in the history of music it came to be recognised that the chorus might be treated as an orchestra - that is to say, the independence of the various 'voices' in an eight-part chorus, for instance, might be pushed to the extreme which is found in the different instruments composing the modern orchestra. It was seen that 'perpendicular' writing inevitably makes for monotony of expression; that to treat the chorus as static rather than fluid is to abandon complex effects that make for dramatic exactitude and reality; and that to confine the melody for long periods to one 'voice' is to create a feeling of mechanical artificiality. These discoveries, and many others, were incorporated in a large amount of new work which British composers quickly wrote, and Sir Edward Elgar, Professor Granville Bantock, Mr Rutland Boughton, Mr Frederick Delius and Mr Havergal Brian all proved within the space of a few years that they had received a strong and lasting impetus in the creation of this form of art...Those who...have had the opportunity of attending many competitive festivals, and have followed closely the action and reaction of composers upon singers, have been able to gauge the depth and scope of the inspiration that is the source of this new movement, and they have seen it spread to the Continent and manifest itself in the work of such representative composers as Claude Debussy in France, Richard Strauss in Germany, and Jan Sibelius in Finland...That, then, is the new movement, and the more closely we regard it the more astonishing does it appear that it should have had its origin in England, the most artistically backward, because the most isolated, of all European countries. Its inception, as I have shown, was largely due to the enthusiasm and organising genius of Mary Wakefield; but for very many years before this lady became actively interested in choral singing England (and particularly Northern England) had been famous for its wonderful choirs, and unless abundant material had been lying ready for use the new movement would have died soon after its birth. If, too, there had not been, for the first time for two centuries, a small band of British composers of genius living in the closest possible communion with the life of their own time, choral singing could not have made its unexpected leaps and bounds to the goal of perfection, nor could the flame of enthusiasm have been kept burning so purely and so steadily.

Well might William McNaught say in a speech that same year: "I question whether the country would be in its present position musically but for the Morecambe Festival, which has led the way to others". And in 1925 the Blackpool Festival programme confirmed Morecambe's seminal role:

> The introduction of these choral songs [of Brahms] at the festivals of Morecambe twenty-five years ago may be regarded as the starting point of the choral renaissance which has been witnessed, first in the north and then spreading gradually throughout the land.

In February 1911 Elgar accepted the conductorship of the London Symphony Orchestra, on the announcement of Richter's retirement. This meant that a permanent move to London was now essential, and by July Alice had found an imposing house (which they renamed 'Severn House') in a fashionable part of Hampstead. In June Elgar had been awarded the Order of Merit in the coronation honours list. Gorton's telegram of 20 June read:

> Honour to whom honour is due. Heartfelt congratulations. Gorton[202].

Elgar's reply made mention of the impending move, and of various "troubles" - the lukewarm reception accorded to his new symphony, financial problems, and continuing difficulties with his publishers, Novello.

> 75, Gloucester Place, Portman Square, W.
> July 16.1911
>
> My dear Canon Gorton:
>
> I was deeply touched by your letter & love to have your congratulations: I wish you gave a better account of yourself & early in next week I hope to see you & find you better than your letter allows me to think & hope you are at the present moment.

---

202. EBML 4963. He followed this with a letter (which is missing).

It has been a very, very busy & eventful time since I landed from America & I have had really no time for anything except 'official' (more or less) work: now the 'tumult & the shouting'[203] dies & the net gain is little. I have my Star (which you shall see) & that is something, but troubles manifold dog me & it is *by no means* in sunshine that I walk - quite the reverse, alas!

We have fixed on a house, but this & other news I will tell you when I come down.

I ape royal state, under my wife's kindly direction, so far that my family precedes me by a day or two in order to prepare the dwelling!

My love to you.
Ever your friend
Edward Elgar

Elgar was unsettled. It was 26 July before he arrived back in Hereford and within a fortnight he had fled to Schuster's house at Maidenhead, even missing his daughter's twenty-first birthday on 14 August. Not until 25 September did he manage to call on the Canon at Vaga House. Thirteen-year-old Priscilla remembered the visit well: "Elgar came to see [my father] dressed in blue [his court dress] & Order of Merit to give him pleasure"[204]. It was the last time the two men met. Early in October Elgar left Hereford for good and moved to London, followed later by Alice. Their move into Severn House was delayed until 1 January 1912, and almost immediately afterwards Elgar began work on *The Crown of India*, a masque written to celebrate the Indian Durbar held for George V in December 1911. But the composer was far from well, and still had many conducting engagements to fulfil. The first performance of the masque took place at the London Coliseum on 11 March, and Elgar agreed to conduct it twice every day for the first fortnight. When this commitment was completed, he managed to find time to write to Gorton.

[Severn House, Hampstead]
25 March [1912]

Dear Canon Gorton,

I have no news only a record of rather a strenuous life for the last six months - trying to keep engagements (& succeeding in doing so save once) - between rather severe attacks of gout. I go in for a cure now soon - so enough of myself

203. Amos 2: 2.
204. Letter to the writer, 1983.

We have heard tolerably regularly of you from one friend or another & I hope the feeling of spring is about you & cheering you - I long for a sight of my own country &, if only trains were running in decent order, should come down for a day or two - but in this chaos it is too much of an undertaking.

Send me a line sometime
& with my love to you believe me to be
Yours v sincerely
Edward Elgar[205]

Despite the artistic success of the 'Coming-of-Age' festival in 1911, the Morecambe executive decided against holding a festival in 1912, but agreed to put on a bazaar instead, in order to establish a firmer financial base for the future. The *Manchester Guardian* summed up the views of many when it commented:

This year for the first time the annual sequence of the Festivals has been broken, and it is hard to believe that had Canon Gorton retained his health and energies this lapse would have taken place.

However, two significant events in the history of the competition movement took place in May that year. The first was the Midland Competition Festival, organised by Granville Bantock and held in Birmingham on 14-18 May. Bantock had deliberately avoided using the name of the city in the title in order to prevent confusion with the triennial Festival in the autumn (which that year saw the première of Elgar's cantata *The Music Makers*). The new competition was an enormous event - the largest in England up to that time, comprising ninety-five classes. There were 6500 competitors, including ten orchestras and 150 choirs. The *Competition Festival Record*, in reporting the success of this festival, acknowledged the debt owed to its models:

The first inquiry was into the plans and management of the most successful existing Festival of the kind held in the country, namely, Blackpool, which in its turn had modelled its scheme on that of Morecambe[206].

Then two weeks later, on 26-28 May, an International Musical Festival was held in Paris. The 'Comité d'Honneur' contained many famous names including Elgar, Debussy, Puccini, Fauré and Saint-

205. Young (1956), 205
206. June 1912, 1

Saëns. Nearly 25,000 competitors took part, and some forty choirs came from England, of which about half were school choirs sponsored by the London County Council. English members of the jury included McNaught, Coward, Herman Klein and Arthur Fagge. Each choir had to sing two pieces: one set by the organisers, and a second of their own choice. Elgar was well represented in this latter category, the pieces being *The Snow* and *Fly, singing bird* for female choirs; *My love dwelt in a northern land, Weary wind of the west* and *Go, song of mine* for mixed choirs; and *After many a dusty mile, Yea, cast me from heights of the mountain,* and *The Reveille* for male voice choirs. The English choirs between them won about £2000 in prize money, but had spent between four and five times that figure in attending. Sadly the festival was marred by poor organisation, chiefly an insufficient number of stewards, and bad accommodation for some of the choirs. The Habergham Glee Union won their class (having sung *The Reveille* as their choice), and the *Burnley Gazette* reported:

> The choir returned to Burnley...and had a great reception. Soon after their arrival several members expressed dissatisfaction at the lack of organisation of the contest, one member remarking that Paris, before she attempted anything of the sort again, should send a committee to see how the Morecambe Festival is worked. In other words, Paris had bit [sic] off more than she could chew.

On 20 April 1912 *The Times* carried an article entitled 'Competitive Festivals: Dangers and Suggestions'. Admitting that the movement was now "permanently established", the writer continued:

> It should be well worth our while to examine some of the more obvious merits and faults of such festivals as they now exist; since in a few years' time the institution will be a stereotyped tradition, and...sacrosanct from the unholy criticism of those who would reform or rebuild.

The unhealthy aspects of competition had been eradicated. "The only question of interest to competitors used to be 'Have we won?' In the majority of cases this is now superseded by the question, 'Are we better than we were last year?'...Even in the choral contests...petty local pride is crumbling before the knowledge that the value lies, not in the prize, but in the work".

Another favourable element was the development of public taste in music. "There can be very few places...which have not already developed a body of sound judgment, capable of appreciating merit and detecting charlatanry".

However, the article ended on a cautionary note. "The greatest friends of the Festival movement, those who, though not pulling the strings, think they see therein a real chance for the regeneration of English musical taste, have serious fears for it". There were five of these "fears": the need to encourage instrumental, and not just vocal, music: the selection of music of worth as test pieces: the avoidance of music publishers' interests: the importance of allowing the judges to address the conductors: and the need to end each festival with the combined performance of a work.

Elgar was now preparing for publication a setting of Psalm 48 (*Great is the Lord*) which he had composed two years earlier.

> Severn House, 42 Netherhall Gardens, Hampstead, N.W.
> Sunday [June 1912]
>
> My dear Canon Gorton:
>
> I venture to send you a very rough proof - which is not worth returning - of the new Anthem. I believe it is to be done first at Westminster Abbey which I shall like very much in view of the dedication[207]. I hope you are having nice flowers & summer things to look at - the rain spoils everything at present but the benefit will be apparent later. I am working very hard at all sorts of things. I have not another copy of the anthem or I wd. send it to Dr.Sinclair - perhaps he or Mr.Hull wd. be able to give you some idea of the anthem in the Cathedral?
>
> My love to you
> Yours ever
> Edward Elgar
>
> That dear good fellow Walford Davies has revised the organ part very lovingly & tenderly for me:

On 3 June Elgar had been to the Temple Church where Walford Davies played over his revision of the accompaniment. The rest of the summer was taken up by the completion and then the orchestration of *The Music Makers*, which Elgar had had in his mind for over eight years, and which Gorton had hoped to première at Morecambe.

Canon Gorton was continuing to deteriorate in health. He was in constant pain, and the simplest movement was slow and difficult. A nurse was now employed to be with him at all times. On 5 June

---

207. To 'The Very Rev J Armitage Robinson, DD, Dean of Wells'. Robinson was Dean of Westminster when he first met Elgar in Italy in 1903-4.

Neville wrote to his mother from Oxford: "I was sorry to get back & find your sad little letter & father's note. I am afraid he must be very poorly. I know how much it means to you". Neville was about to leave Oxford and hoped to spend the summer in Germany before joining the Community of the Resurrection at Mirfield in September. In the end, though, he stayed at Hereford and was able to record in his diary a remark of his father's which showed the Canon's courage and resilience: "Of late when so very poorly I have been enabled to feel that sickness is not the most favourable time to seek for repentance, but I was at times enabled to look unto Him Who alone can help in sickness or in health with desire that if I lived I might be enabled to serve Him, & my mind was mercifully preserved in a good degree of peace". His son later commented: "His humanity became more wide and more tender as his spiritual faculties grew in depth and power. This upward wresting came not without its cost right to the last. He was often greatly depressed at the seeming ineffectiveness of his work. Now and then he felt as if he had lost all power of helping others. He would then turn resolutely to some other line of service or plunge into some hard reading. He would not allow slackness to prevail against him."

The summer of 1912 was unusually cold and very wet. On 20 August Elgar wrote to a friend: "I cannot live much longer in this weather". That same day the River Wye was in flood at Hereford, running six feet higher than normal past the garden at Vaga House. Even so the garden (from where a flight of stone steps led down to the river) was still fourteen feet above the water. Around midday, Charles Gorton was in a deck chair at the top of the steps, which was where he usually sat. His nurse, Sarah Pugh, was with him, and Neville was reading to him. Nurse Pugh went into the house, and shortly after the Canon complained of severe pain at the back of his head. He asked Neville to fetch a hot water bottle to bring him relief. Neville, glad to oblige, also went into the house; and what happened next is not clear. When the nurse looked out of the bedroom window she could see no one in the garden. With growing alarm, she rushed out to find that Canon Gorton was in the river, being swept downstream. She called out for help, and soon Neville was bravely diving in after his father. But before he was able to reach the Canon, the body had disappeared. Despite the dangerous state of the river, Neville swam on for some distance, but could see no further trace. The police were informed and the river dragged and searched carefully, but to no avail.

The shock and distress of the residents of Vaga House can be well imagined. Ella Gorton was distraught; her son recorded her reactions in his notebook. "My darling - gone. And I loved him - oh I loved him - he knows I loved him. He wanted me - oh, he wanted me". Emotions were mixed. Neville Gorton experienced feelings of guilt as he reflected on "the suffering of my father on the last day and moments":

> God has shewn me I must not look to Him alone & mystical union, but also to others for their own sake - not merely for God's sake, as souls to be saved. This has been my sin against my father. I never or seldom went out to him in sympathy with his sufferings, with his weakness, as Christ did & does.

A rumour quickly spread that the Canon had used the nurse's absence to dismiss Neville on a pretext, so that he could be alone and free to do away with himself. This the family firmly and consistently denied. As Priscilla Gorton said, more than seventy years later:

> It would have been completely against his character - a denial of his principles and all he ever stood for[208].

Eleven days later, on the morning of Sunday 1 September, a fisherman at the village of Hampton Bishop (more than three miles downstream from Vaga House) discovered a body lying on a bank of shingle. The corpse was taken to the nearest inn, and soon identified as that of Canon Gorton. An inquest was held the following day at the inn. Dr Du Buisson gave evidence of identification, and said that there was every appearance of death having been caused by drowning. The most important witness was nurse Pugh, and she was closely questioned by both the coroner and the foreman of the jury. She said that the Canon could often get out of his deck chair without assistance, and being very fond of the river he would sometimes stand and watch it.

> "He could see it better standing, I suppose?" asked the coroner.
> "Yes", she replied. Nurse Pugh proceeded to describe what Canon Gorton was wearing at the time; and then the foreman of the jury asked:
> "What was his disposition generally - cheerful or despondent?"
> "He varied, sometimes one and sometimes the other".
> "Had he ever said anything about destroying himself?"

208. In conversation with the writer, 1983.

"No, not that I am aware of".

"What fence is there there?"

"One about two feet high".

"Was there a gate to the steps?"

"Yes".

"Was it opened or closed?"

"It was open".

"Had it been opened previously?"

"Yes, it was nearly always open".

"Could he have overbalanced and fallen into the river?"

"Yes, quite easily".

"When you saw him in the river did he struggle or cry out?"

"No, I think he was dead when I saw him".

After further evidence from the fisherman and the police, the coroner said he thought that the jury would be satisfied with the evidence of identity, and that the Canon came by his death by drowning. There was no evidence whatever as to how he came to be drowned, he said, and if they sat there longer they would probably have no better evidence that what they had had before them. A verdict of "found drowned" was duly returned.

The funeral took place on the Monday evening immediately after the inquest. The body was taken from Hampton Bishop direct to Breinton, a village three miles upstream from Hereford, where the churchyard stands high above the river Wye. The Canon had been particularly fond of the spot, and was often driven there.

After the interment, which was conducted by the Dean of Hereford assisted by two clergymen from the Morecambe area, there was a memorial service in Hereford Cathedral, during which Percy Hull played some of Gorton's favourite passages from *The Apostles*.

There were many tributes. The obituary in *The Times* referred to Gorton's friendship with Elgar, and their first meeting which led to the composition of *Weary wind of the west*. The *Manchester Guardian* emphasised the Canon's contribution to the musical life of the nation:

> It is a very few years since Sir Edward Elgar, while wintering in Rome, wrote for the Festival...the finest set of part-songs that has ever been written by an English composer. It is not at all likely that their scope and difficulty would have been ventured on if the composer's imagination had not been fired by the singing which he had heard at the Morecambe Festival. Looking back it can be seen that the

improved standard of part-singing is largely due to the influence of
Brahms' unaccompanied choral works on their introduction at the
Northern Festivals. The serene beauty of these works created the
greatest enthusiasm and admiration among the singers and a delight
in choral singing such as had never before been felt. Canon Gorton
helped forward this movement by making many painstaking
translations...in all of which he displayed, for an amateur in music,
an unusual perception of the composers' aims. He had a severe taste,
with the moral courage to adhere to it, and it is the reward of that faith
and determination that there are no more staunch adherents to what
is noble in music to be found in England today than the singers of our
North-country choirs.

One of Gorton's former curates, John Drury (himself now a canon)
paid a moving tribute in a sermon preached at his church in
Cheshire. Canon Gorton, he said, was the best man he ever knew.
Describing him as "the ideal priest", Drury said:

> I was his curate for two years, and for twenty-two years it has been my
> privilege to count him my adviser and friend...To the end of my life I
> shall thank God that I went to Morecambe, and was brought into
> contact with such a fine personality, such an inspiring spiritual force.
> To know Canon Gorton was to love him - to reverence him...He
> appealed to us from many standpoints: some delighted to hear his
> sermons, for they were always earnest, thoughtful and original: others
> were attracted by that robust manhood that would tolerate nothing
> mean, coarse or ungenerous: others revelled in his piquant epigrams
> when he belaboured snobbery and 'priggism' whether it was found in
> the county magnate or the local tradesman.

The Canon's death was particularly distressing for his daughter
Helen, who was due to be married to Arthur Walker of Ben Rhydding
on 18 September. The wedding was postponed for four weeks.

On the Saturday after the funeral the Elgars arrived in Hereford for
the Three Choirs Festival. Alice visited Vaga House and found Mrs
Gorton "very calm and wonderful". But the circumstances of the
Canon's death meant that Ella Gorton was now keen to quit not just
the house but the area as soon as could be conveniently arranged.
She decided to return to her home town of Bowdon, and Vaga House
was put on the market immediately.

The Blackpool Festival that year took place on 8 - 12 October. The
programme book contained this generous tribute:

The almost tragic death of Canon Gorton came as a shock to all those who remember the well-known presence at the Morecambe Festival, of which he was almost the life and soul. Up to the last he was deeply interested in all that affected the movement. It was only in the spring of this year that he undertook the translation of one of Brahms' part-songs "Nightwatch (No 2)" for this Festival...the words of which seem to sound like a paean to the memory of a man who while he lived gave of his best.

The Blackpool Festival was immensely popular. In the mezzo-soprano class there were no less than sixty-six entries to sing the test piece - the 'Angel's Song'("My work is done") from Elgar's *The Dream of Gerontius*. The *Competition Festival Record* remarked:

Again we have to record the marvellous success of this great event. As we have on previous occasions remarked, the working of the competition festival movement in all its phases can be studied with better advantage here than anywhere else in the country.[209]

Vaga House was vacated on 6 November. That day Neville wrote to his mother:

You will feel nearer Father at Altrincham & be able to think of him as we believe he now is - a weapon being used by God after a hard fashioning of so many years & such pain. I always think of that part of the Dream of Gerontius as the ideal statement of the possibilities of the future life when God shews Himself in a way to the soul directly & awakens the faculty by which we can fully grasp His love & the personal relationship with Him.

In her reply Ella Gorton wrote:

I went out to Breinton yesterday. It was such a lovely morning. I thought it best to go & not to wait...I taxied out & walked back. It all looked so lovely. I felt full of thankfulness for dear Father. I took some flowers & also made an evergreen cross...which will last some time fresh there.

After the Gortons' departure from Hereford it was left to Percy Hull to arrange for a permanent headstone to be installed on Canon Gorton's grave. Mrs Gorton had remembered that on Robert Howson's gravestone was engraved the opening phrase from Cornelius's *O Death, thou art the tranquil night*, with both words and music. She suggested that something from *The Apostles* might be appropriate for the Canon. Hull suggested the 'Fellowship' theme, and wrote to Elgar about the idea. On 14 May 1913 Elgar replied:

209. *Competition Festival Record*, November 1912, 1

I feel very much honoured that there should be a wish to engrave on my friend's memorial some notes of mine, if it is decided to do so, I cannot think of anything more appropriate than your choice: I was not aware that anything of the kind had been done in Mr Howson's case - I *may* have known - but I do not remember anything of it - so your reference to that does not help me to judge.

I do not think it wd. be possible to add the 'title' of the motive & I do not feel that my name should be added either: would it not be best to put simply (*The Apostles*) in paren[thesis]: -...Of course if Mrs.Gorton wd. prefer my name to be added I am only too glad & proud to be associated with Canon Gorton's name & memory & to give the slightest gratification to her & the family would willingly run the risk of being misunderstood by the unthinking.[210]

Ella Gorton wrote to Elgar herself, formally asking permission for the theme to be used.

Severn House, Hampstead N.W.
May 26 1913

My dear Mrs.Gorton:

Many thanks for your letter: it was most kind of you to write: I am only too happy that my theme shd. be associated with my dear friend & I thank you for allowing it

With very kind regards
Believe me to be
Yrs very sincly
Edward Elgar

Alice Elgar was moved to write the following day.

Severn House, 42 Netherhall Gardens, Hampstead N.W.
27 May 1913

My dear Mrs.Gorton

I was so sorry to hear that you had been through so many anxieties of illness & hope Olive and Alice Elgar are now nearly well. I do hope you find the new house comfortable & answering your purpose but I know "our own Country" has a great claim on your affections.

I have been much troubled by Edward having been so long unwell - I think & hope he is now somewhat better -

210. Young (1956), 210-11

The Gorton grave (left), Breinton churchyard, with detail of the inscription (below) and motto from The Apostles *(above).*

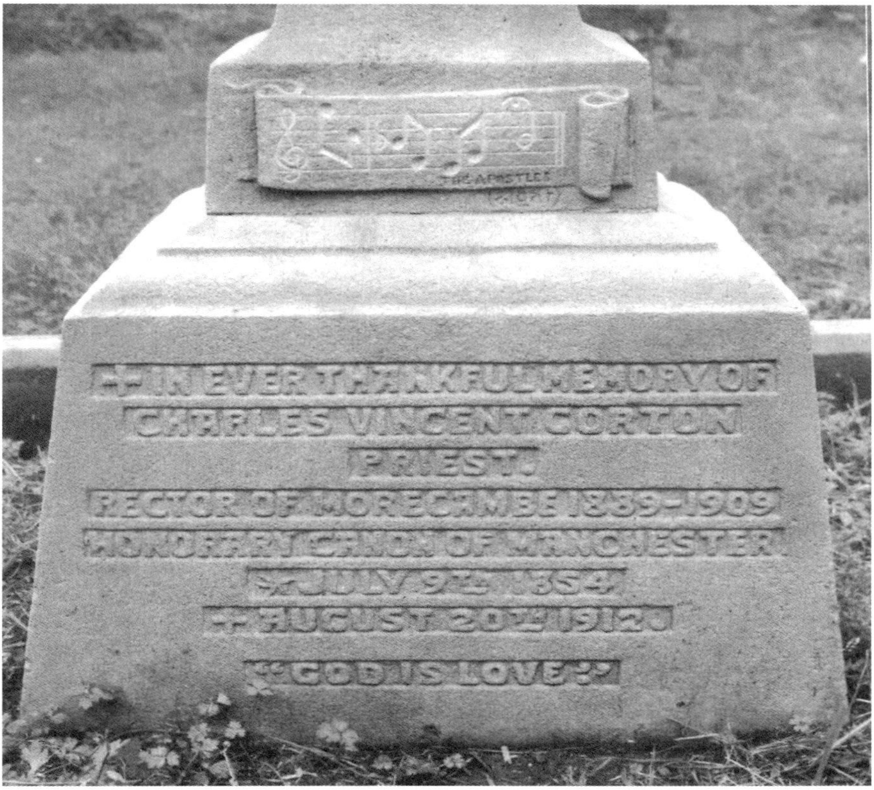

✝ IN EVER THANKFUL MEMORY OF
CHARLES VINCENT GORTON
PRIEST
RECTOR OF MORECAMBE 1889-1909
HONORARY CANON OF MANCHESTER
✱ JULY 9th 1854
✝ AUGUST 20th 1912

"GOD IS LOVE"

I do not know if you have heard anything regarding our beloved friend Mrs.Worthington - We have been so strictly charged to say nothing disquieting as she was to be kept as hopeful as possible that we have not liked to write about her even to friends but it is deep grief to us to know that she is very very ill. We have the most beautiful & sweetest letters from her - & we dare not allude to her, in any way disquieting & nobody must - We miss her usual summer visit terribly.

With love & hoping all will now be well with your children
V. affectionately
C A Elgar

Elgar's letter to Hull had included a harmonised version of the 'Fellowship' theme set on two staves. It had been transposed from E flat into C to avoid the need for leger lines, although a flat sign would still be needed for the third note. But this was too complicated for the engraver, and so Elgar was asked to provide a simpler version - just the theme on a single stave. He omitted the bar line and inverted the stems of the first two quavers.

Saturday [June 1913]

Dear Mrs.Gorton:

I have redrawn the first two or three notes & made suggestions which will improve the look of the music & make it look less rigid. If the engraver is in any doubt as to my meaning will he send to me here.

We all send love to you
Ever sincy yours
Edward Elgar

The theme was engraved on a scroll design at the foot of a celtic cross, above the plinth which carried the details of the Canon's life. Under the music was written 'Apostles', and beneath that, 'Elgar'. It was entirely fitting that 'Fellowship' should stand as the final word on a friendship which had been so valuable and enriching to both men.

EPILOGUE

The Morecambe Musical Festival resumed in 1913. The financial deficit of over £600 which remained after the 1911 Festival was more than met by the proceeds from the great bazaar in 1912. Over £1000 had been raised, and with the excess a reserve fund was set up. As the President, John Hatch, was able to write: "The Morecambe Festival had its birth at a Bazaar in 1891; its fortunes were retrieved by a Bazaar in 1912". His preface began with a tribute to his predecessor:

> Since I last addressed you Charles Vincent Gorton has passed away. Not again will his inspiring enthusiasm hearten us to our task; not again his cheery welcome encourage to success, his open-hearted sympathy make failure seem almost a reward. But the spirit of his views and his ideals remains with us. Evermore must it be the motive power of our efforts to maintain worthily that high heritage of noble achievement with which to enrich us he gave the finest of his intellect, the tenderest emotions of his heart. Gorton! Howson! Together they started this great Festival movement. Together they brought it to a fullness undreamt of in the beginning. Together now - and we? We who are left! We have set up a memorial that shall keep their names for ever in men's eyes.

This last remark is a reference to a new prize in the open male voice class, the Gorton Howson Challenge Shield (and still competed for). The *Competition Festival Record* also paid tribute to the two men:

> A Festival at Morecambe irresistibly awakens memories of former gatherings at this Lancashire seaside resort. Those of us who have long been associated with the event, and are proud of the record, cannot but see Gorton and Howson reincarnated as it were in all his doings. Today, when the Festival movement has made such strides as an exponent of all the best *a capella* music by the old and the most modern masters, the work of these two men who dreamed dreams and realised them is not sufficiently recognised. At the right moment they broke through shackling conditions and boldly forged new paths, and practically created the particular type of competitive festival which is now followed at the greatest events held in this country.

On the Friday evening, the Festival concert began with the chorus 'All flesh doth perish' from Brahms's *Requiem*. It was given in memory of Canon Gorton, and the audience stood throughout as a mark of

The Gorton-Howson Memorial Shield (detail)

respect. Several local choirs and the Nelson Orchestra were conducted by Harry Evans. "It was a touching tribute", said the *Competition Festival Record*, "and all the more pathetic because it was submitted not by outsiders, but by those who knew him well".

Saturday's open classes were poorly attended initially - possibly a combination of the effect of the break in the sequence of festivals in 1912, and the dismal weather. However the hall was packed in the evening as usual, and Blackpool won the Challenge Shield for the first time in eleven years. Nelson Arion Glee Union were successful in the open male voice class, defeating strong opposition from Southport and Habergham: and Barrow won the female voice class, where one of the test pieces - Hegar's *Whitsun Song* - was Charles Gorton's last translation from the German.

Although overtaken by Blackpool in size and prestige, the reputation of the Morecambe Festival was such that its recommencement merited an inclusion in *Punch*. The magazine received, it said, a letter from a correspondent who had attended:

He is full of admiration of the prodigies of musical valour achieved by infants, boys, girls and adults, whether individually or collectively, for the patience of adjudicators, and the splendid results of a movement which will always be associated with the name of the late Mary Wakefield. Yet he cannot resist the temptation of indulging in a little criticism in the form of suggestions for a series of supplementary prizes on the following lines:-

Prize I. For the adjudicator who gives his award with the minimum of sumptuous comment and irrelevant facetiousness.

Prize II. For the composer of a new madrigal or part-song which is not suggestive of an equal admixture of treacle and olives.

Prize III. For the referee in the tenor solo competition who listens to more than fifteen competitors with the least loss of equanimity.

Prize IV. For the conductor who thinks more of poetry than pitch.

Prize V. For any song writer who will set to appropriate music a lyric more futile than the following:-

> *Bobby's secret*
> Nursie told me this morning
> Something that made me feel sore,
> For nursie said that, unless I wed,
> I should die an old bachelor!
> Now I've a secret I'll tell to you,
> Though it makes me feel rather blue:
> I don't love anyone but my granny,
> And she's already Mrs.Mulvaney,
> So that, only for grandpa, don't you see,
> Why, granny might have waited for me!

Neville Gorton was able to attend the last two days at Morecambe, and wrote to his mother: "It is a great thing the Festival - I wish there was someone big & obviously the person to take it on - a local Walford Davies. I distrust these London Fuller-Maitland & co & the superior Sammy [Langford]..."

J A Fuller-Maitland had been music critic of *The Times* for twelve years until 1911, when he retired to live near Carnforth. He was a champion of Stanford, and at best had always been lukewarm towards Elgar. Now he was elected to serve on the Morecambe Executive, and his advocacy of the new generation of English composers bore fruit immediately. The following year at Morecambe saw the first performances of Vaughan Williams' choral suite *Five English Folk Songs*, and Holst's *The Homecoming*, a part-song for male voices. Other new works were by Hathaway, Walford Davies, Nicholson and Julius Harrison: and a pamphlet containing notes on all the new pieces was written by Fuller-Maitland and published by the Festival executive. Lancaster won the Challenge Shield that year, from Blackpool and Carlisle: Padiham Ladies Choir won the female voice class: and Todmorden won a hard fought contest among the male voices, where Elgar's *The Reveille* was one of the tests.

Elgar had recently completed five more large-scale part-songs similar to the Opus 53 set of 1907. They were finished in early 1914, and using a suggestion of McNaught, Elgar gave them the collective title 'Choral Songs'. Writing to McNaught on 13 February, Elgar said: "The dedications are fixed & Blackpool may change colour before I write another pt song"[211]. At the end of March that year, Elgar paid a visit to the competition festival on the Isle of Man. He and Alice were accompanied by Granville Bantock, a fellow-adjudicator. During the festival there *The Banner of St George* was given. This work had marked Elgar's introduction to large-scale choral competition at Morecambe in 1903. Now this visit was to be his last to such a festival.

Elgar's music was still extremely popular at such gatherings, however. After the Lytham Festival in June 1914 William McNaught wrote to Elgar: "At last I have heard 'Go, song of mine' sung to perfection"[212]. He was speaking of the Blackpool Glee & Madrigal Society, which had just received the rare distinction of full marks for its performance. The same choir had also won the top honours at the third Midland Festival in May, where Bach's *Sing ye to the Lord* was given by the combined forces of the best five choirs under McNaught. The audience included Ernest Newman who, according to a report, "sat spellbound for fifteen minutes"[213].

1914 represents the peak in competitive choral singing in this country. Over thirty years later the great musical historian, Reginald Nettel, spoke of an era that had clearly passed:

> I can remember the enthusiasm that surrounded choral activities before the first World War. The crowded trains on concert nights, the respect paid to choir conductors, although they spoke with the local dialect and were never too happy with an orchestra. The town was proud of them, and they in turn tried to uphold the prestige of their town wherever they went to sing. There was a sense of civic

211. Moore, 780
212. Quoted in the Blackpool Glee & Madrigal Society *Retrospect* (privately published, 1921)
213. ibid.

responsibility about our choirs that had no thought for political or class
distinctions - it was a sense of local patriotism, and it had its effect[214].

Obviously the Great War accounted for many tenors and basses.
However, when things began to return to normal there was just as
much interest as before - at first. In 1924 the Midland Festival in
Birmingham reached its peak with a total of 13,285 competitors. Yet
within two years it had collapsed. Choral singing, on the scale on
which it had existed before the war, went into decline. This was
particularly true in country districts and partly reflected the
continuing drift of the population to the towns. In 1945 the
musicologist and scholar E H Fellowes said: "Twenty or thirty years
ago there was a choral society in almost every village. Now there are
hardly any. The choral society has almost disappeared"[215].

Several factors contributing to this state of affairs can be identified.
First, the generation of philanthropic reformers such as Charles
Gorton and Mary Wakefield had gone. The promotion of music among
working class children in order to breed contentment and diminish the
threat of anti-social behaviour was a thing of the past. Despite a decline
in certain basic industries, which kept unemployment high throughout
the inter-war years, real poverty was gradually being eliminated,
thanks in part to an increase in social services and benefits.

Second, increased affluence and leisure for many people was
accompanied by a development in entertainment. Dance halls
became popular, reflecting the interest in the various 'crazes' from
America, such as the Charleston. The music hall, with its shady
reputation, declined as the cinema increased in popularity. Domestic
entertainment, especially the 'wireless' and the gramophone,
encouraged a 'stay-at-home' mentality. The twenties was generally a
time of superficiality - epitomised by the flapper - a good deal of
which was a reaction against the horrors of the war. There was a
corresponding criticism and rejection of the mores of the period
leading up to that war: Elgar himself suffered from this, most notably
in the words of Edward Dent in 1924: "For English ears Elgar's
music is too emotional and not quite free from vulgarity. His
orchestral works...are animated in colour but pompous in style and
of a too deliberate nobility of expression"[216].

214. *Proceedings of the Royal Musical Association*, vol 72 (1945), 31.

215. *op cit.*, 38

216. Quoted in Maine, *Elgar: His Life & Works* (Bell, 1933), vol ii, 278

To those delighted with the piquancy and wit of Walton's *Facade*, part-songs about the charms of Corinna and Phoebe must have seemed laughably unsophisticated and dated. Taste among the musical public was moving away from choral towards orchestral music: here again wireless and gramophone opened up a whole new world to millions of listeners. This change in attitude can be measured by the number of publications in the Novello Part-Song Book. Four hundred new songs were published in the eleven years between Elgar's *Weary wind of the west* in 1903 and his five choral songs in 1914. Yet in the next fifteen years there were only one hundred and fifty additions. The continuing success of those competitive festivals which survived was therefore due less to choral singing than to solo contests, be they vocal, instrumental, or terpsichorean. The North of England, which had taken the lead in establishing competitions, continued to thrive more than other regions, but even here the choral emphasis was away from competition towards the large oratorio chorus. The festivals at Morecambe and Blackpool persevered (and still do). Walford Davies still continued to attend, and other famous adjudicators to go to Morecambe during the interwar years included Thomas Beecham, Malcolm Sargent, and Hugh Roberton (conductor of the famous Glasgow Orpheus Choir). The young Kathleen Ferrier came to prominence when winning at Blackpool in the mid 'thirties.

Neville Cardus wrote in 1930:

> A few years ago I was on the way to a Blackpool Musical Festival and, not having then seen or heard one, I was feeling the musician's usual prejudice against the competitive aspects of it. At Bolton a young man got in the railway carriage; he was a typical Lancashire toiler under the sun - perhaps under the earth! He sat down, lighted a cigarette, and proceeded to study the Michelangelo songs of Hugo Wolf.
>
> My prejudices against these North of England musical festivals immediately began to weaken. In a flash of imagination I saw all the fine and brave work which leads up to that hour of ordeal when a lad or a lass from some hinterland of Lancashire or Yorkshire stands face to face with the adjudicator and tries to give an account of Schubert and Brahms. I saw innumerable Tom Smiths and Maggie Hancocks in the setting of winding streets, narrow and cobbled; I saw them at home on Sunday mornings with Beethoven on the piano, in parlours hidden from the outer world by lace curtains; I saw them all at practice, coming home late on winter nights, tired of body but eager of spirit, eager to have a run through the test piece...

Competitors at the festivals are not attracted primarily by lust for spoils. My experience amongst them convinces me that though they all hope to win, it is their singing or playing, and their pride in it, that spurs them on and gives them courage as they submit to the jurisdiction of the various and visible Beckmessers.

It is a mistake to look at these festivals exclusively as affairs of music-making. It is beside the question to say that they do not provide unalloyed æsthetic satisfaction...But the man in the railway carriage, reading his Hugo Wolf, made the purist point of view of a competitive festival seem paltry and narrow...A competitive festival must be looked at with eyes other than those of the musician who stands detached from the ordinary world. They must be seen as things Institutional, as parts of the great activities whereby the North of England lets the world know how it lives when it is not in the factory, the pit, the office, the mill.

Indirectly, the festivals have done immense pioneer work in the music of this country.[217]

In these days when such a wide variety of good music is available to all, through radio and recordings especially, it is easy to forget the painstaking way in which our present musical base was built up: by people such as the North country rector whose concern for his parishioners extended beyond their souls to their bodies, minds, and spirits: and by the Worcester piano-tuner's son who, when on the brink of fame, was not ashamed to identify himself with such as mill-girls from Ancoats and miners from Habergham.

217. 'Pioneers of Music in the North – 3'; *Radio Times*, 28 November 1930, 636.

APPENDIX

The following is a list of the winners in the five major open classes at Morecambe from the first four-day festival in 1899 to the outbreak of war. During the first ten years of this period, the Morecambe Festival was the most prestigious in the country.

*   *   *

1. OPEN MIXED-VOICE CHOIR (The Challenge Shield)

1899	1. Blackburn (163)	2. Morecambe (162)	3. Blackpool (161)
1900	1. Blackpool (175)	2. Morecambe (166)	3. Colne (158)
1901	1. Blackpool (174)	2. Blackburn (164)	3. Nottingham (163)
1902	1. Blackpool (233)	2. Morecambe (226)	3. Nottingham (223)
1903	1. Hanley (232)	2. Blackpool (231)	3. Morecambe (229)
1904	1. Nottingham (296)	2. Southport (295)	3. Hanley (294)
1905	1. Hanley (316)	2. Blackpool (311)	3. Morecambe (310)
1906	1. Barrow (309)	2. Blackpool (308)	3. Isle of Man (300)
1907	1. Isle of Man (301)	2. Barrow (300)	3. Blackpool (299)
1908	1. Lancaster (368)	2. Southport (363)	3. Barrow (362)
1909	1. Lancaster (382)	2. Morecambe (381)	3. Barrow (380)
1910	1. Lancaster (378)	2. Barrow (371)	3. Blackpool (361)
1911	1. Barrow (356)	2. Blackpool (354)	3. Sale (348)
1912	No competition		
1913	1. Blackpool (379)	2. Lancaster (370)	3. Carlisle (368)
1914	1. Lancaster (363)	2. Blackpool (362)	3. Carlisle (354)

NB. The discrepancy in the marks is caused by the differing number of test pieces (three up to 1901, four from 1902 onwards): and an upward revision of the marking system (out of sixty to 1903, out of eighty 1904-07), out of one hundred from 1908).

2. OPEN MALE-VOICE CHOIRS

1899	1. Manchester (110)	2. Morley (108)	3. Nelson (107)
1900	1. Manchester (171)	2. Nelson (156)	3. Colne (147)
1901	1. Colne (105)	2. Nelson (92)	3. Workington (88)
1902	1. Southport (56)	2. Manchester (55)	3. Sheffield (54)
1903	1. Southport (160)	2. Manchester (159)	3. Sheffield (155)
1904	1. Southport (111)	2. Habergham (110)	3. Lancaster (109)
1905	1. Manchester (313)	2. Southport (304)	3. Harrogate (289)
1906	1. Southport (229)	2. Habergham (228)	3. Manchester (221)
1907	1. Habergham (234)	2= Manchester (231)	2= Southport (231)
1908	1. Newcastle (283)	2. Manchester (280)	3. Habergham (278)
1909	1. Habergham (392)	2. Southport (383)	3. Lancaster (372)
1910	1. Manchester (286)	2. Colne (279)	3. Lancaster (261)
1911	1. Habergham (478)	2. Todmorden (454)	3. Lancaster (428)
1912	No competition		
1913	1. Nelson (371)	2. Southport (358)	3. Habergham (357)
1914	1. Todmorden (267)	2. Nelson (266)	3. Habergham (257)

3. OPEN FEMALE-VOICE CLASS

1899	1. Blackpool (54)	2. Barrow (51)	3. Earlestown
1900	1. Barrow (117)	2. Blackpool (104)	3. Ancoats (94)
1901	1. Blackpool (108)	2. Barrow (107)	3. Bendemeer (102)
1902	1. Southport (118)	2. Ancoats (110)	3. Blackpool (109)
1903	1. Blackpool (113)	2. Barrow (112)	3. Ancoats 9107)
1904	1. Hanley (58)	2. Blackpool (54)	3= Harrogate (53)
			3= Lancaster (53)
1905	1. Colne (118)	2. Padiham (114)	3. Barrow (109)
1906	1. Blackpool (152)	2. Barrow (150)	3. Padiham (148)
1907	1. Barrow (149)	2. Padiham (144)	3. Penrith (143)
1908	1. Lancaster (187)	2. Barrow (185)	3. Padiham (180)
1909	1. Barrow (190)	2. Lancaster (185)	3. Morecambe (180)
1910	1. Lancaster (178)	2. Penrith (171)	3. Barrow (155)
1911	1. Barrow (378)	2. Carlisle (343)	3. Penrith (341)
1912	No competition		
1913	1. Barrow (193)	2. Padiham (184)	3. Blackpool (183)
1914	1. Lancaster (179)	2. Ancoats (174)	3. Blackpool (168)

4. FULL ORCHESTRA

1899	1. Colne	2. Accrington	3. Lancaster
1900	1. Nelson (52)	2. Colne (47)	
1901	1. Colne (53)	2. Nelson (47)	
1902	1. Colne (52)	2. Nelson (49)	3. Lancaster (48)
1903	1. Nelson (112)	2. Colne (111)	
1904	1. Nelson (50)	2. Colne (49)	3. Rochdale (48)
1905	1. Colne	2. Lancaster	3. Nelson
1906	1. Nelson	2. Potteries	
1907	1. Nelson (73)	2. Colne (71)	
1908	1. Nelson (86)	2. North Staffs (84)	
1909	1. Nelson		
1910	1. Nelson (99)	2. Altrincham (90)	
1911	1. Nelson (91)	2. Brackenburgh (86)	
1912	No competition		
1913	1. Slaithwaite	2. Nelson	3. Lancaster
1914	1. Nelson (86)	2. Slaithwaite (80)	

5. STRING ORCHESTRA

1899	1. Furness (52)	2. Lancaster (48)	3. Accrington
1900	1. Lancaster (53)	2. Hollinwood (51)	
1901	1. Lancaster (57)	2. Colne (53)	
1902	1. Nelson (50)	2. Colne (41)	
1903	1. Colne (58)	2. Nelson (54)	
1904	1=. Nelson, Colne and Rochdale (each 50)		
1905	1. Colne (50)	2. Lancaster (49)	3. Nelson (46)
1906	1. Nelson (148)	2= Colne (141)	2= Lancaster (141)
1907	1. Colne (70)	2. Nelson (66)	
1908	1. Nelson (86)	2. North Staffs (77)	
1909	1. Nelson	2. Cumberland	
1910	1. Nelson (95)	2. Altrincham (90)	
1911	1. Nelson (88)	2. Brackenburgh (85)	
1912	No competition		
1913	1. Nelson		
1914	1. Huddersfield (93)	2. Nelson	3. Padiham (82)

TEST PIECES

 * First public performance
 † English version by Canon Gorton

OPEN MIXED-VOICE CLASS

Bach	*Death, I do not fear thee* (1909)
Bantock	*Music, when soft voices die* (1913)*
Bath	*Spring wind* (1914)
Bennett	*To Mary in heaven* (1901)
Brahms	*Night Watch* (1900)†
	Autumn (1901)†
	The Maiden (1902)†
	O Lovely May (1902)† (1911)
	Dim-lit woods (1903)†
	The Dirge of Darthula (1903)
	Memories (1904)†
	Abendständchen (1910)
Brian	*Shall I compare thee to a summer's day?* (1906)
Corder	*I love the jocund dance* (1901)
Cornelius	*O Death, thou art the tranquil night* (1905)† (1911)
	The Tempest (1907)
	Love and Youth (1910)
Davies, Walford	*England* (1908)*
	The green fields of England (1908)*
	And did those feet (1908)*
	These sweeter far than lilies are (1914)*
Elgar	*O Happy eyes* (1902)
	Weary wind of the west (1903)*
	On the Alm (1904)
	Evening Scene (1906)* (1907) (1911)
	There is Sweet Music (1909)*
	Deep in my Soul (1909)*
	Go, Song of Mine (1910)
Faning	*There is dew* (1899)
Gibbons	*What is our life* (1914)
Hathaway	*Justice* (1908)*
	Spring (1913)*
Holbrooke	*Through groves sequestered* (1913)
King	*Soldier, rest* (1900)
Leslie	*Charm me asleep* (1899)
McEwen	*Let Me the Canakin Clink* (1907)
Marenzio	*So saith my fair* (1903)
Marson	*The Nymphs and Shepherds Danced* (1910)

Möllendorf	*Night Whispers* (1905)
	Welcome to Spring (1906)‡
Morley	*Fire, fire, my heart* (1900) (1911)
	I follow, lo, the footing (1906)
	Arise, Awake (1907)
	Stay, heart (1914)
Munday	*Lightly she tripped* (1909)
Parry	*Come, pretty wag* (1899)
	There Rolls the Deep (1904)
	Tell me, O love (1905)
Tomkins	*Fusca, in thy starry eyes* (1905)
Vecchi	*Phillida, come tell to me* (1904)
Ward	*Hope of my heart* (1902)
Wilbye	*Ye that do live* (1913)

OPEN MALE-VOICE CHOIRS

Bantock	*Boot and saddle* (1905)
Berger	*The Hunter, the Rabbit and the Moon* (1909)‡
Bridge	*Bold Turpin* (1899)
	With thee, sweet hope (1901)
Bruch	*Media Vita* (1908)‡
Coerne	*Sadly the moon* (1909)
Davies, Walford	*Dominus illuminatio mea* (1913)*
Delius	*Wanderer's song* (1913)
Elgar	*It's oh to be a wild wind* (1904) (1911)
	Feasting I Watch (1904) (1911)
	After Many a Dusty Mile (1906)
	Yea, Cast me from Heights of the Mountain (1907)
	The Reveille (1914)
Fauth	*Storm song* (1908)‡
Fletcher	*The sailor's return* (1913)
Goss	*T'other day as I sat* (1901)
	Hark! heard ye not (1902)
Hegar	*The Phantom Host* (1906)‡ (1911)
	The Desert March (1907)‡
	Walpurga (1909)‡
Holst	*The Homecoming* (1914)*
Küchen	*The Northman's Song* (1900)
	The Young Musicians (1904)
MacDowell	*From the Sea* (1907) (1911)
Mackenzie	*A Franklyn's Dogge* (1905)
Mendelssohn	*To the sons of art* (1903)
Pitt	*Sunset* (1903)
Reger	*Call of Spring* (1910)
Scharwenka	*Happy light, happy day* (1908)‡ (1911)
	When shadows flee away (1909)
Schubert	*Song of the Spirits* (1905)
Schumann	*The Lotus Flower* (1900)
	Battle song (1903)
Selby	*The Roysterers* (1910)
Sibelius	*Hail! O Moon* (1910)
Spohr	*Counsel* (1906)
Stainer	*Bind my brows* (1900)
Strauss, Richard	*Love* (1905)
Weingartner	*Song of the Robbers* (1913)
	New Year's song (1914)
Wesley, S S	*I wish to tune* (1899)

OPEN FEMALE-VOICE CHOIRS

Bantock	*The Happy Isle* (1914)
Bishop	*Welcome to this place* (1901)
Brahms	*Questions* (1900)
	A March Night (1902)
	A Love Song (1903) (1911)
	Weep on the rocks (1909)
Buck	*Weep you no more* (1901)
Coleridge-Taylor	*The Pixies* (1910)
Corder	*The Siren's Chorus* (1903) (1911)
	Song of the Spirits (1908)
Davidson	*Love's Requiem* (1909)
Hathaway	*In the heart of a dreaming rose* (1914)*
Hegar	*Evening* (1907)‡
	Whitsun Song (1913)‡
Jensen	*The Mountain Spirit* (1904)
	Eglantine (1906)
Lassen	*Spanish Gypsy Girl* (1913)
Schumann	*Sinks the night* (1900)
	The Mermaid (1902)
	The Tambourine Player (1905)
Vaughan Williams	*Sound Sleep* (1906)
Wolstenholme	*The three fishers* (1910)
Woyrsch	*Love's influence* (1905)
	The sleeping beauty (1908)
Wurm	*Some strain that once* (1899)
Young	*How the ripples gurgle* (1907)

FULL ORCHESTRA

Beethoven	Overture *Leonora* no 3 (1908)
	Overture *The Creatures of Prometheus* (1910)
Cherubini	Overture *Anacreon* (1901)
Humperdinck	Overture *Hansel and Gretel* (1907)
Mendelssohn	Overture *Ruy Blas* (1905)
Mozart	Overture *The Magic Flute* (1904) (1911)
Reissiger	Overture *Die Felsenmühle* (1900)
Schubert	Overture *Rosamunde* (1899)
	Symphony no.8 (*Unfinished*): Andante (1903)
Sibelius	*Karelia* Suite (exc) (1909)
Wagner	*Lohengrin*: Introduction Act III (1903)
	Siegfried Idyll (1914)
Weber	Overture *Oberon* (1902)
	Overture *Euryanthe* (1906)

STRING ORCHESTRA

Dvořák	*Nocturne* (1904)
Elgar	Serenade (exc) (1901) (1911)
Gade	*Novelletten* (exc) (1905) (1909) (1910)
Glazunov	*Quatuor Slav* Suite (1913)
Goetz	Serenade (1902)
Grieg	*Holberg* Suite (1900)
Herbert	Suite for strings (exc) (1906) (1907)
Parry	*Lady Radnor* Suite (1908)
Sibelius	*Romance* in C (1914)
Tchaikovsky	Serenade for strings: Waltz (1899); Elegy (1903)

Other works translated by Canon Gorton and performed at Morecambe are as follows:

Brahms	*Dear, canst thou tell* (1903)
	The Falcon (1903)
	The Hump-backed fiddler (1906)
Cornelius	*The Hero's Rest* (1903)
Humperdinck	*The Pilgrimage to Kevlaar* (1906)
Schillings	*New Year's Greeting* (1909)
Berger	*Song of the Pied Piper* (1910)
Kaun	*Praise God* (1910)
Tinel	*The Angelus* (1910)

INDEX

There are no separate entries for the Morecambe Festival, Canon Charles Gorton, or Sir Edward Elgar, although the latter's compositions are included.